WORK

by Cathy Guisewite

**Andrews McMeel
Publishing**

Kansas City

01 02 03 04 05 BAE 10 9 8 7 6 5 4 3 2 1

Library of Congress Catalog Card Number: 2001090619

ISBN: 0-7407-2062-7

Cathy® may be viewed on the Internet at:
www.uexpress.com

─────── **ATTENTION: SCHOOLS AND BUSINESSES** ───────

Andrews McMeel books are available at quantity discounts with bulk purchase for educational, business, or sales promotional use. For information, please write to: Special Sales Department, Andrews McMeel Publishing, 4520 Main Street, Kansas City, Missouri 64111.

Contents

Introduction

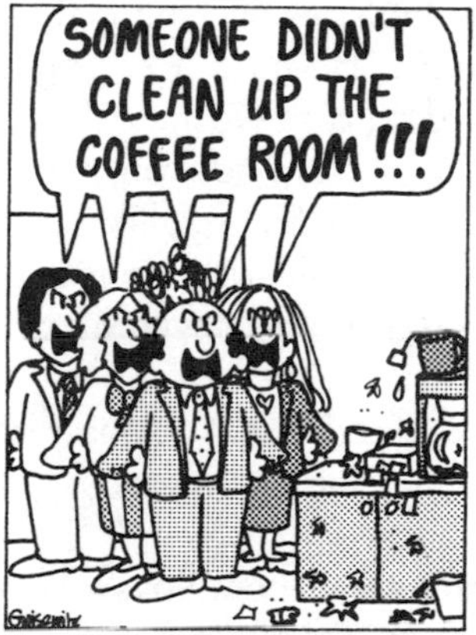
SOMEONE DIDN'T CLEAN UP THE COFFEE ROOM!!!

Nothing sums up the last quarter century's explosion of social and technological change in the workforce like the heap of dirty dishes in the office coffee room sink.

It's all right there.

The enlightenment: "I am woman. Wash your own dishes."

The expansion: "Filthy dinner plates must not be piled on top of the filthy latte pot and the filthy food processor."

The restructuring: "Here's a 300-page manual on office policy regarding dish washing."

The streamlining: "From now on, one filthy mug will be allowed per employee."

The prioritizing: "I will wash the mugs, but I'm not touching the microwave platter with Bruce's breakfast burrito welded to it."

The teamwork: "Fred didn't do the dishes on his day so I'm not doing the dishes on my day."

The sink in the coffee room links who we used to be (people too busy to do the dishes) to who we have become (people too busy to do the dishes).

It links what we dreamed of having then (a multibillion dollar corporation with a staff of people to handle the coffee cups) to what we dream of having now (time to sit down and have a cup of coffee).

It's the one area where—after 25 years of research, seminars, workshops, training sessions, retreats, and heated legal debate—men and women actually have an equal voice in business: "It's not my turn to do the dishes."

Twenty-five years of evolution is written all over our unwashed mugs.

From thinking of others ("Have a Nice Day") to thinking unpleasant things about others ("Men Are Pigs") to ordering others ("Get a Life") to cheering others ("Go Girl!") to affirming we are worthy of others ("I Believe in Me") to pleas for contact with others ("Visit me at www.aack.org").

Look on the counter next to the sink and you see a microcosm of where all the time went that we saved with the invention of Wite-Out.

Where there was once a little container of coffee cream there are now 42 options: nondairy creamer; low-fat, fat-free, and/or lactose-free nondairy creamer; hazelnut, fat-free nondairy creamer; vanilla bean, cholesterol-free low sodium creamer; powdered mocha creamer-like substitute; skim milk, 1 percent milk, 2 percent milk, whole milk, half and half, soy milk, lite soy milk, vanilla soy milk; four types of fake sugar; two kinds of real sugar; and six types of organically harvested honey.

Look at the lineup of coffee makers in a big office and see where all the time went that we saved when Wite-Out got replaced by the "self-correcting" typewriter.

Regular? Decaf? Espresso? Latte? Mocha latte? Mocha latte decaf? Tea? Herbal? Homeopathic? Yogi? Chinese? Chai? Bag? Leaves? Mulberry? Mango? Lemon Spice? Chamomile? Spearmint? Ginkgo biloba?

Look how we grew.

The classic coffee room guilt-ridden doughnut box (140 calories per doughnut) became the self-righteous giant bagel (400 calories), giant croissant (500 calories), giant fat-free, cranberry-bran muffin (600 calories), and giant chocolate-chip scone (800 calories) platter.

Look at the empty wrappers on the floor: Once there were 25-cent, fabulously satisfying, gooey chocolate vending machine candy bars. Now we have $3.50 mega-protein-boost, calcium-enriched, high-fiber nutrition bars that taste like dried grout.

Look at the abandoned water cooler—grand symbol of office peer togetherness, the gathering point, the common meeting ground . . . literally, the original "think" tank.

Abandoned because those puny four-ounce cups are a joke for the modern 2.5 liter thirst.

Abandoned because water is now divided up into individual hydration systems and strapped like extra appendages on people whose only human contact in the workday may be getting an IM on their PDA re: the IPO.

Open the office refrigerator and simultaneously experience the brave new and brave old worlds linked with very familiar and unfamiliar aromas.

Two-week-old doggie bags from swank three-hour, two-martini lunches are now two-week-old delivery bags from the order-in vegan Thai place.

Stale, half-eaten pastrami sandwiches are now stale, half-eaten nine-grain buns with lite soy cheese and nonfat mayo-like spread sandwiches.

Old, wilted, fermenting salads are now new wilted, fermenting salads. At some point in the late '80s, we ran out of time to chew, so order-in salads all started being "chopped." This still required lifting a fork to the mouth, unless you were a real overachiever and ordered your chopped salad stuffed in a pita, in which case you could eat, work and never even look down at the plate.

Ancient, moldy cottage cheese is now ancient, moldy artificially sweetened, reduced fat yogurt.

Now, look back at the sink full of dirty dishes. A monument to how far we have and haven't come. A reminder that "we will always need our people," even if it's just someone to get the mug from the sink to the dishwasher.

A symbol of the fact that the there are some challenges too big for technology: that the warp-speed Pentium Processor down the hall never has and never will have one nanosecond of impact on how fast Harold gets around to scraping the petrified drippings from his nuked pizza off his plate.

The sink is the exact same problem in giant conglomerates as it is in one-person home offices. The sink is the same in hip dot-coms as it is in funky mom and pops.

The sink represents 25 years of grandiose human potential, leveled by a really gross cup.

Twenty-five years of struggling to be, to achieve, to prove, to create, to enlighten, to prosper . . . a frantic, high-powered rat race that comes to a screeching halt at an "icky" Tupperware container.

Twenty-five years of looking at the exact same sink and believing—with one grand team spirit—that tomorrow's system will get it under control.

When I look back at our history, I see a comforting common thread. Unless it's my turn to do the dishes, I've always found something very reassuring about that sink.

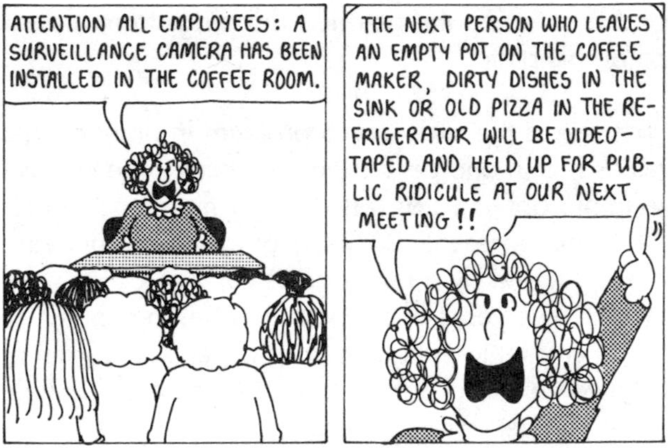
ATTENTION ALL EMPLOYEES: A SURVEILLANCE CAMERA HAS BEEN INSTALLED IN THE COFFEE ROOM.
THE NEXT PERSON WHO LEAVES AN EMPTY POT ON THE COFFEE MAKER, DIRTY DISHES IN THE SINK OR OLD PIZZA IN THE REFRIGERATOR WILL BE VIDEOTAPED AND HELD UP FOR PUBLIC RIDICULE AT OUR NEXT MEETING!!

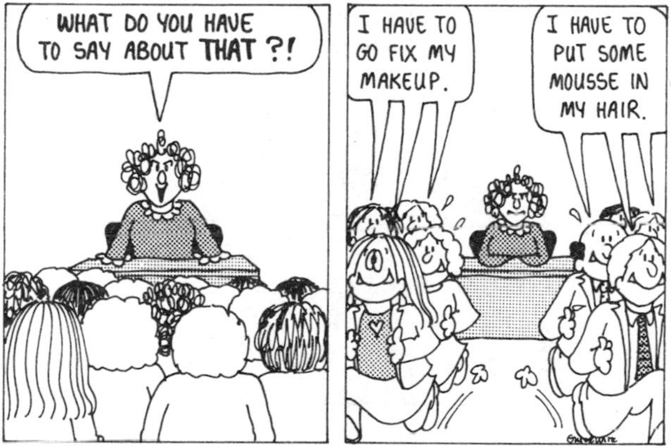
WHAT DO YOU HAVE TO SAY ABOUT THAT ?!
I HAVE TO GO FIX MY MAKEUP.
I HAVE TO PUT SOME MOUSSE IN MY HAIR.

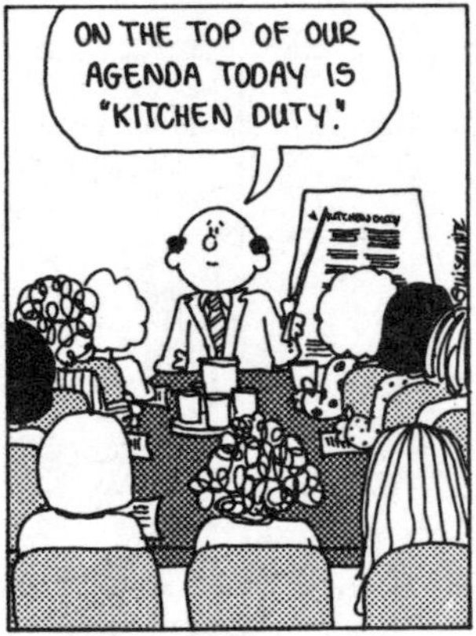
ON THE TOP OF OUR AGENDA TODAY IS "KITCHEN DUTY."

The Late '70s

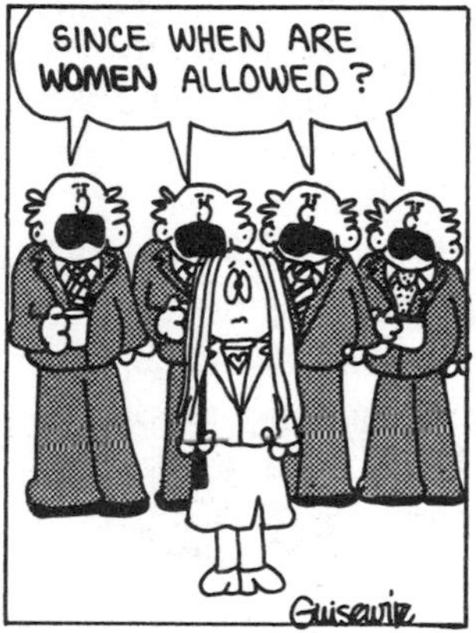
SINCE WHEN ARE WOMEN ALLOWED?

June Cleaver.
Gloria Steinem.
June Cleaver.
Gloria Steinem.

Mine was the first generation to have a full set of conflicting fantasies presented to us on TV.

Years before anyone was talking about multitasking and overachieving, I was in the frustrated little fringe group who completely agreed and disagreed with two exact opposite life role models at once—and on some level, wanted to be both of them.

We were just annoyed enough with Mrs. Cleaver to want more for ourselves and just empowered enough by Ms. Steinem to believe we could do everything— including having a nice, hot supper on the table for our own version of Ward, after launching our own billion-dollar conglomerate.

Work was the center of it all. Work took women out of the discussion phase and gave us actual freedom. Work gave us confidence and choices. Work gave us dreams. Work ruined our love lives.

It was a tumultuous phase. Exhilarating and confusing. Inspiring and depressing.

I gained 45 pounds of liberation weight between my freshman year of college and my first job. Perfect for the time. If I look back and remember what it was like to want to be an independent, self-sufficient career woman until the boyfriend left . . . and to want to just get married and have children until I read the *Ms.* magazine article . . . the truest thing I can say about the late '70s is this: My closet was an exact clone of my mental state.

Nothing fit anymore.

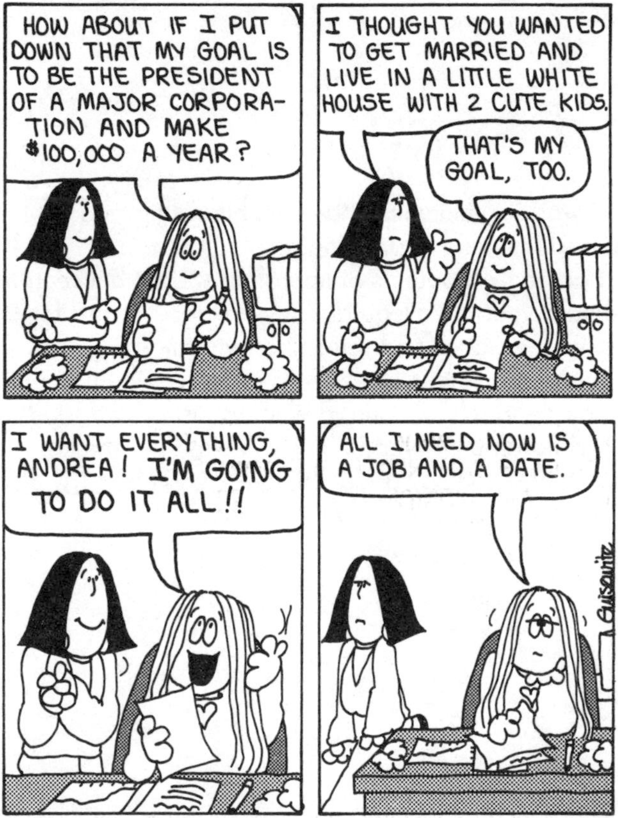
HOW ABOUT IF I PUT DOWN THAT MY GOAL IS TO BE THE PRESIDENT OF A MAJOR CORPORATION AND MAKE $100,000 A YEAR?
I THOUGHT YOU WANTED TO GET MARRIED AND LIVE IN A LITTLE WHITE HOUSE WITH 2 CUTE KIDS.
THAT'S MY GOAL, TOO.
I WANT EVERYTHING, ANDREA! I'M GOING TO DO IT ALL!!
ALL I NEED NOW IS A JOB AND A DATE.
Guisewite

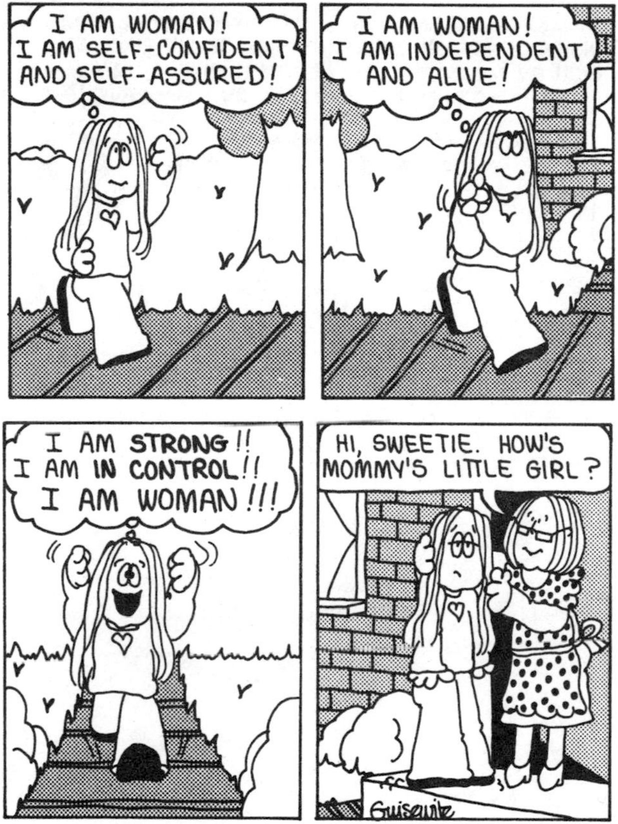
I AM WOMAN! I AM SELF-CONFIDENT AND SELF-ASSURED!
I AM WOMAN! I AM INDEPENDENT AND ALIVE!
I AM STRONG!! I AM IN CONTROL!! I AM WOMAN!!!
HI, SWEETIE. HOW'S MOMMY'S LITTLE GIRL?
Guisewite

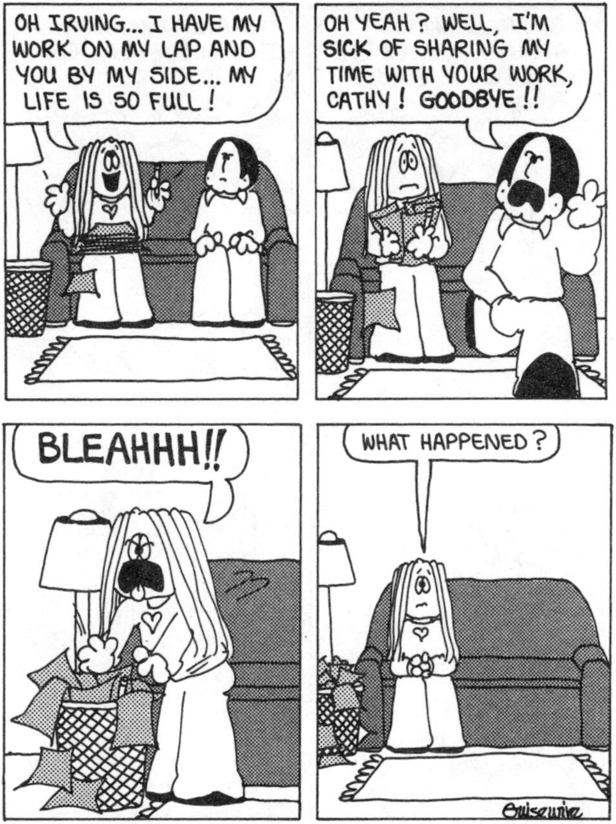
OH IRVING... I HAVE MY WORK ON MY LAP AND YOU BY MY SIDE... MY LIFE IS SO FULL!
OH YEAH? WELL, I'M SICK OF SHARING MY TIME WITH YOUR WORK, CATHY! GOODBYE!!
BLEAHHH!!
WHAT HAPPENED?
Guisewite

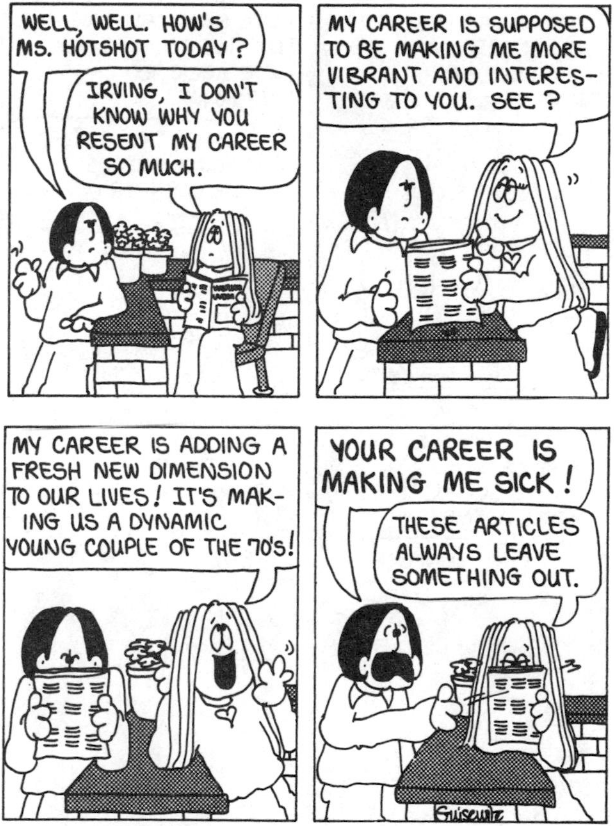
WELL, WELL. HOW'S MS. HOTSHOT TODAY?
IRVING, I DON'T KNOW WHY YOU RESENT MY CAREER SO MUCH.
MY CAREER IS SUPPOSED TO BE MAKING ME MORE VIBRANT AND INTERES-TING TO YOU. SEE?
MY CAREER IS ADDING A FRESH NEW DIMENSION TO OUR LIVES! IT'S MAK-ING US A DYNAMIC YOUNG COUPLE OF THE 70'S!
YOUR CAREER IS MAKING ME SICK!
THESE ARTICLES ALWAYS LEAVE SOMETHING OUT.
Guisewite

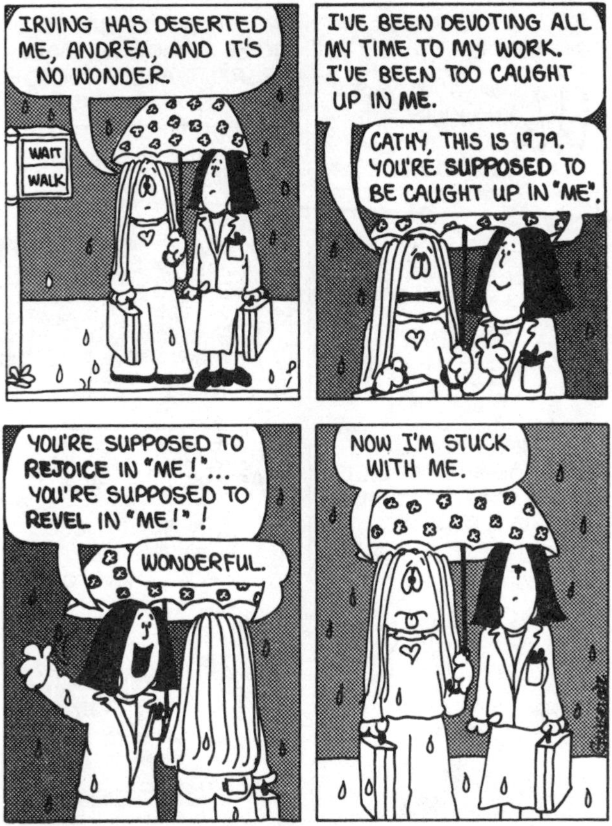
IRVING HAS DESERTED ME, ANDREA, AND IT'S NO WONDER.
WAIT
WALK
I'VE BEEN DEVOTING ALL MY TIME TO MY WORK. I'VE BEEN TOO CAUGHT UP IN ME.
CATHY, THIS IS 1979. YOU'RE SUPPOSED TO BE CAUGHT UP IN "ME".
YOU'RE SUPPOSED TO REJOICE IN "ME!"... YOU'RE SUPPOSED TO REVEL IN "ME!"!
WONDERFUL.
NOW I'M STUCK WITH ME.

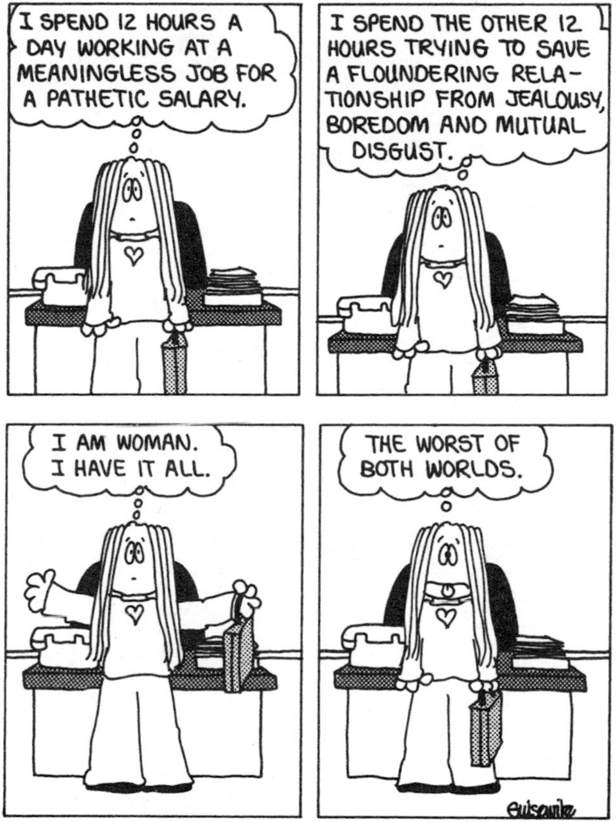
I SPEND 12 HOURS A DAY WORKING AT A MEANINGLESS JOB FOR A PATHETIC SALARY.
I SPEND THE OTHER 12 HOURS TRYING TO SAVE A FLOUNDERING RELATIONSHIP FROM JEALOUSY, BOREDOM AND MUTUAL DISGUST.
I AM WOMAN. I HAVE IT ALL.
THE WORST OF BOTH WORLDS.
Guisewite

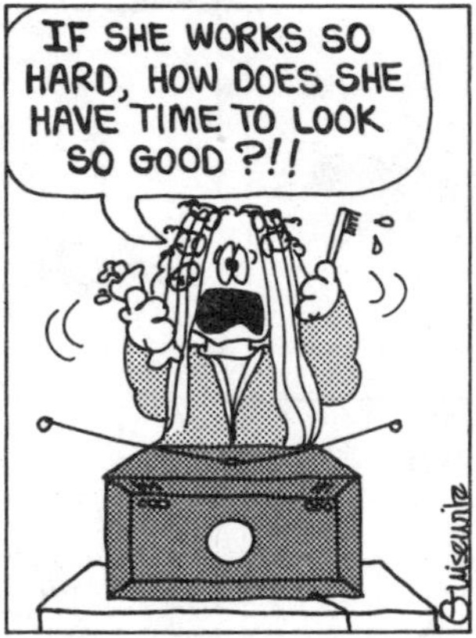
IF SHE WORKS SO HARD, HOW DOES SHE HAVE TIME TO LOOK SO GOOD?!!

The Early '80s

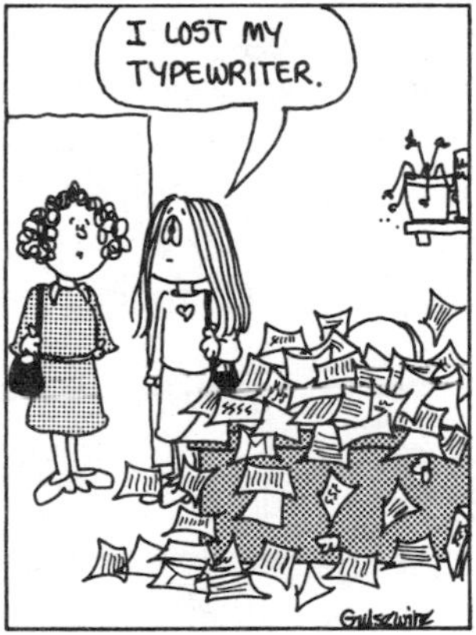
I LOST MY TYPEWRITER.
Gulsewite

Remember typewriters?
Remember the busy signal?
Remember needing to be near a wall to talk on the phone?

Remember having to go inside the bank during "banking hours," wait in a line, speak to a human, and write a check to get cash?

Remember when cooking dinner required food, a pan, a stove and/or an oven, and at least an hour?

Remember how getting new glasses took a month, getting a roll of film developed took a week, and getting a page copied took three minutes?

Remember dropping really, really rush things in the mailbox?

Remember how "filling up the tank" took ten minutes because the nice man doing it also checked your oil, water, brake fluid, windshield washer fluid, and tire pressure, washed every single window and asked you about your day?

Remember having to walk across the room to change the channel? Having to use your whole arm to roll up a window? Having to get up to turn the record over to listen to the other side?

Remember walking down the hall to deliver a phone message?

Remember having to drive to a store to buy something?

Remember how if someone wasn't there, you had to keep redialing at all different times to try to reach him?

The early '80s.
We were so busy.
So very, very busy.
So many dreams.
So much to prove.
So many doors to pry open.
And all without 99 percent of the modern time-saving devices that are now critical to our lives.

Remember having about five more hours a day of time than we do now?

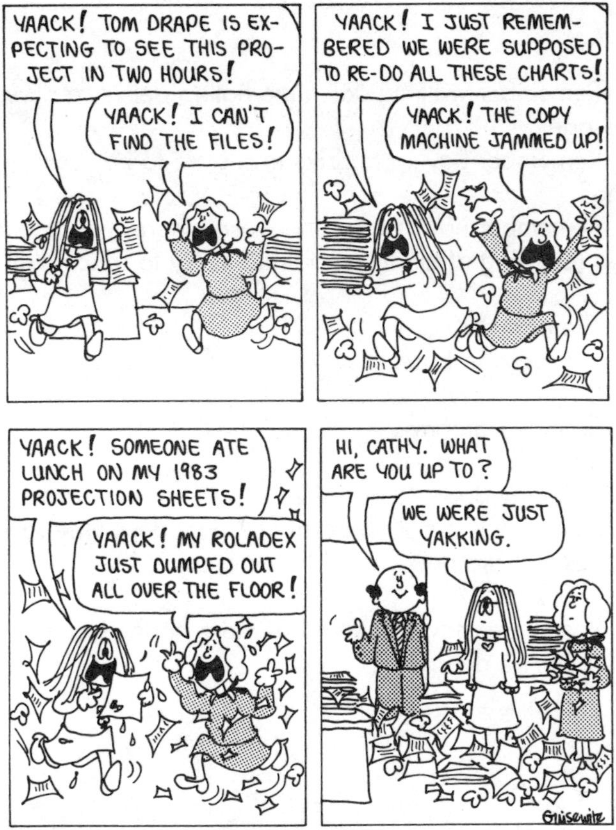
YAACK! TOM DRAPE IS EXPECTING TO SEE THIS PROJECT IN TWO HOURS!
YAACK! I CAN'T FIND THE FILES!
YAACK! I JUST REMEMBERED WE WERE SUPPOSED TO RE-DO ALL THESE CHARTS!
YAACK! THE COPY MACHINE JAMMED UP!
YAACK! SOMEONE ATE LUNCH ON MY 1983 PROJECTION SHEETS!
YAACK! MY ROLADEX JUST DUMPED OUT ALL OVER THE FLOOR!
HI, CATHY. WHAT ARE YOU UP TO?
WE WERE JUST YAKKING.
Guisewite

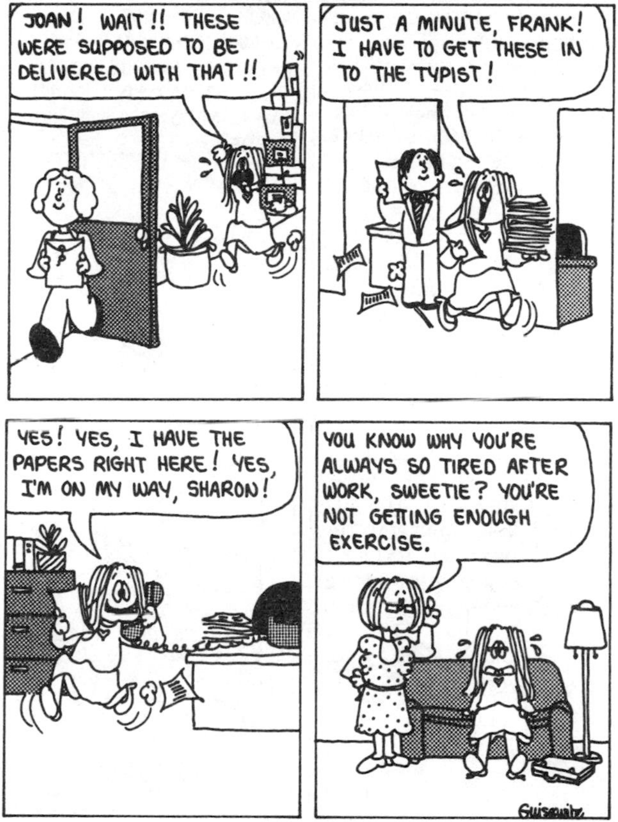
JOAN! WAIT!! THESE WERE SUPPOSED TO BE DELIVERED WITH THAT!!
JUST A MINUTE, FRANK! I HAVE TO GET THESE IN TO THE TYPIST!
YES! YES, I HAVE THE PAPERS RIGHT HERE! YES, I'M ON MY WAY, SHARON!
YOU KNOW WHY YOU'RE ALWAYS SO TIRED AFTER WORK, SWEETIE? YOU'RE NOT GETTING ENOUGH EXERCISE.
Guisewite

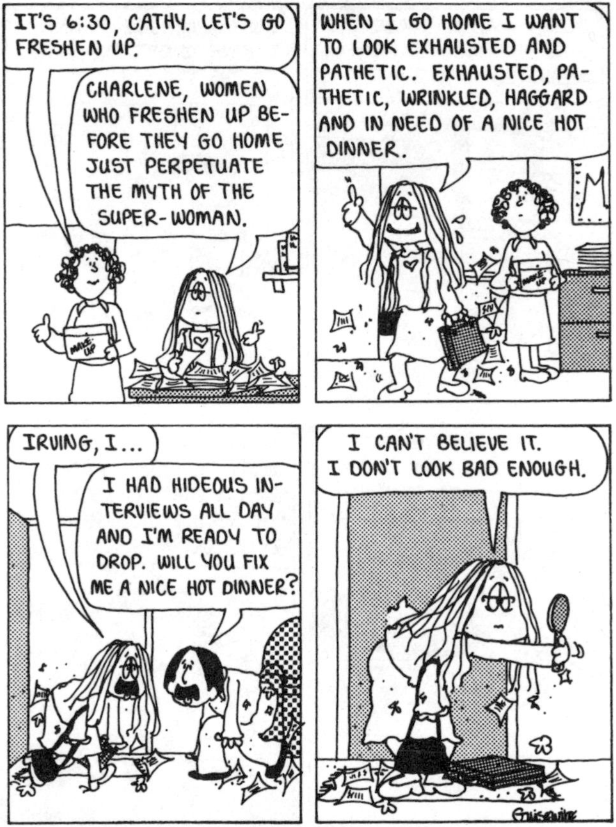
IT'S 6:30, CATHY. LET'S GO FRESHEN UP.
CHARLENE, WOMEN WHO FRESHEN UP BEFORE THEY GO HOME JUST PERPETUATE THE MYTH OF THE SUPER-WOMAN.
MAKE-UP
WHEN I GO HOME I WANT TO LOOK EXHAUSTED AND PATHETIC. EXHAUSTED, PATHETIC, WRINKLED, HAGGARD AND IN NEED OF A NICE HOT DINNER.
IRVING, I...
I HAD HIDEOUS INTERVIEWS ALL DAY AND I'M READY TO DROP. WILL YOU FIX ME A NICE HOT DINNER?
I CAN'T BELIEVE IT. I DON'T LOOK BAD ENOUGH.
Guisewite

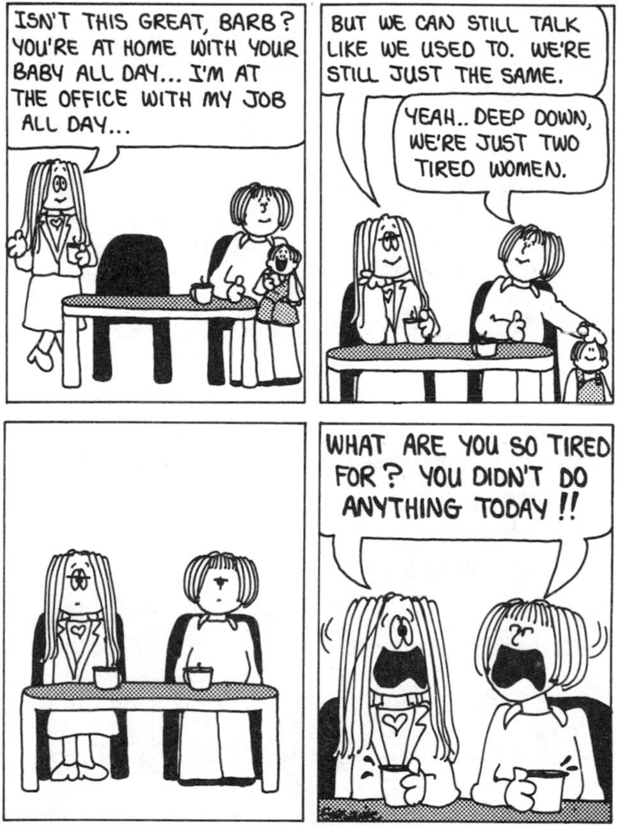
ISN'T THIS GREAT, BARB? YOU'RE AT HOME WITH YOUR BABY ALL DAY... I'M AT THE OFFICE WITH MY JOB ALL DAY...
BUT WE CAN STILL TALK LIKE WE USED TO. WE'RE STILL JUST THE SAME.
YEAH.. DEEP DOWN, WE'RE JUST TWO TIRED WOMEN.
WHAT ARE YOU SO TIRED FOR? YOU DIDN'T DO ANYTHING TODAY!!

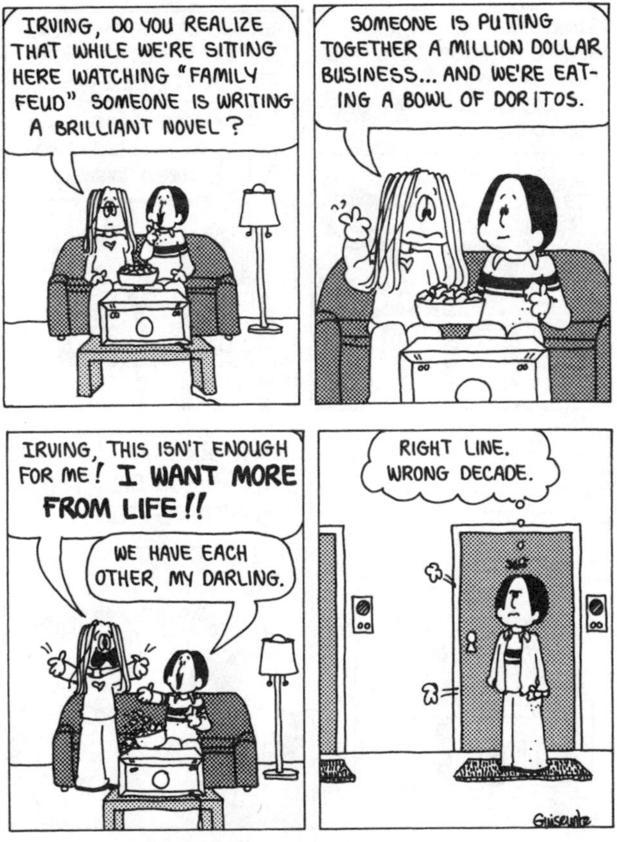
IRVING, DO YOU REALIZE THAT WHILE WE'RE SITTING HERE WATCHING "FAMILY FEUD" SOMEONE IS WRITING A BRILLIANT NOVEL?
SOMEONE IS PUTTING TOGETHER A MILLION DOLLAR BUSINESS... AND WE'RE EATING A BOWL OF DORITOS.
IRVING, THIS ISN'T ENOUGH FOR ME! I WANT MORE FROM LIFE!!
WE HAVE EACH OTHER, MY DARLING.
RIGHT LINE. WRONG DECADE.
GUISEWITE

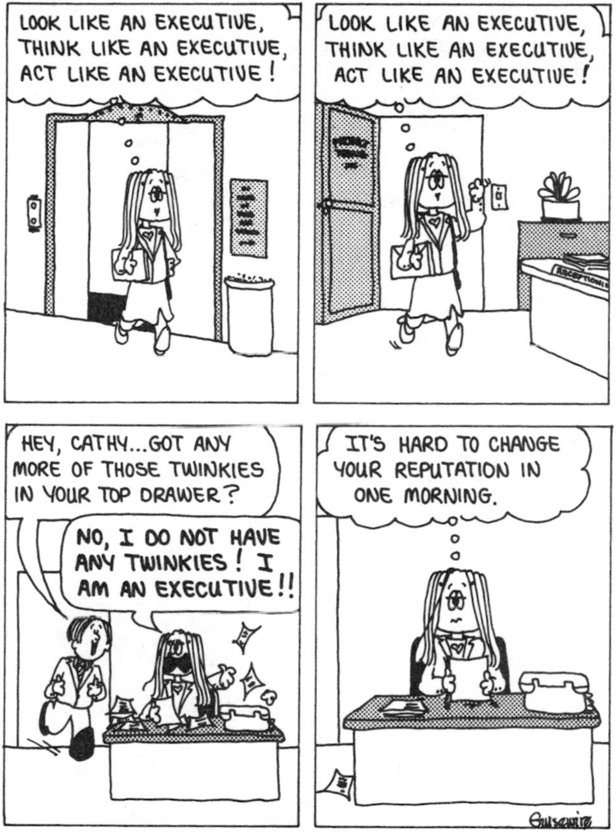
LOOK LIKE AN EXECUTIVE, THINK LIKE AN EXECUTIVE, ACT LIKE AN EXECUTIVE!
LOOK LIKE AN EXECUTIVE, THINK LIKE AN EXECUTIVE, ACT LIKE AN EXECUTIVE!
HEY, CATHY...GOT ANY MORE OF THOSE TWINKIES IN YOUR TOP DRAWER?
NO, I DO NOT HAVE ANY TWINKIES! I AM AN EXECUTIVE!!
IT'S HARD TO CHANGE YOUR REPUTATION IN ONE MORNING.
Guisewite

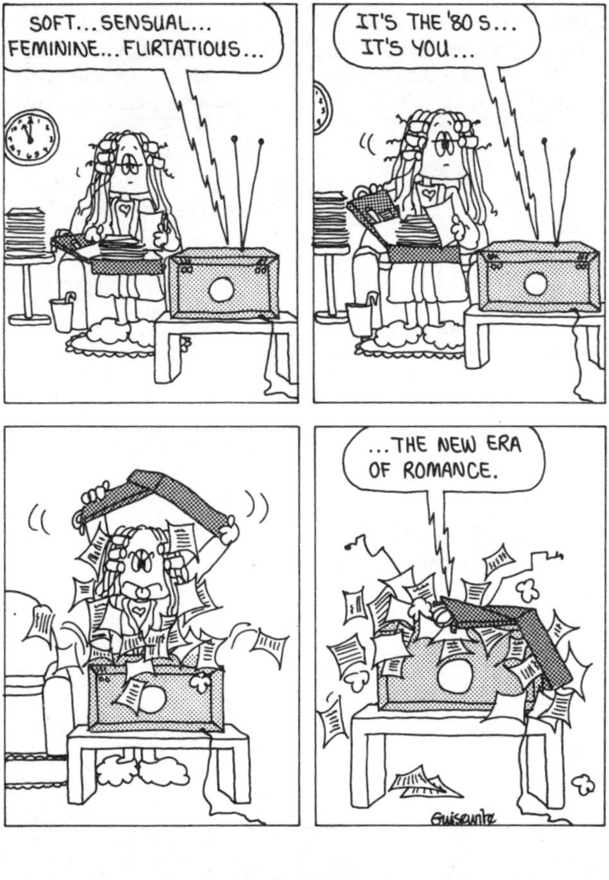
SOFT... SENSUAL... FEMININE... FLIRTATIOUS...
IT'S THE '80 S... IT'S YOU...
...THE NEW ERA OF ROMANCE.
Guisewite

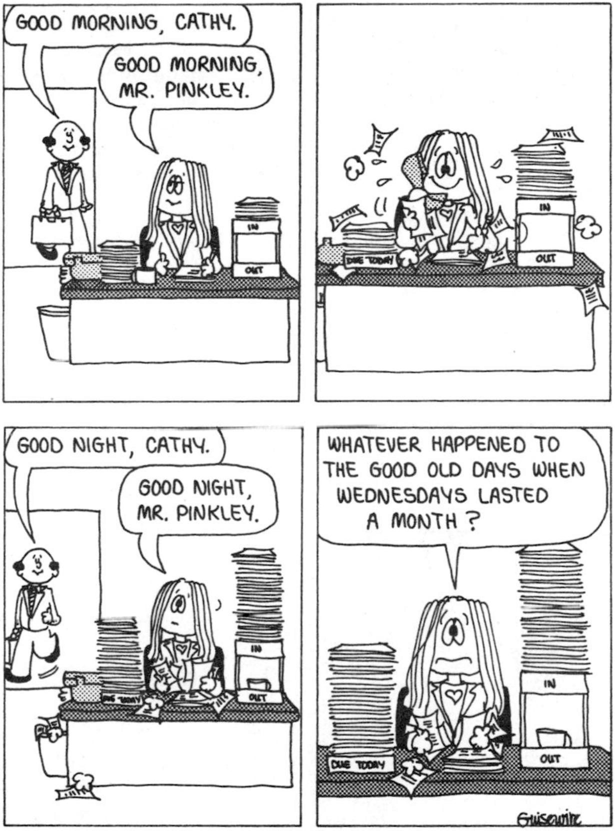
GOOD MORNING, CATHY.
GOOD MORNING, MR. PINKLEY.
IN
OUT
DUE TODAY
IN
OUT
GOOD NIGHT, CATHY.
GOOD NIGHT, MR. PINKLEY.
DUE TODAY
IN
OUT
WHATEVER HAPPENED TO THE GOOD OLD DAYS WHEN WEDNESDAYS LASTED A MONTH?
DUE TODAY
IN
OUT
Guisewite

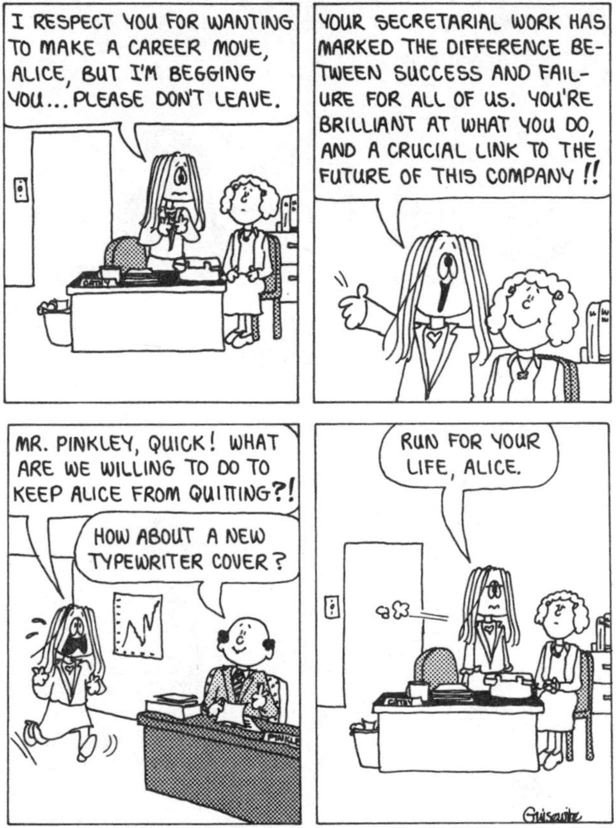
I RESPECT YOU FOR WANTING TO MAKE A CAREER MOVE, ALICE, BUT I'M BEGGING YOU... PLEASE DON'T LEAVE.
CATHY
YOUR SECRETARIAL WORK HAS MARKED THE DIFFERENCE BETWEEN SUCCESS AND FAILURE FOR ALL OF US. YOU'RE BRILLIANT AT WHAT YOU DO, AND A CRUCIAL LINK TO THE FUTURE OF THIS COMPANY!!
MR. PINKLEY, QUICK! WHAT ARE WE WILLING TO DO TO KEEP ALICE FROM QUITTING?!
HOW ABOUT A NEW TYPEWRITER COVER?
RUN FOR YOUR LIFE, ALICE.
CATHY
Guisewite

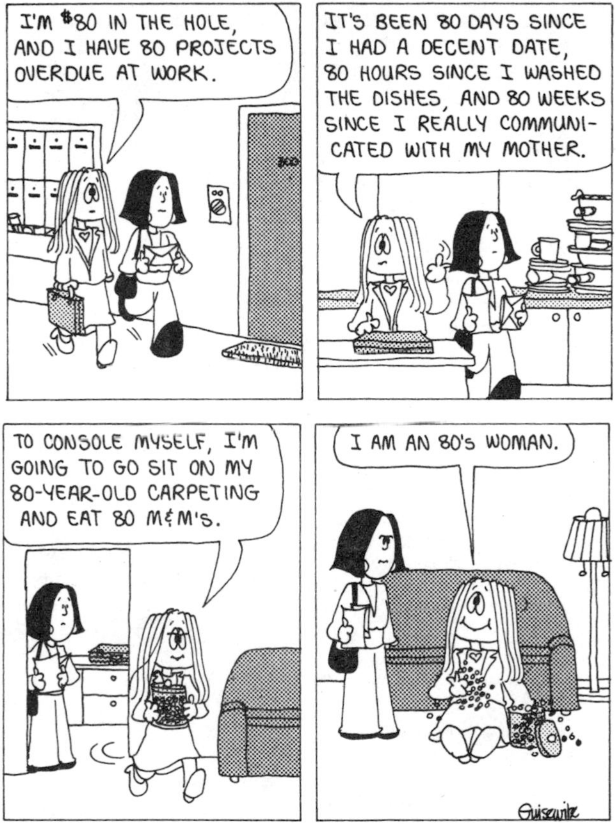
I'M $80 IN THE HOLE, AND I HAVE 80 PROJECTS OVERDUE AT WORK.
IT'S BEEN 80 DAYS SINCE I HAD A DECENT DATE, 80 HOURS SINCE I WASHED THE DISHES, AND 80 WEEKS SINCE I REALLY COMMUNICATED WITH MY MOTHER.
TO CONSOLE MYSELF, I'M GOING TO GO SIT ON MY 80-YEAR-OLD CARPETING AND EAT 80 M&M'S.
I AM AN 80's WOMAN.
Guisewite

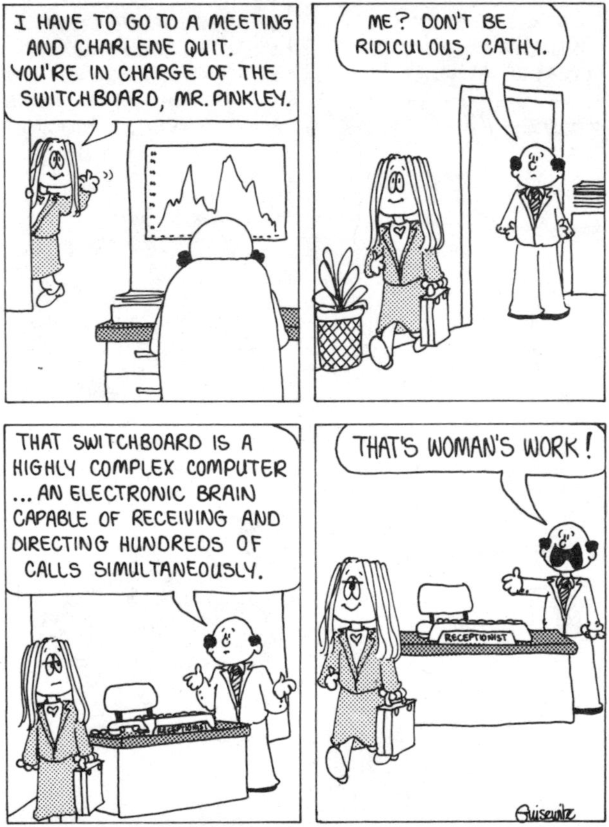
I HAVE TO GO TO A MEETING AND CHARLENE QUIT. YOU'RE IN CHARGE OF THE SWITCHBOARD, MR. PINKLEY.
ME? DON'T BE RIDICULOUS, CATHY.
THAT SWITCHBOARD IS A HIGHLY COMPLEX COMPUTER ... AN ELECTRONIC BRAIN CAPABLE OF RECEIVING AND DIRECTING HUNDREDS OF CALLS SIMULTANEOUSLY.
RECEPTIONIST
THAT'S WOMAN'S WORK!
RECEPTIONIST
Guisewite

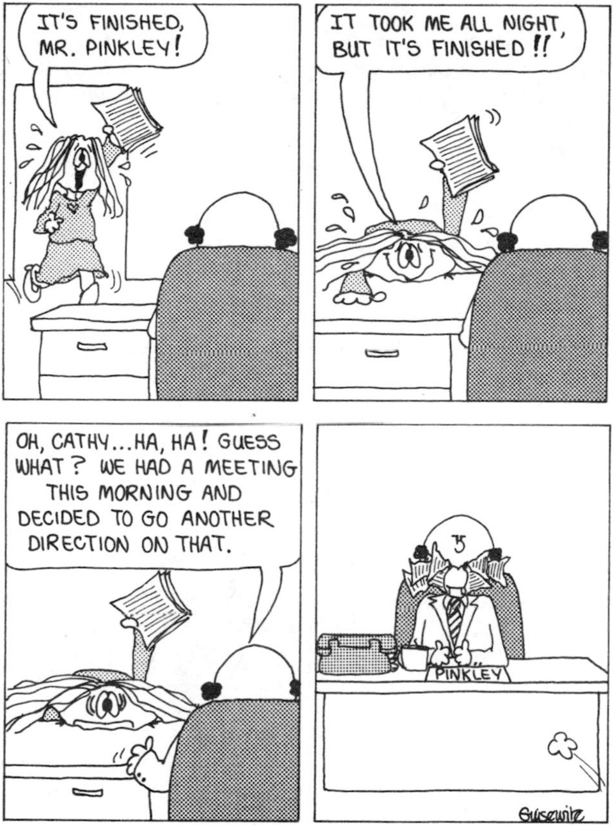
IT'S FINISHED, MR. PINKLEY!
IT TOOK ME ALL NIGHT, BUT IT'S FINISHED!!
OH, CATHY...HA, HA! GUESS WHAT? WE HAD A MEETING THIS MORNING AND DECIDED TO GO ANOTHER DIRECTION ON THAT.
PINKLEY
Guisewite

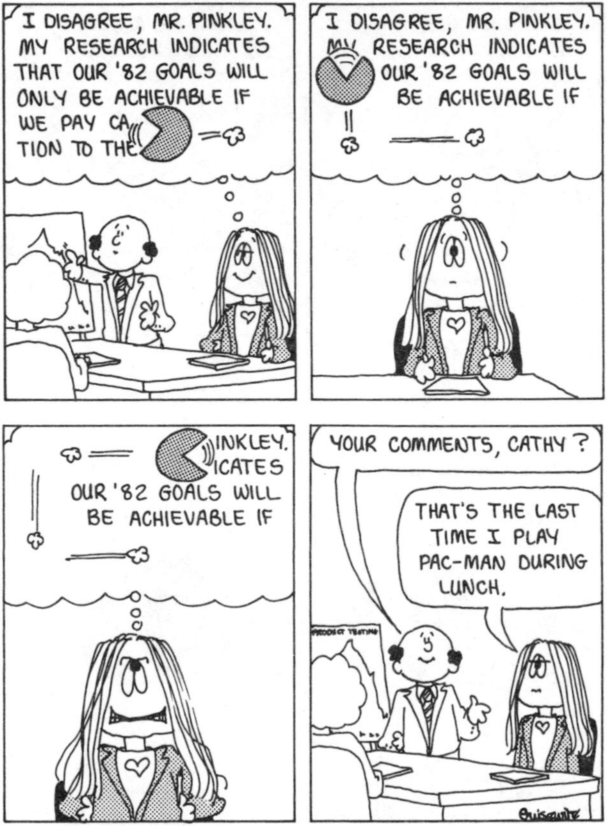
I DISAGREE, MR. PINKLEY. MY RESEARCH INDICATES THAT OUR '82 GOALS WILL ONLY BE ACHIEVABLE IF WE PAY CA TION TO THE
I DISAGREE, MR. PINKLEY. MY RESEARCH INDICATES OUR '82 GOALS WILL BE ACHIEVABLE IF
INKLEY. ICATES OUR '82 GOALS WILL BE ACHIEVABLE IF
YOUR COMMENTS, CATHY?
THAT'S THE LAST TIME I PLAY PAC-MAN DURING LUNCH.

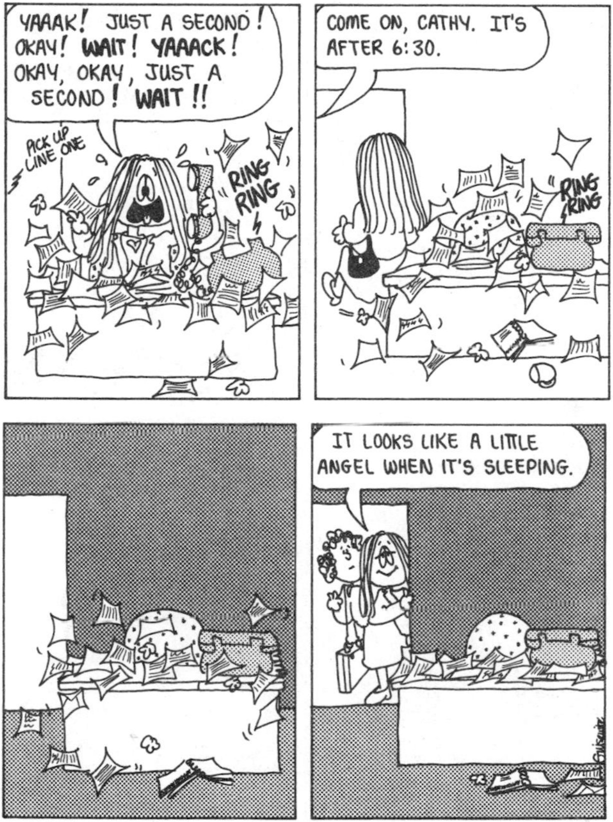
YAAAK! JUST A SECOND! OKAY! WAIT! YAAACK! OKAY, OKAY, JUST A SECOND! WAIT!!
PICK UP LINE ONE
RING RING
COME ON, CATHY. IT'S AFTER 6:30.
RING RING
IT LOOKS LIKE A LITTLE ANGEL WHEN IT'S SLEEPING.

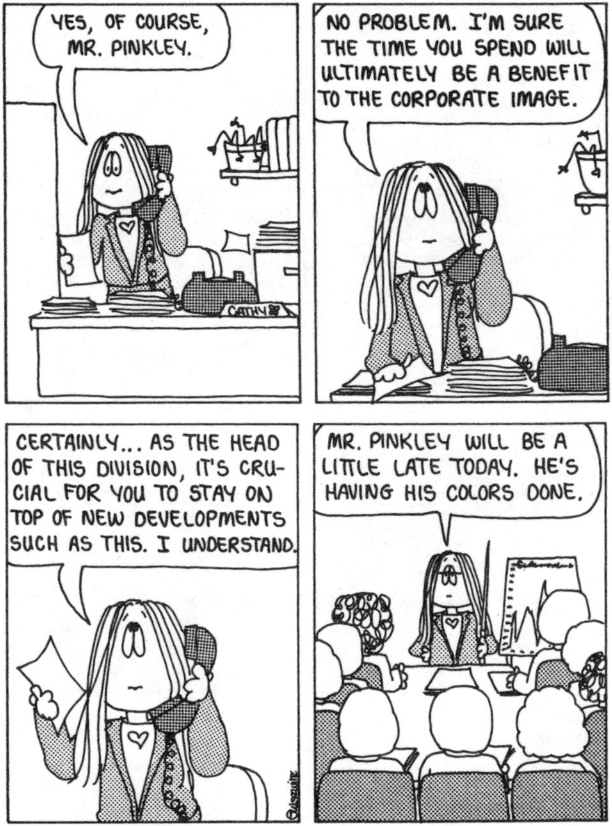

YES, OF COURSE, MR. PINKLEY.
CATHY
NO PROBLEM. I'M SURE THE TIME YOU SPEND WILL ULTIMATELY BE A BENEFIT TO THE CORPORATE IMAGE.
CERTAINLY... AS THE HEAD OF THIS DIVISION, IT'S CRUCIAL FOR YOU TO STAY ON TOP OF NEW DEVELOPMENTS SUCH AS THIS. I UNDERSTAND.
MR. PINKLEY WILL BE A LITTLE LATE TODAY. HE'S HAVING HIS COLORS DONE.

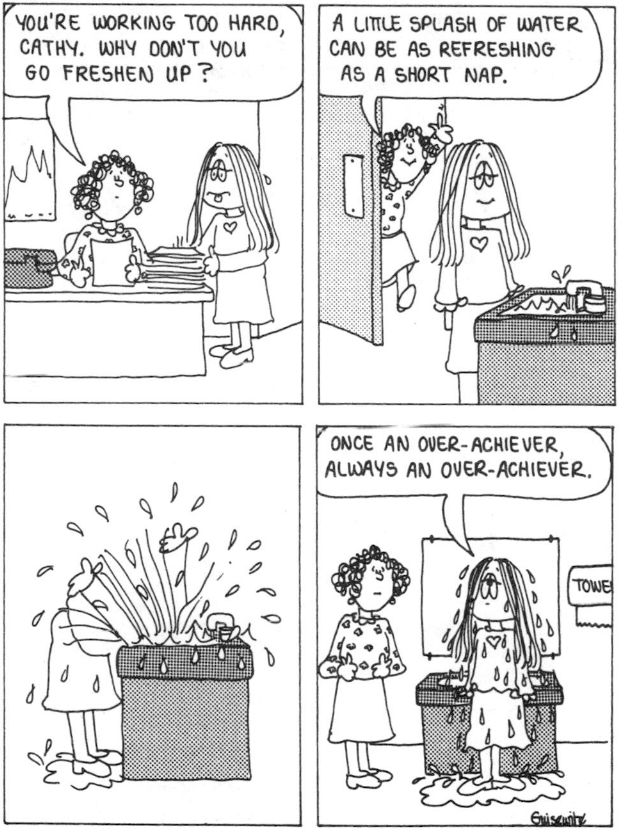
YOU'RE WORKING TOO HARD, CATHY. WHY DON'T YOU GO FRESHEN UP?
A LITTLE SPLASH OF WATER CAN BE AS REFRESHING AS A SHORT NAP.
ONCE AN OVER-ACHIEVER, ALWAYS AN OVER-ACHIEVER.
TOWE
Guisewite

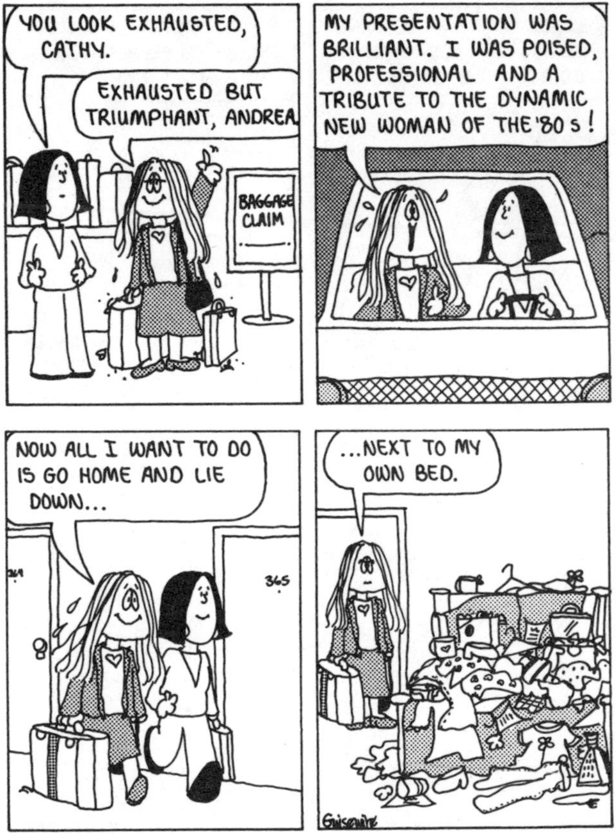
YOU LOOK EXHAUSTED, CATHY.
EXHAUSTED BUT TRIUMPHANT, ANDREA.
BAGGAGE CLAIM
MY PRESENTATION WAS BRILLIANT. I WAS POISED, PROFESSIONAL AND A TRIBUTE TO THE DYNAMIC NEW WOMAN OF THE '80s!
NOW ALL I WANT TO DO IS GO HOME AND LIE DOWN...
365
...NEXT TO MY OWN BED.
Guisewite

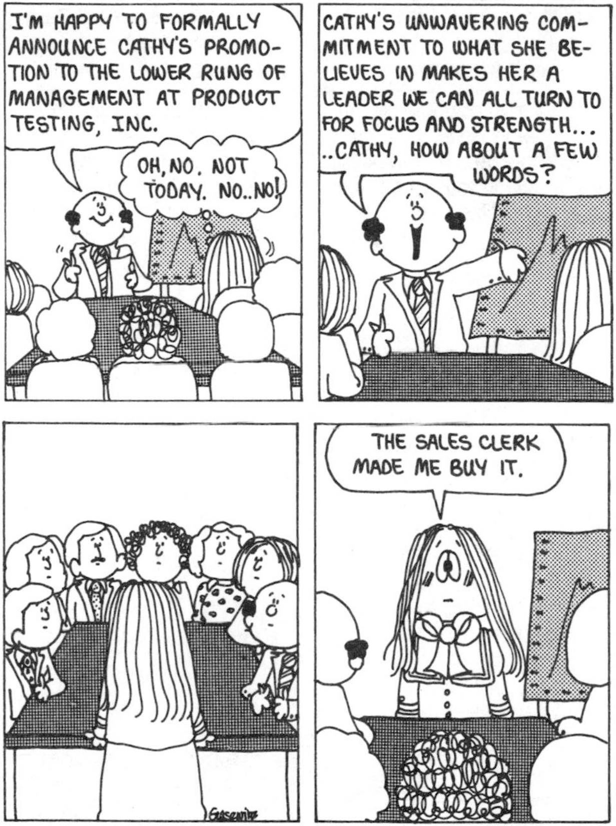
I'M HAPPY TO FORMALLY ANNOUNCE CATHY'S PROMOTION TO THE LOWER RUNG OF MANAGEMENT AT PRODUCT TESTING, INC.
OH, NO. NOT TODAY. NO..NO!
CATHY'S UNWAVERING COMMITMENT TO WHAT SHE BELIEVES IN MAKES HER A LEADER WE CAN ALL TURN TO FOR FOCUS AND STRENGTH...
..CATHY, HOW ABOUT A FEW WORDS?
THE SALES CLERK MADE ME BUY IT.

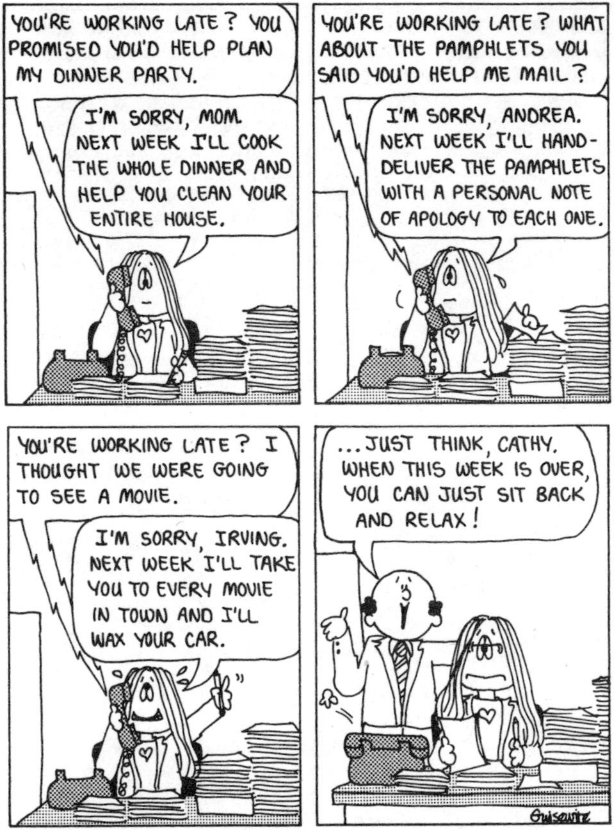
YOU'RE WORKING LATE? YOU PROMISED YOU'D HELP PLAN MY DINNER PARTY.
I'M SORRY, MOM. NEXT WEEK I'LL COOK THE WHOLE DINNER AND HELP YOU CLEAN YOUR ENTIRE HOUSE.
YOU'RE WORKING LATE? WHAT ABOUT THE PAMPHLETS YOU SAID YOU'D HELP ME MAIL?
I'M SORRY, ANDREA. NEXT WEEK I'LL HAND-DELIVER THE PAMPHLETS WITH A PERSONAL NOTE OF APOLOGY TO EACH ONE.
YOU'RE WORKING LATE? I THOUGHT WE WERE GOING TO SEE A MOVIE.
I'M SORRY, IRVING. NEXT WEEK I'LL TAKE YOU TO EVERY MOVIE IN TOWN AND I'LL WAX YOUR CAR.
...JUST THINK, CATHY. WHEN THIS WEEK IS OVER, YOU CAN JUST SIT BACK AND RELAX!
Guisewite

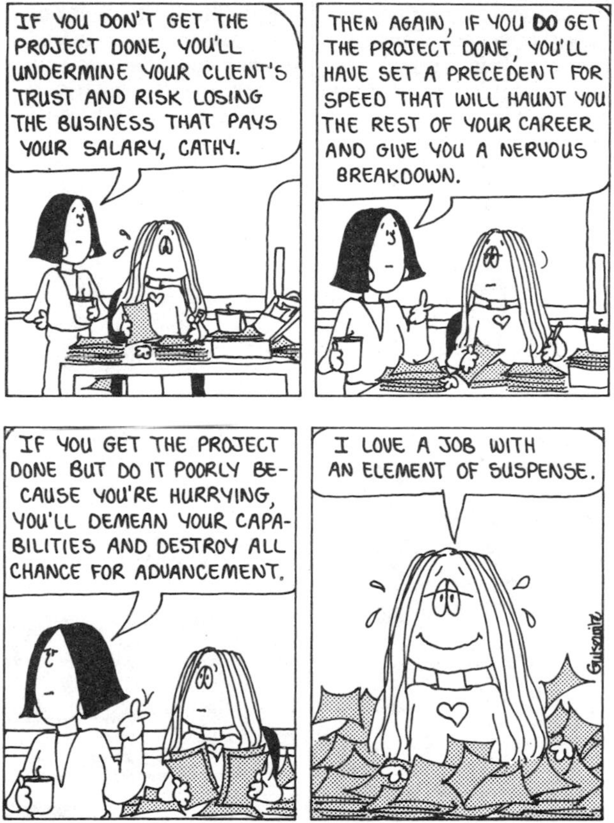
IF YOU DON'T GET THE PROJECT DONE, YOU'LL UNDERMINE YOUR CLIENT'S TRUST AND RISK LOSING THE BUSINESS THAT PAYS YOUR SALARY, CATHY.
THEN AGAIN, IF YOU **DO** GET THE PROJECT DONE, YOU'LL HAVE SET A PRECEDENT FOR SPEED THAT WILL HAUNT YOU THE REST OF YOUR CAREER AND GIVE YOU A NERVOUS BREAKDOWN.
IF YOU GET THE PROJECT DONE BUT DO IT POORLY BE-CAUSE YOU'RE HURRYING, YOU'LL DEMEAN YOUR CAPA-BILITIES AND DESTROY ALL CHANCE FOR ADVANCEMENT.
I LOVE A JOB WITH AN ELEMENT OF SUSPENSE.
Guisewite

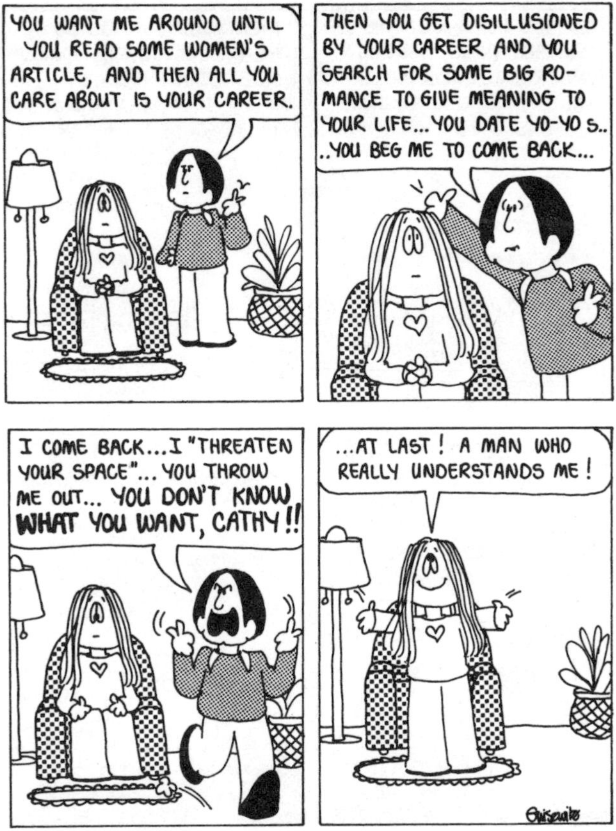
YOU WANT ME AROUND UNTIL YOU READ SOME WOMEN'S ARTICLE, AND THEN ALL YOU CARE ABOUT IS YOUR CAREER.
THEN YOU GET DISILLUSIONED BY YOUR CAREER AND YOU SEARCH FOR SOME BIG RO- MANCE TO GIVE MEANING TO YOUR LIFE... YOU DATE YO-YO S.. ..YOU BEG ME TO COME BACK...
I COME BACK... I "THREATEN YOUR SPACE"... YOU THROW ME OUT... YOU DON'T KNOW WHAT YOU WANT, CATHY!!
...AT LAST! A MAN WHO REALLY UNDERSTANDS ME!
Guisewite

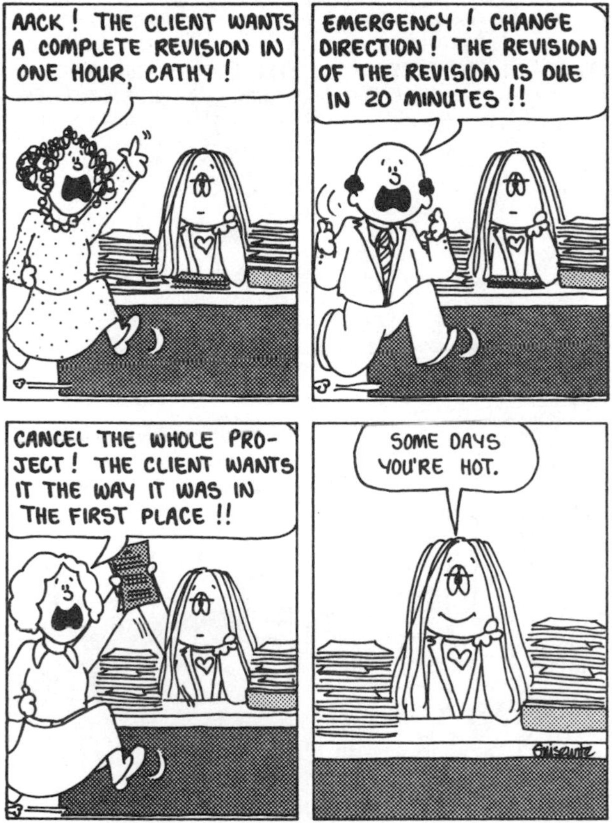
AACK ! THE CLIENT WANTS A COMPLETE REVISION IN ONE HOUR, CATHY !
EMERGENCY ! CHANGE DIRECTION ! THE REVISION OF THE REVISION IS DUE IN 20 MINUTES !!
CANCEL THE WHOLE PROJECT ! THE CLIENT WANTS IT THE WAY IT WAS IN THE FIRST PLACE !!
SOME DAYS YOU'RE HOT.

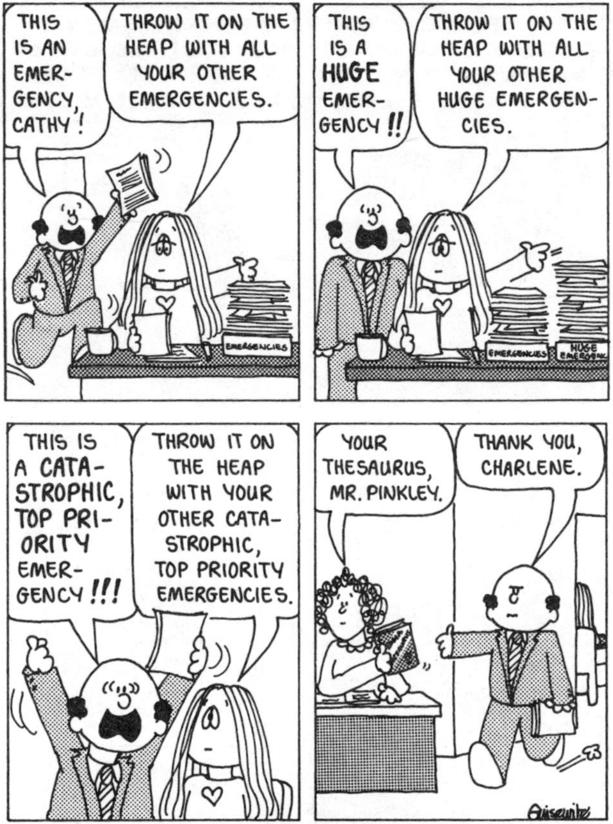
THIS IS AN EMERGENCY, CATHY!
THROW IT ON THE HEAP WITH ALL YOUR OTHER EMERGENCIES.
THIS IS A HUGE EMERGENCY!!
THROW IT ON THE HEAP WITH ALL YOUR OTHER HUGE EMERGENCIES.
THIS IS A CATASTROPHIC, TOP PRIORITY EMERGENCY!!!
THROW IT ON THE HEAP WITH YOUR OTHER CATASTROPHIC, TOP PRIORITY EMERGENCIES.
YOUR THESAURUS, MR. PINKLEY.
THANK YOU, CHARLENE.

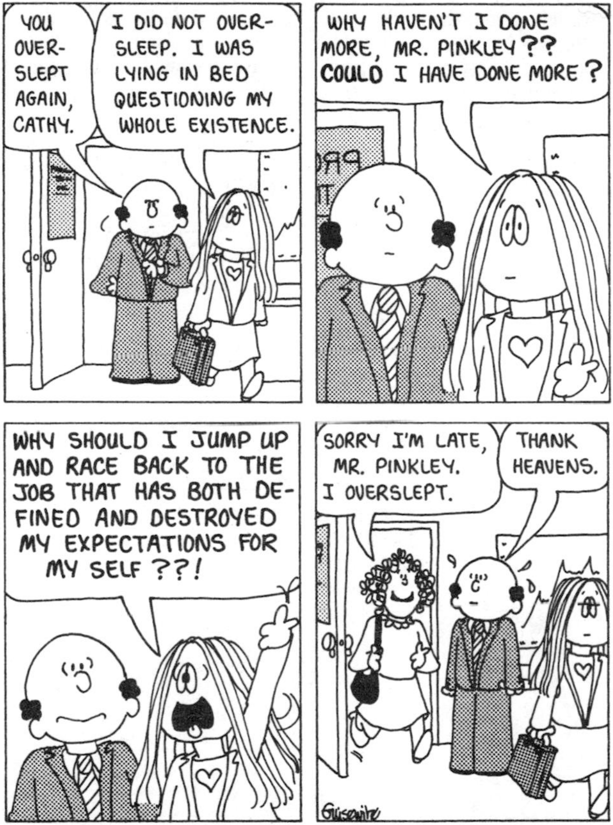
YOU OVER-SLEPT AGAIN, CATHY.
I DID NOT OVER-SLEEP. I WAS LYING IN BED QUESTIONING MY WHOLE EXISTENCE.
WHY HAVEN'T I DONE MORE, MR. PINKLEY?? COULD I HAVE DONE MORE?
WHY SHOULD I JUMP UP AND RACE BACK TO THE JOB THAT HAS BOTH DE-FINED AND DESTROYED MY EXPECTATIONS FOR MY SELF??!
SORRY I'M LATE, MR. PINKLEY. I OVERSLEPT.
THANK HEAVENS.
Guisewite

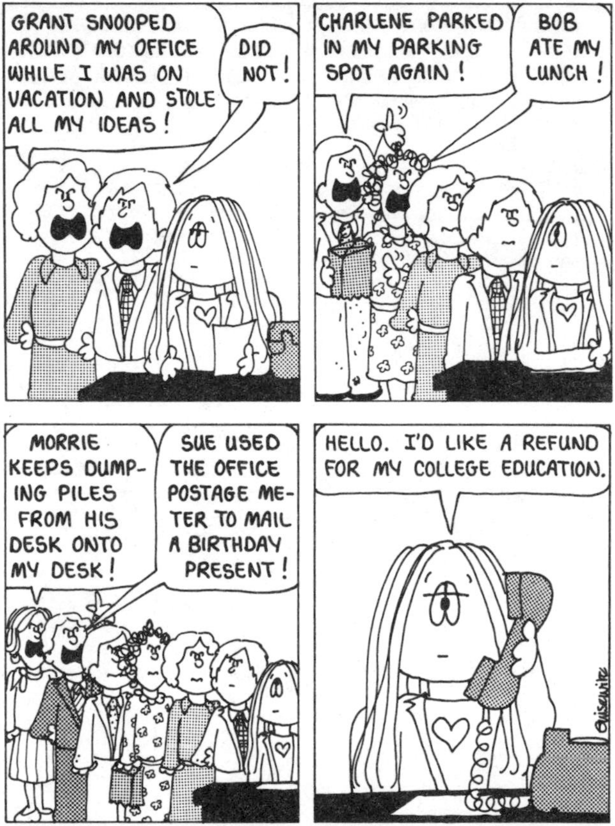
GRANT SNOOPED AROUND MY OFFICE WHILE I WAS ON VACATION AND STOLE ALL MY IDEAS!
DID NOT!
CHARLENE PARKED IN MY PARKING SPOT AGAIN!
BOB ATE MY LUNCH!
MORRIE KEEPS DUMPING PILES FROM HIS DESK ONTO MY DESK!
SUE USED THE OFFICE POSTAGE METER TO MAIL A BIRTHDAY PRESENT!
HELLO. I'D LIKE A REFUND FOR MY COLLEGE EDUCATION.
Guisewite

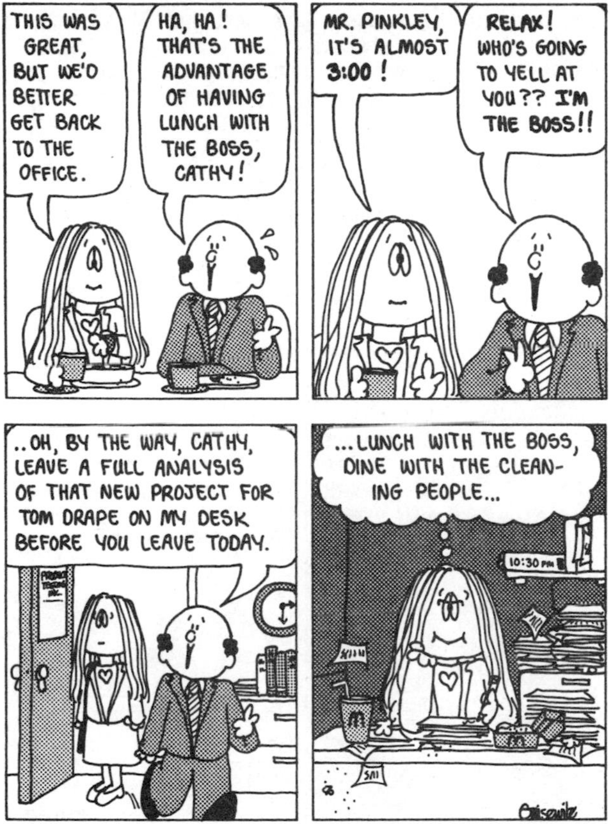
THIS WAS GREAT, BUT WE'D BETTER GET BACK TO THE OFFICE.
HA, HA! THAT'S THE ADVANTAGE OF HAVING LUNCH WITH THE BOSS, CATHY!
MR. PINKLEY, IT'S ALMOST 3:00!
RELAX! WHO'S GOING TO YELL AT YOU?? I'M THE BOSS!!
..OH, BY THE WAY, CATHY, LEAVE A FULL ANALYSIS OF THAT NEW PROJECT FOR TOM DRAPE ON MY DESK BEFORE YOU LEAVE TODAY.
...LUNCH WITH THE BOSS, DINE WITH THE CLEANING PEOPLE...
10:30 PM
Guisewite

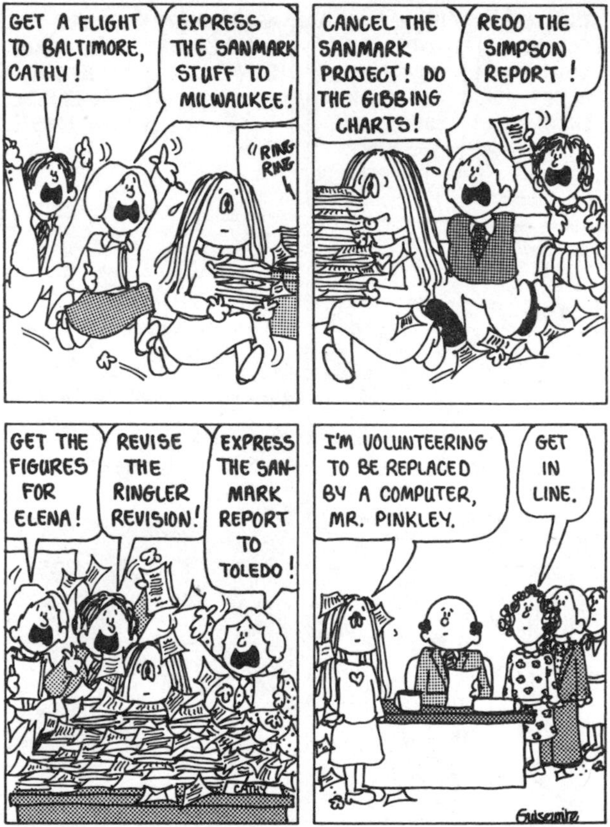
GET A FLIGHT TO BALTIMORE, CATHY!
EXPRESS THE SANMARK STUFF TO MILWAUKEE!
"RING RING
CANCEL THE SANMARK PROJECT! DO THE GIBBING CHARTS!
REDO THE SIMPSON REPORT!
GET THE FIGURES FOR ELENA!
REVISE THE RINGLER REVISION!
EXPRESS THE SAN-MARK REPORT TO TOLEDO!
CATHY
I'M VOLUNTEERING TO BE REPLACED BY A COMPUTER, MR. PINKLEY.
GET IN LINE.
Guisewite

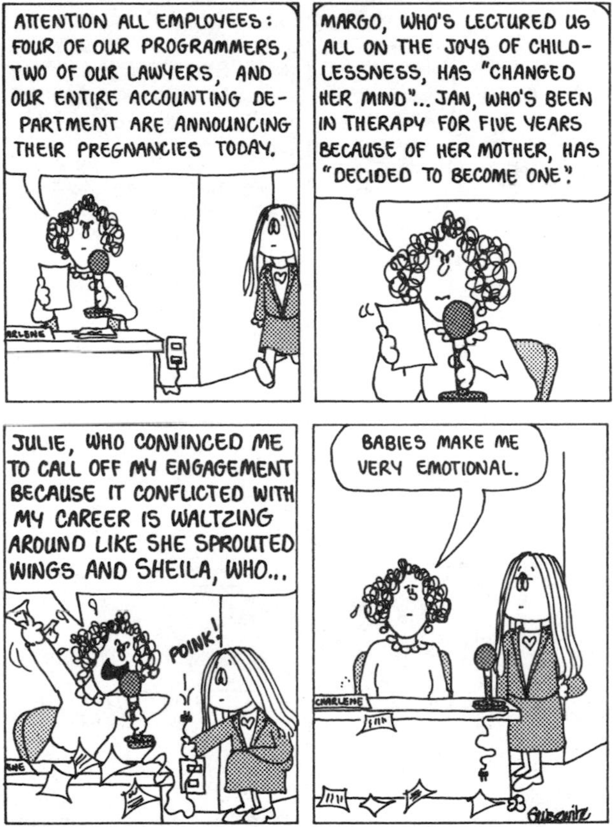
ATTENTION ALL EMPLOYEES: FOUR OF OUR PROGRAMMERS, TWO OF OUR LAWYERS, AND OUR ENTIRE ACCOUNTING DE-PARTMENT ARE ANNOUNCING THEIR PREGNANCIES TODAY.
MARGO, WHO'S LECTURED US ALL ON THE JOYS OF CHILD-LESSNESS, HAS "CHANGED HER MIND"... JAN, WHO'S BEEN IN THERAPY FOR FIVE YEARS BECAUSE OF HER MOTHER, HAS "DECIDED TO BECOME ONE."
JULIE, WHO CONVINCED ME TO CALL OFF MY ENGAGEMENT BECAUSE IT CONFLICTED WITH MY CAREER IS WALTZING AROUND LIKE SHE SPROUTED WINGS AND SHEILA, WHO...
POINK!
BABIES MAKE ME VERY EMOTIONAL.
CHARLENE
Guisewite

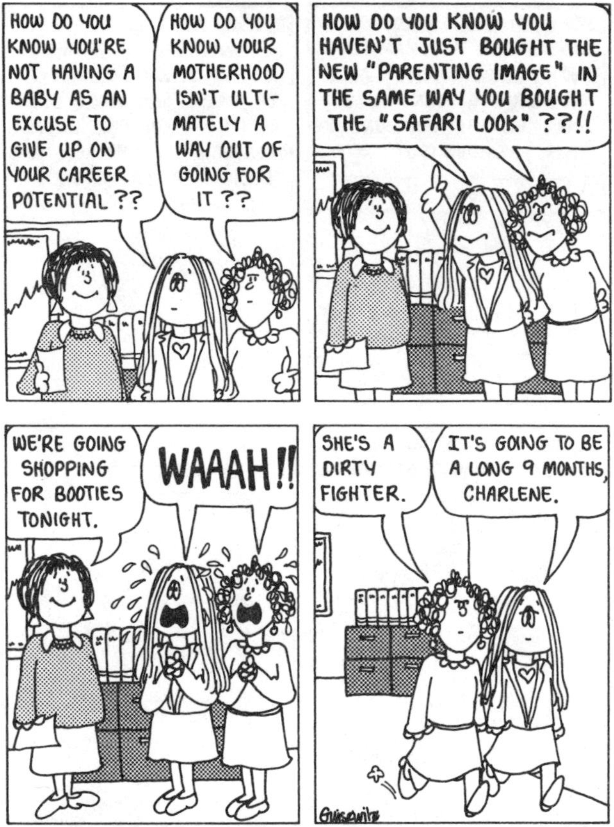
HOW DO YOU KNOW YOU'RE NOT HAVING A BABY AS AN EXCUSE TO GIVE UP ON YOUR CAREER POTENTIAL??
HOW DO YOU KNOW YOUR MOTHERHOOD ISN'T ULTI-MATELY A WAY OUT OF GOING FOR IT??
HOW DO YOU KNOW YOU HAVEN'T JUST BOUGHT THE NEW "PARENTING IMAGE" IN THE SAME WAY YOU BOUGHT THE "SAFARI LOOK"??!!
WE'RE GOING SHOPPING FOR BOOTIES TONIGHT.
WAAAH!!
SHE'S A DIRTY FIGHTER.
IT'S GOING TO BE A LONG 9 MONTHS, CHARLENE.

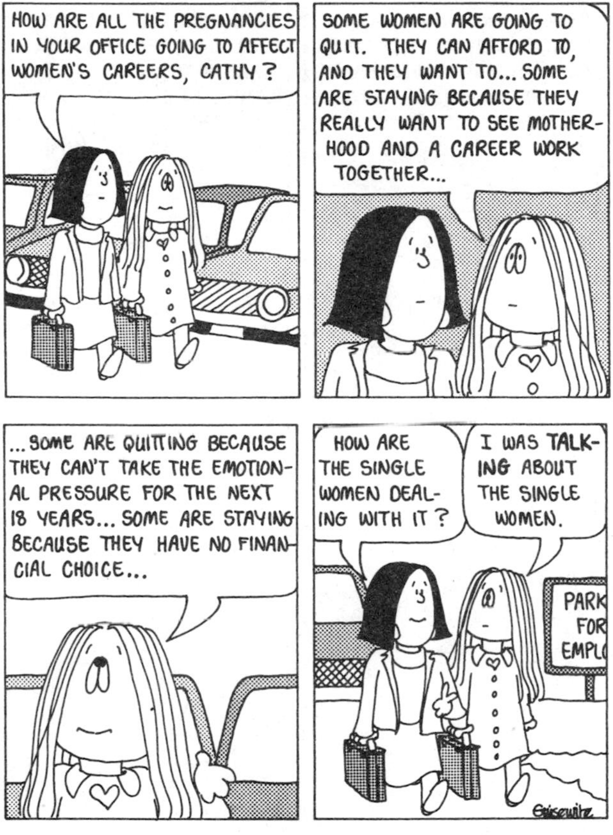
HOW ARE ALL THE PREGNANCIES IN YOUR OFFICE GOING TO AFFECT WOMEN'S CAREERS, CATHY?
SOME WOMEN ARE GOING TO QUIT. THEY CAN AFFORD TO, AND THEY WANT TO... SOME ARE STAYING BECAUSE THEY REALLY WANT TO SEE MOTHERHOOD AND A CAREER WORK TOGETHER...
...SOME ARE QUITTING BECAUSE THEY CAN'T TAKE THE EMOTIONAL PRESSURE FOR THE NEXT 18 YEARS... SOME ARE STAYING BECAUSE THEY HAVE NO FINANCIAL CHOICE...
HOW ARE THE SINGLE WOMEN DEALING WITH IT?
I WAS TALKING ABOUT THE SINGLE WOMEN.
PARK
FOR
EMPL
Guisewite

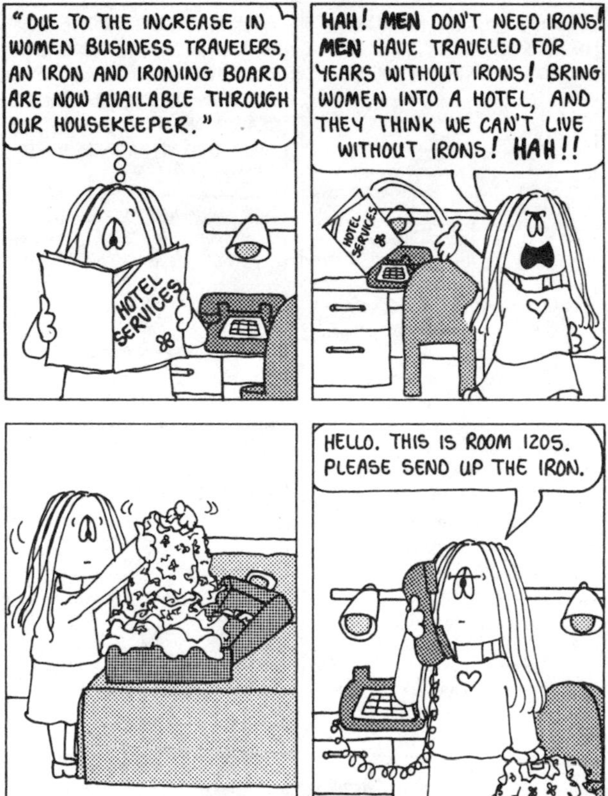
"DUE TO THE INCREASE IN WOMEN BUSINESS TRAVELERS, AN IRON AND IRONING BOARD ARE NOW AVAILABLE THROUGH OUR HOUSEKEEPER."
HOTEL SERVICES
HAH! MEN DON'T NEED IRONS! MEN HAVE TRAVELED FOR YEARS WITHOUT IRONS! BRING WOMEN INTO A HOTEL, AND THEY THINK WE CAN'T LIVE WITHOUT IRONS! HAH!!
HOTEL SERVICES
HELLO. THIS IS ROOM 1205. PLEASE SEND UP THE IRON.
Guisewite

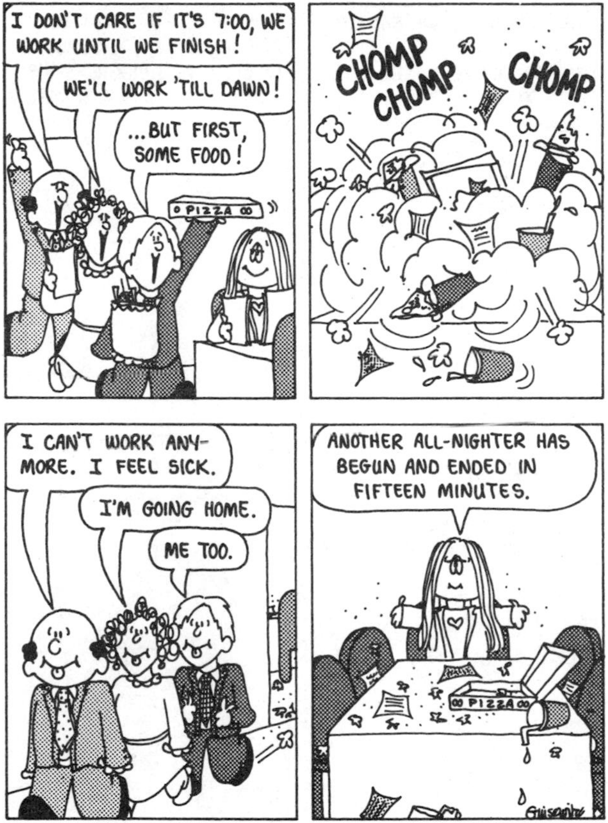
I DON'T CARE IF IT'S 7:00, WE WORK UNTIL WE FINISH!
WE'LL WORK 'TILL DAWN!
...BUT FIRST, SOME FOOD!
PIZZA
CHOMP
CHOMP
CHOMP
I CAN'T WORK ANY-MORE. I FEEL SICK.
I'M GOING HOME.
ME TOO.
ANOTHER ALL-NIGHTER HAS BEGUN AND ENDED IN FIFTEEN MINUTES.
PIZZA

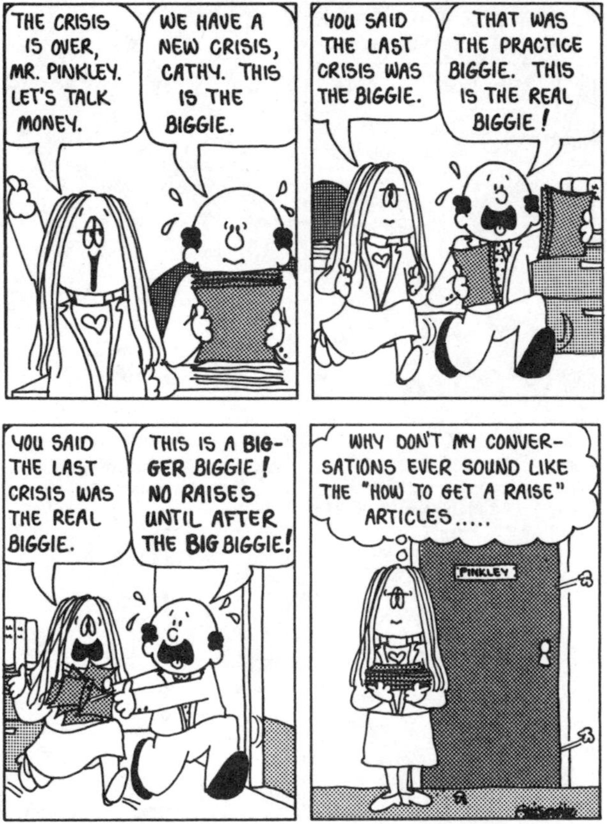
THE CRISIS IS OVER, MR. PINKLEY. LET'S TALK MONEY.
WE HAVE A NEW CRISIS, CATHY. THIS IS THE BIGGIE.
YOU SAID THE LAST CRISIS WAS THE BIGGIE.
THAT WAS THE PRACTICE BIGGIE. THIS IS THE REAL BIGGIE!
YOU SAID THE LAST CRISIS WAS THE REAL BIGGIE.
THIS IS A BIGGER BIGGIE! NO RAISES UNTIL AFTER THE BIG BIGGIE!
WHY DON'T MY CONVERSATIONS EVER SOUND LIKE THE "HOW TO GET A RAISE" ARTICLES.....
PINKLEY

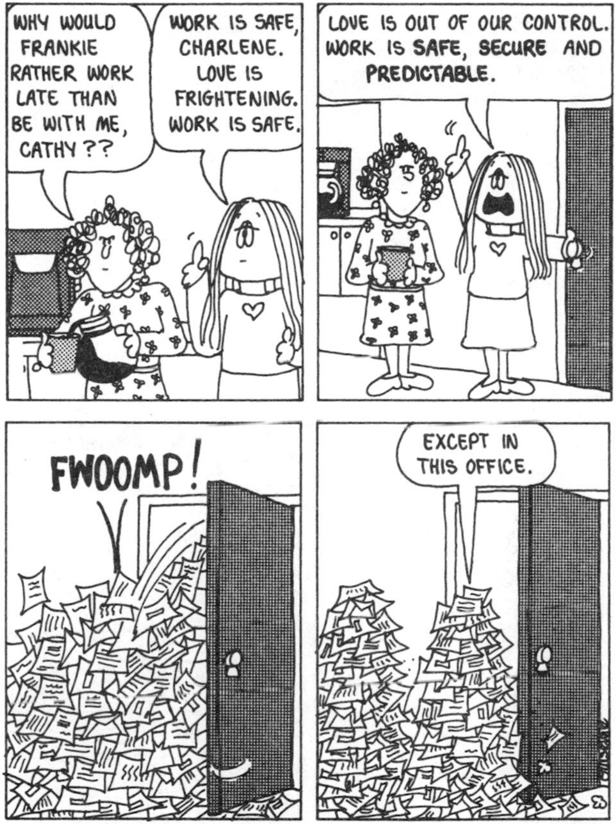
WHY WOULD FRANKIE RATHER WORK LATE THAN BE WITH ME, CATHY??
WORK IS SAFE, CHARLENE. LOVE IS FRIGHTENING. WORK IS SAFE.
LOVE IS OUT OF OUR CONTROL. WORK IS SAFE, SECURE AND PREDICTABLE.
FWOOMP!
EXCEPT IN THIS OFFICE.

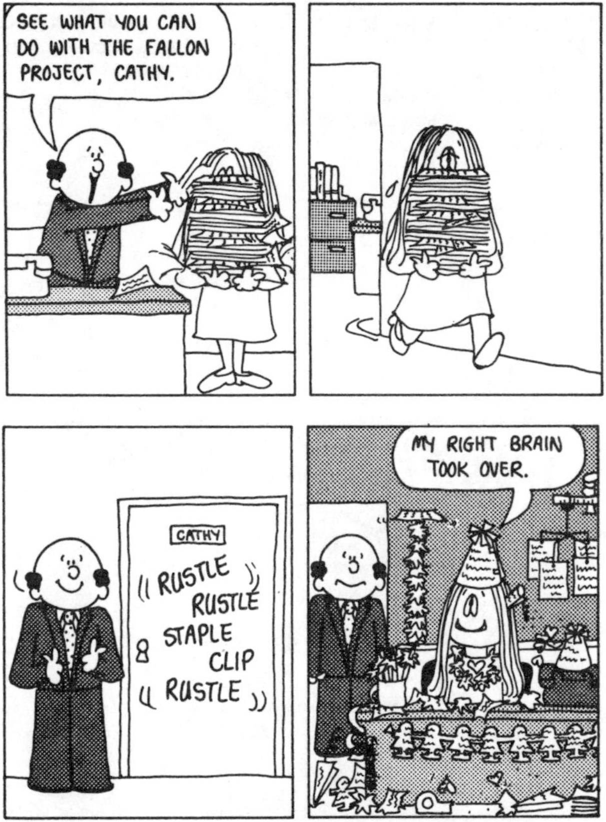
SEE WHAT YOU CAN DO WITH THE FALLON PROJECT, CATHY.
CATHY
RUSTLE RUSTLE STAPLE CLIP RUSTLE
MY RIGHT BRAIN TOOK OVER.

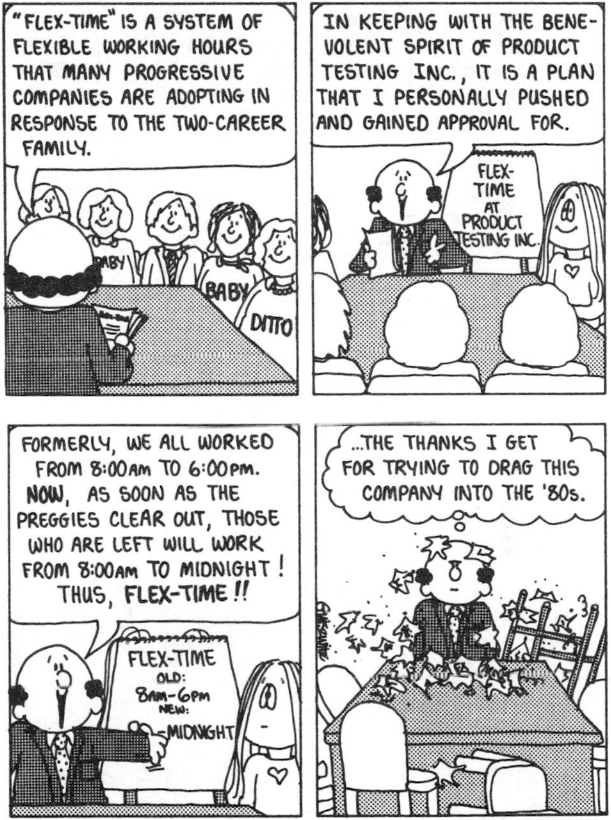
"FLEX-TIME" IS A SYSTEM OF FLEXIBLE WORKING HOURS THAT MANY PROGRESSIVE COMPANIES ARE ADOPTING IN RESPONSE TO THE TWO-CAREER FAMILY.
BABY
BABY
DITTO
IN KEEPING WITH THE BENEVOLENT SPIRIT OF PRODUCT TESTING INC., IT IS A PLAN THAT I PERSONALLY PUSHED AND GAINED APPROVAL FOR.
FLEX-TIME AT PRODUCT TESTING INC.
FORMERLY, WE ALL WORKED FROM 8:00AM TO 6:00PM. NOW, AS SOON AS THE PREGGIES CLEAR OUT, THOSE WHO ARE LEFT WILL WORK FROM 8:00AM TO MIDNIGHT! THUS, FLEX-TIME!!
FLEX-TIME
OLD:
8AM-6PM
NEW:
-MIDNIGHT
...THE THANKS I GET FOR TRYING TO DRAG THIS COMPANY INTO THE '80s.

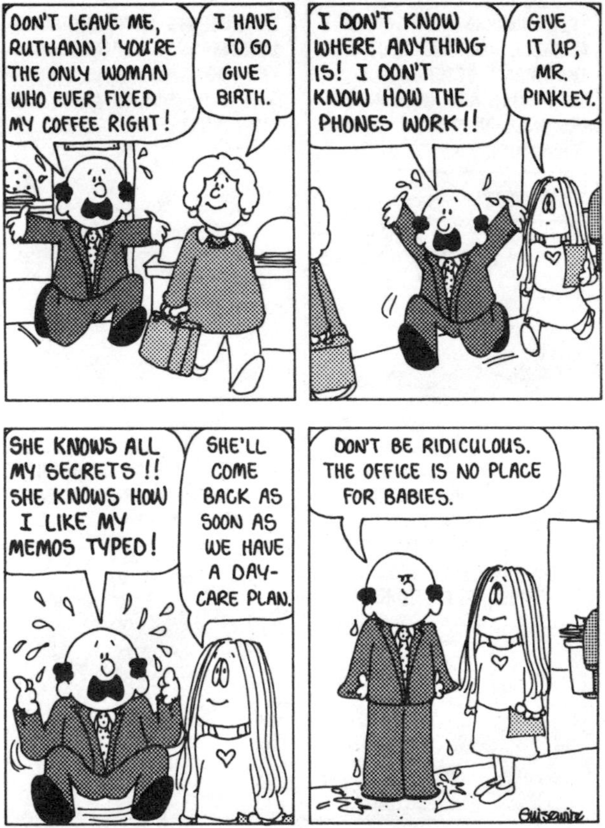
DON'T LEAVE ME, RUTHANN! YOU'RE THE ONLY WOMAN WHO EVER FIXED MY COFFEE RIGHT!
I HAVE TO GO GIVE BIRTH.
I DON'T KNOW WHERE ANYTHING IS! I DON'T KNOW HOW THE PHONES WORK!!
GIVE IT UP, MR. PINKLEY.
SHE KNOWS ALL MY SECRETS!! SHE KNOWS HOW I LIKE MY MEMOS TYPED!
SHE'LL COME BACK AS SOON AS WE HAVE A DAY-CARE PLAN.
DON'T BE RIDICULOUS. THE OFFICE IS NO PLACE FOR BABIES.
Guisewite

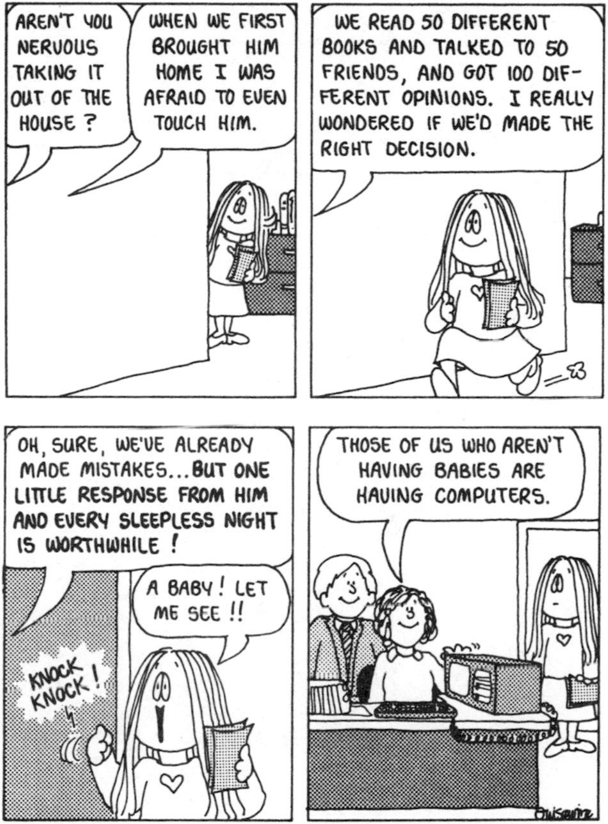

AREN'T YOU NERVOUS TAKING IT OUT OF THE HOUSE ?
WHEN WE FIRST BROUGHT HIM HOME I WAS AFRAID TO EVEN TOUCH HIM.
WE READ 50 DIFFERENT BOOKS AND TALKED TO 50 FRIENDS, AND GOT 100 DIFFERENT OPINIONS. I REALLY WONDERED IF WE'D MADE THE RIGHT DECISION.
OH, SURE, WE'VE ALREADY MADE MISTAKES...BUT ONE LITTLE RESPONSE FROM HIM AND EVERY SLEEPLESS NIGHT IS WORTHWHILE !
KNOCK KNOCK !
A BABY ! LET ME SEE !!
THOSE OF US WHO AREN'T HAVING BABIES ARE HAVING COMPUTERS.
GUISEWITE

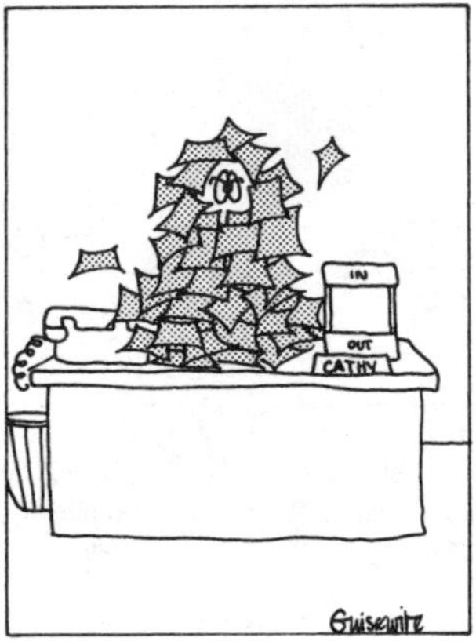
IN
OUT
CATHY
Guisewite

The Late '80s

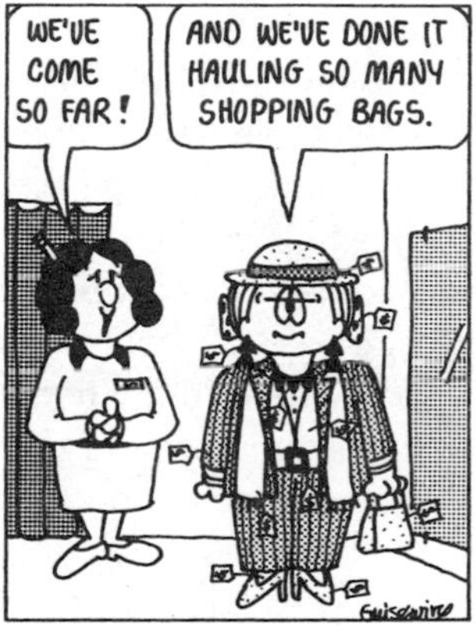
WE'VE COME SO FAR!
AND WE'VE DONE IT HAULING SO MANY SHOPPING BAGS.

In the late '80s, I came to think of corporate America as one great big salesclerk who had just convinced me to invest my life savings in the wrong outfit.

While I had "put off marriage and children to pursue my career," as instructed by page 243 of New Woman magazine, everyone else had snatched up all the single men and were starting families.

I had committed to massive obligations and endless deadlines, approximately five minutes before everyone decided to quit and become organic fruit farmers.

I had pointed myself down the career fast-track, fueled by 10 years of business-savvy seminars, self-help books, liberation manifestos, and a 12-hour workday schedule— only to learn that, somewhere in my heap of unread reading material was the article informing me that "we had decided to go a different direction on that."

I had sewn great big shoulder pads in my mental power suit the night before everyone showed up soft, feminine, and ready to flirt again.

In the late '80s, I had nine dates and accumulated 47,000 frequent-flier business travel miles.

The other problem many of us had was that we hadn't exactly amassed enough of a fortune during our self-absorbed workaholic years to be able to go into the new, "simple" life with the luxuries to which we now felt we were entitled.

I liked the idea of forsaking the stress-filled materialistic rat race for life in a cabin making inspirational greeting cards of pressed forest leaves, but by the late '80s, I also needed the cabin to have central air, cable TV, a Jacuzzi, a fax machine, and a gelato maker.

A lot of people hit the late '80s with a lifetime commitment to not much else besides paying off the credit cards, but women, especially, took the hit.

We had proven we could work just as obsessively as men, but we had nowhere near equal pay. We had all the big stress without the big titles. We were still having to prove we were serious without the perks, respect, or admission to the inner circle.

The only women close to breaking the glass ceiling were the ones who were threatening to throw their Windex bottles through it.

Single women who had put everything on hold for our careers—who had achieved massive new self-respect, confidence, and exhilarating financial freedom—were either learning to "downplay our success" so we weren't "intimidating" or "threatening" to men or else just giving up on them all in disgust and deciding to stay single by choice.

The more we were taken seriously in business, the less we were taken seriously as a date.

Career women who had become mothers had to face the shocking new challenge of trying to raise enlightened children in a country that simultaneously cheered the return to good, old-fashioned family values and made it impossible for a woman whose family depended on her income to keep her job.

By the end of the '80s, a lot of us looked in the mirror and had a new, weird feeling that we were wearing the wrong life.

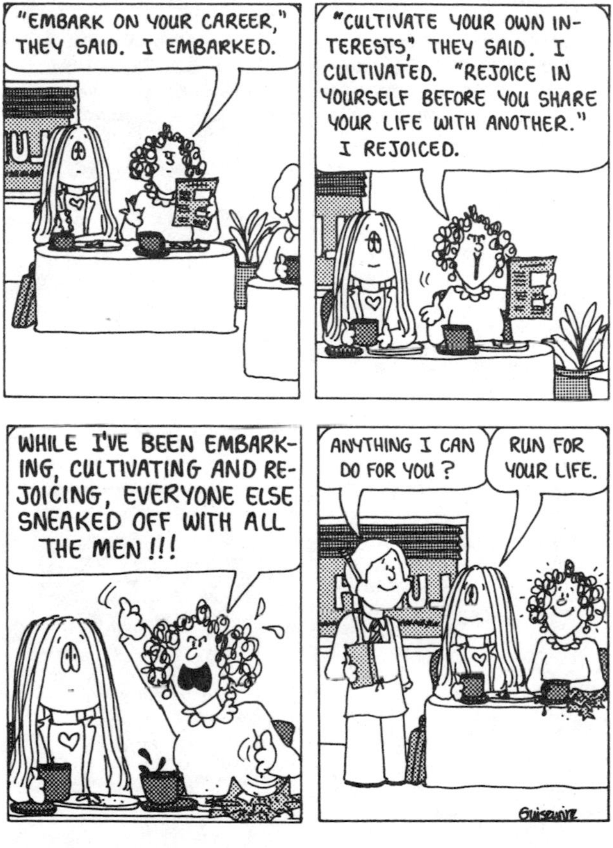
"EMBARK ON YOUR CAREER," THEY SAID. I EMBARKED.
"CULTIVATE YOUR OWN INTERESTS," THEY SAID. I CULTIVATED. "REJOICE IN YOURSELF BEFORE YOU SHARE YOUR LIFE WITH ANOTHER." I REJOICED.
WHILE I'VE BEEN EMBARKING, CULTIVATING AND REJOICING, EVERYONE ELSE SNEAKED OFF WITH ALL THE MEN!!!
ANYTHING I CAN DO FOR YOU?
RUN FOR YOUR LIFE.
Guisewite

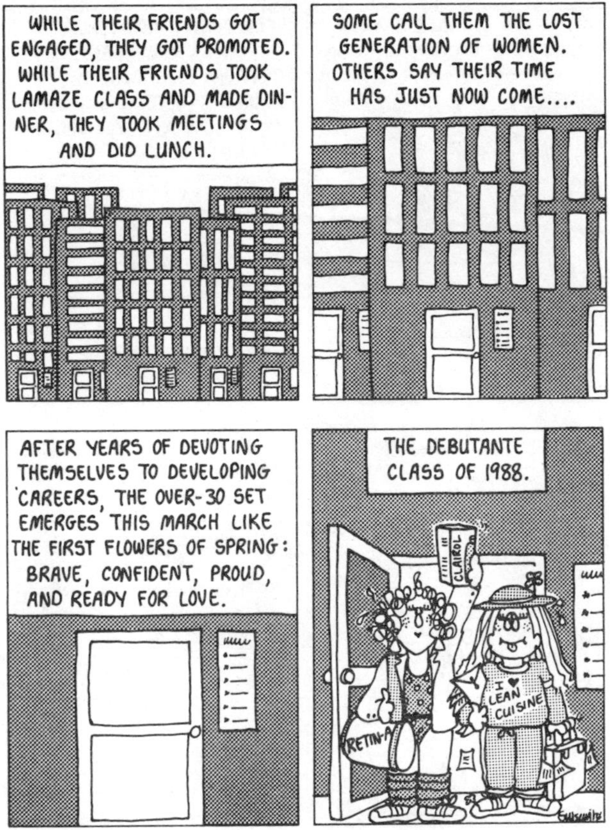
WHILE THEIR FRIENDS GOT ENGAGED, THEY GOT PROMOTED. WHILE THEIR FRIENDS TOOK LAMAZE CLASS AND MADE DINNER, THEY TOOK MEETINGS AND DID LUNCH.
SOME CALL THEM THE LOST GENERATION OF WOMEN. OTHERS SAY THEIR TIME HAS JUST NOW COME....
AFTER YEARS OF DEVOTING THEMSELVES TO DEVELOPING CAREERS, THE OVER-30 SET EMERGES THIS MARCH LIKE THE FIRST FLOWERS OF SPRING: BRAVE, CONFIDENT, PROUD, AND READY FOR LOVE.
THE DEBUTANTE CLASS OF 1988.
CLAIROL
RETIN-A
I ♥ LEAN CUISINE
Guisewite

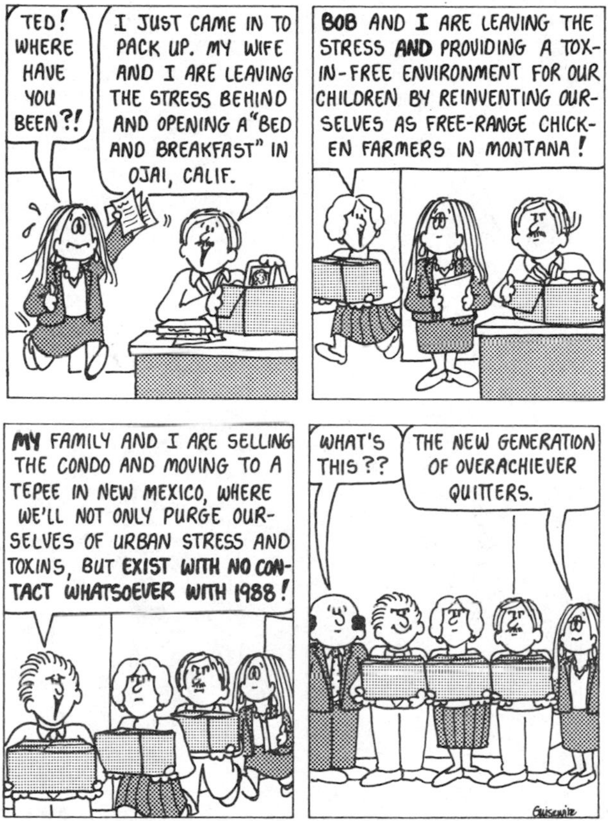
TED! WHERE HAVE YOU BEEN?!
I JUST CAME IN TO PACK UP. MY WIFE AND I ARE LEAVING THE STRESS BEHIND AND OPENING A "BED AND BREAKFAST" IN OJAI, CALIF.
BOB AND I ARE LEAVING THE STRESS AND PROVIDING A TOXIN-FREE ENVIRONMENT FOR OUR CHILDREN BY REINVENTING OURSELVES AS FREE-RANGE CHICKEN FARMERS IN MONTANA!
MY FAMILY AND I ARE SELLING THE CONDO AND MOVING TO A TEPEE IN NEW MEXICO, WHERE WE'LL NOT ONLY PURGE OURSELVES OF URBAN STRESS AND TOXINS, BUT EXIST WITH NO CONTACT WHATSOEVER WITH 1988!
WHAT'S THIS??
THE NEW GENERATION OF OVERACHIEVER QUITTERS.
Guisewite

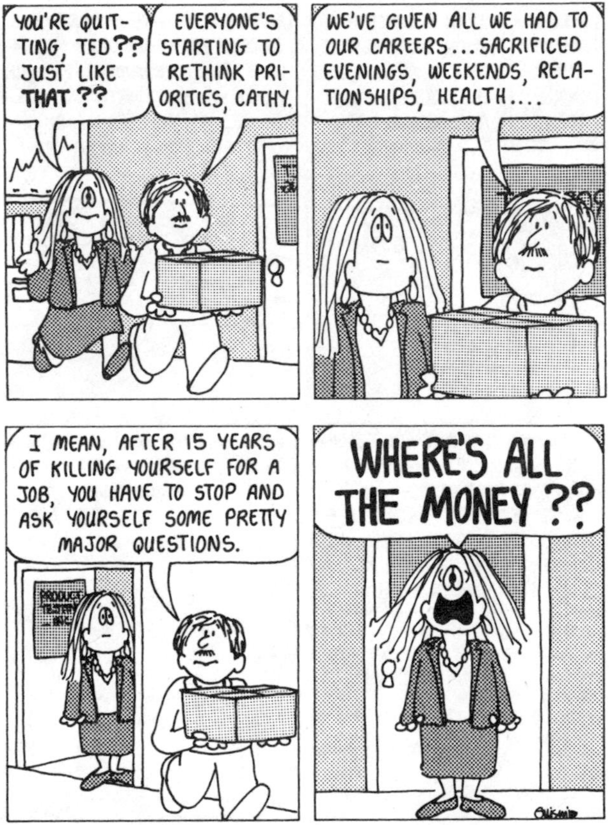
YOU'RE QUITTING, TED?? JUST LIKE THAT??
EVERYONE'S STARTING TO RETHINK PRIORITIES, CATHY.
WE'VE GIVEN ALL WE HAD TO OUR CAREERS... SACRIFICED EVENINGS, WEEKENDS, RELATIONSHIPS, HEALTH....
I MEAN, AFTER 15 YEARS OF KILLING YOURSELF FOR A JOB, YOU HAVE TO STOP AND ASK YOURSELF SOME PRETTY MAJOR QUESTIONS.
WHERE'S ALL THE MONEY??

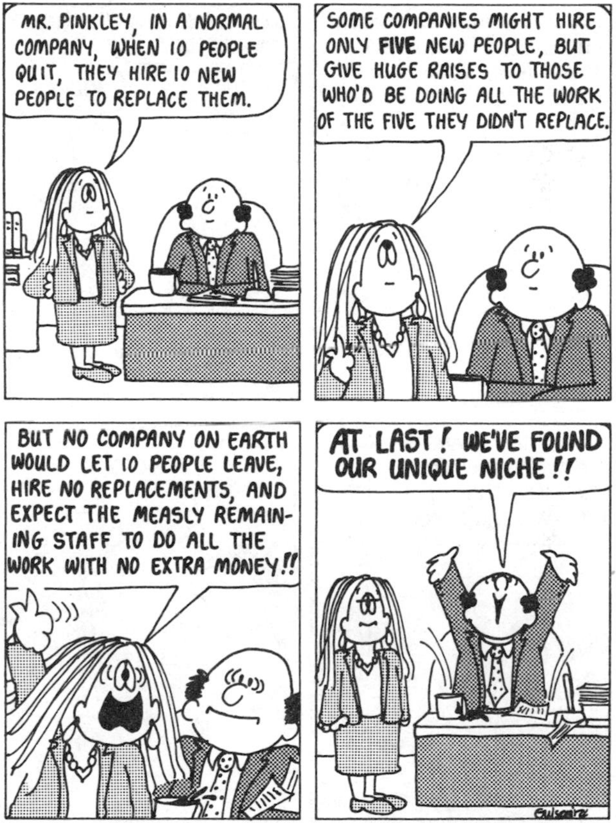
MR. PINKLEY, IN A NORMAL COMPANY, WHEN 10 PEOPLE QUIT, THEY HIRE 10 NEW PEOPLE TO REPLACE THEM.
SOME COMPANIES MIGHT HIRE ONLY FIVE NEW PEOPLE, BUT GIVE HUGE RAISES TO THOSE WHO'D BE DOING ALL THE WORK OF THE FIVE THEY DIDN'T REPLACE.
BUT NO COMPANY ON EARTH WOULD LET 10 PEOPLE LEAVE, HIRE NO REPLACEMENTS, AND EXPECT THE MEASLY REMAINING STAFF TO DO ALL THE WORK WITH NO EXTRA MONEY!!
AT LAST! WE'VE FOUND OUR UNIQUE NICHE!!

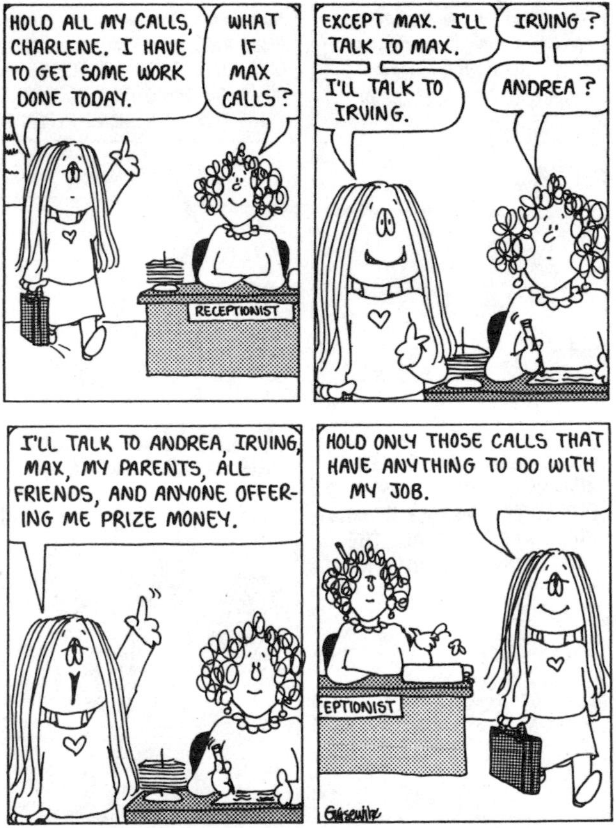
HOLD ALL MY CALLS, CHARLENE. I HAVE TO GET SOME WORK DONE TODAY.
WHAT IF MAX CALLS?
RECEPTIONIST
EXCEPT MAX. I'LL TALK TO MAX.
IRVING?
I'LL TALK TO IRVING.
ANDREA?
I'LL TALK TO ANDREA, IRVING, MAX, MY PARENTS, ALL FRIENDS, AND ANYONE OFFERING ME PRIZE MONEY.
HOLD ONLY THOSE CALLS THAT HAVE ANYTHING TO DO WITH MY JOB.
EPTIONIST

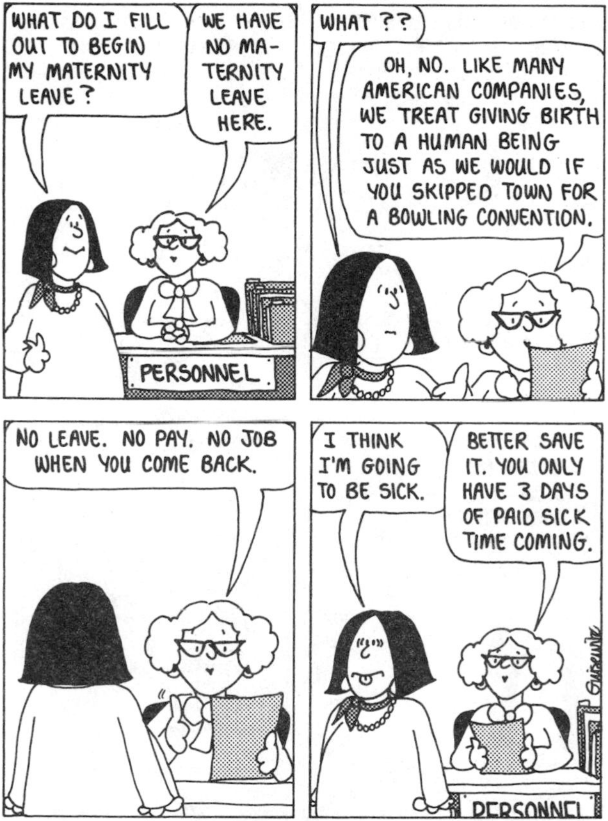
WHAT DO I FILL OUT TO BEGIN MY MATERNITY LEAVE?
WE HAVE NO MATERNITY LEAVE HERE.
PERSONNEL
WHAT??
OH, NO. LIKE MANY AMERICAN COMPANIES, WE TREAT GIVING BIRTH TO A HUMAN BEING JUST AS WE WOULD IF YOU SKIPPED TOWN FOR A BOWLING CONVENTION.
NO LEAVE. NO PAY. NO JOB WHEN YOU COME BACK.
I THINK I'M GOING TO BE SICK.
BETTER SAVE IT. YOU ONLY HAVE 3 DAYS OF PAID SICK TIME COMING.
GUISEWITE

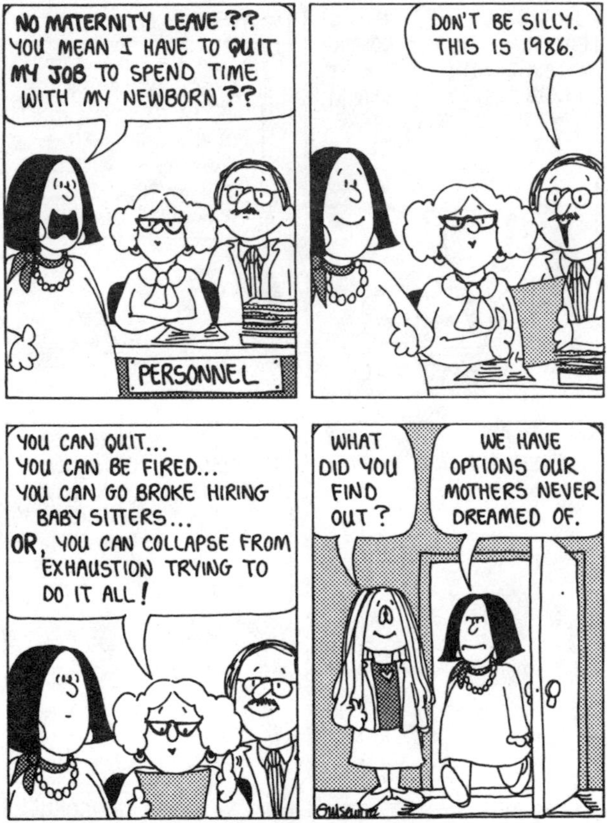
NO MATERNITY LEAVE ?? YOU MEAN I HAVE TO QUIT MY JOB TO SPEND TIME WITH MY NEWBORN ??
PERSONNEL
DON'T BE SILLY. THIS IS 1986.
YOU CAN QUIT... YOU CAN BE FIRED... YOU CAN GO BROKE HIRING BABY SITTERS... OR, YOU CAN COLLAPSE FROM EXHAUSTION TRYING TO DO IT ALL!
WHAT DID YOU FIND OUT?
WE HAVE OPTIONS OUR MOTHERS NEVER DREAMED OF.

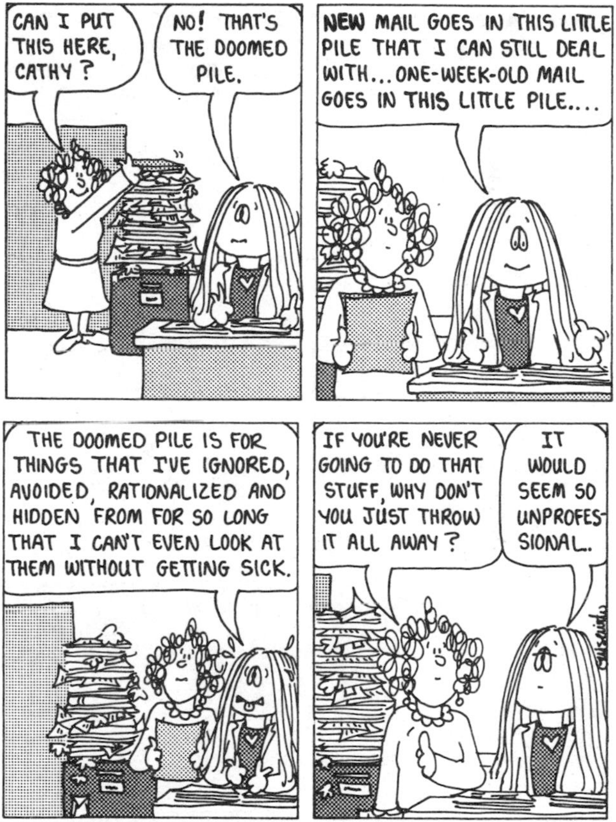
CAN I PUT THIS HERE, CATHY?
NO! THAT'S THE DOOMED PILE.
NEW MAIL GOES IN THIS LITTLE PILE THAT I CAN STILL DEAL WITH... ONE-WEEK-OLD MAIL GOES IN THIS LITTLE PILE....
THE DOOMED PILE IS FOR THINGS THAT I'VE IGNORED, AVOIDED, RATIONALIZED AND HIDDEN FROM FOR SO LONG THAT I CAN'T EVEN LOOK AT THEM WITHOUT GETTING SICK.
IF YOU'RE NEVER GOING TO DO THAT STUFF, WHY DON'T YOU JUST THROW IT ALL AWAY?
IT WOULD SEEM SO UNPROFESSIONAL.

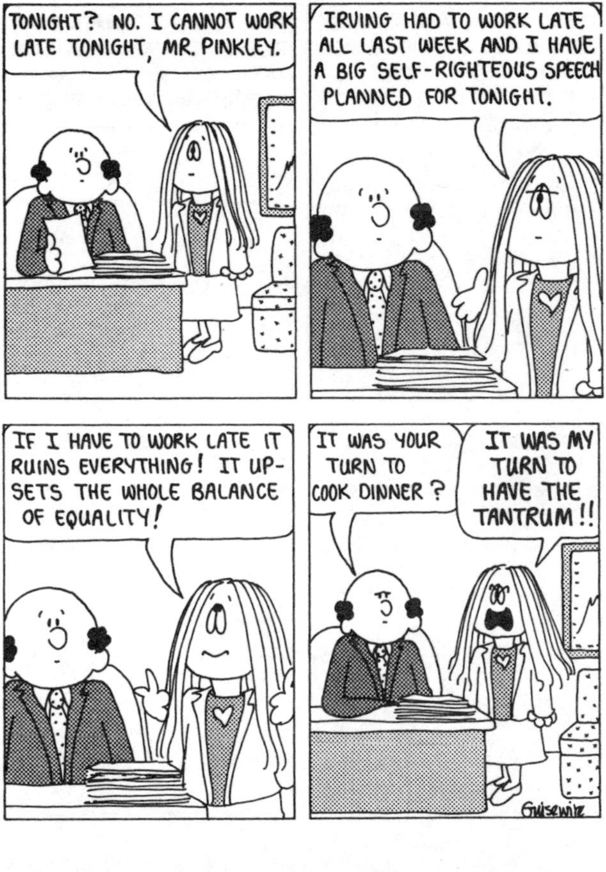

TONIGHT? NO. I CANNOT WORK LATE TONIGHT, MR. PINKLEY.
IRVING HAD TO WORK LATE ALL LAST WEEK AND I HAVE A BIG SELF-RIGHTEOUS SPEECH PLANNED FOR TONIGHT.
IF I HAVE TO WORK LATE IT RUINS EVERYTHING! IT UP-SETS THE WHOLE BALANCE OF EQUALITY!
IT WAS YOUR TURN TO COOK DINNER?
IT WAS MY TURN TO HAVE THE TANTRUM!!
Guisewite

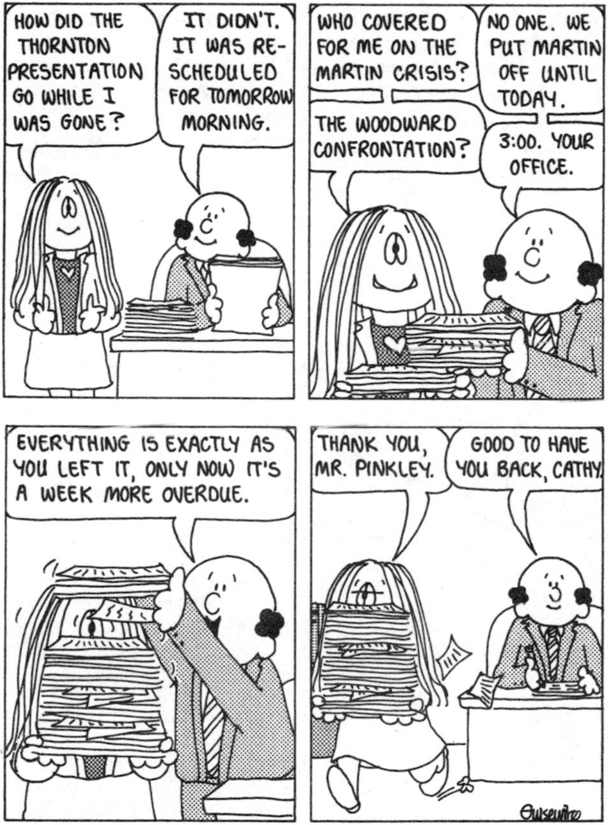
HOW DID THE THORNTON PRESENTATION GO WHILE I WAS GONE?
IT DIDN'T. IT WAS RE-SCHEDULED FOR TOMORROW MORNING.
WHO COVERED FOR ME ON THE MARTIN CRISIS?
NO ONE. WE PUT MARTIN OFF UNTIL TODAY.
THE WOODWARD CONFRONTATION?
3:00. YOUR OFFICE.
EVERYTHING IS EXACTLY AS YOU LEFT IT, ONLY NOW IT'S A WEEK MORE OVERDUE.
THANK YOU, MR. PINKLEY.
GOOD TO HAVE YOU BACK, CATHY.
Guisewite

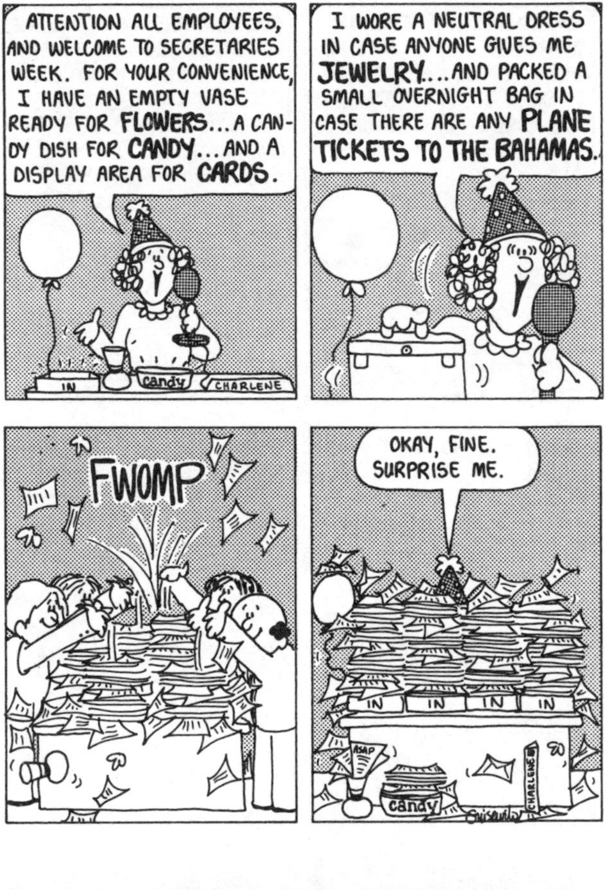
ATTENTION ALL EMPLOYEES, AND WELCOME TO SECRETARIES WEEK. FOR YOUR CONVENIENCE, I HAVE AN EMPTY VASE READY FOR FLOWERS... A CANDY DISH FOR CANDY... AND A DISPLAY AREA FOR CARDS.
IN
candy
CHARLENE
I WORE A NEUTRAL DRESS IN CASE ANYONE GIVES ME JEWELRY.... AND PACKED A SMALL OVERNIGHT BAG IN CASE THERE ARE ANY PLANE TICKETS TO THE BAHAMAS.
FWOMP
OKAY, FINE. SURPRISE ME.
IN
IN
IN
IN
ASAP
candy
CHARLENE

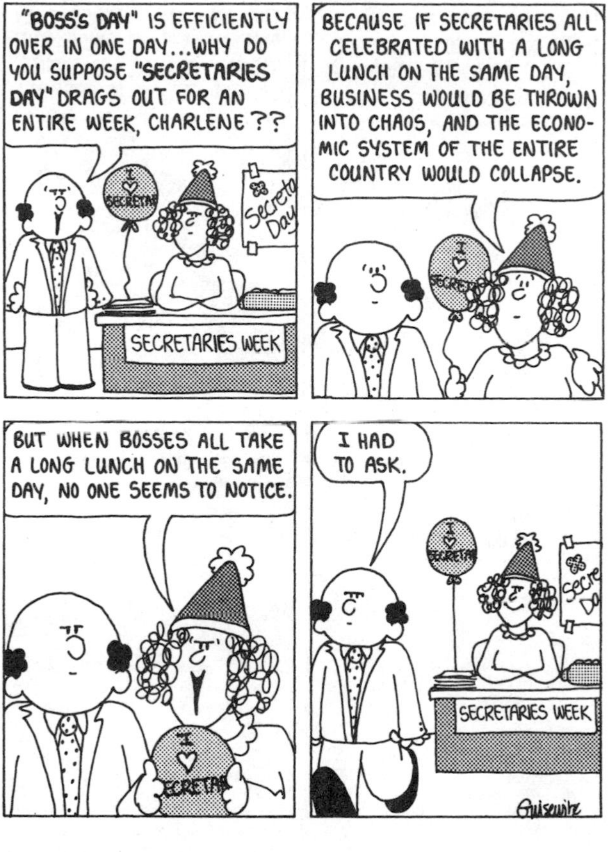
"BOSS'S DAY" IS EFFICIENTLY OVER IN ONE DAY...WHY DO YOU SUPPOSE "SECRETARIES DAY" DRAGS OUT FOR AN ENTIRE WEEK, CHARLENE??
SECRETARIES WEEK
BECAUSE IF SECRETARIES ALL CELEBRATED WITH A LONG LUNCH ON THE SAME DAY, BUSINESS WOULD BE THROWN INTO CHAOS, AND THE ECONOMIC SYSTEM OF THE ENTIRE COUNTRY WOULD COLLAPSE.
BUT WHEN BOSSES ALL TAKE A LONG LUNCH ON THE SAME DAY, NO ONE SEEMS TO NOTICE.
I HAD TO ASK.
SECRETARIES WEEK
Guisewite

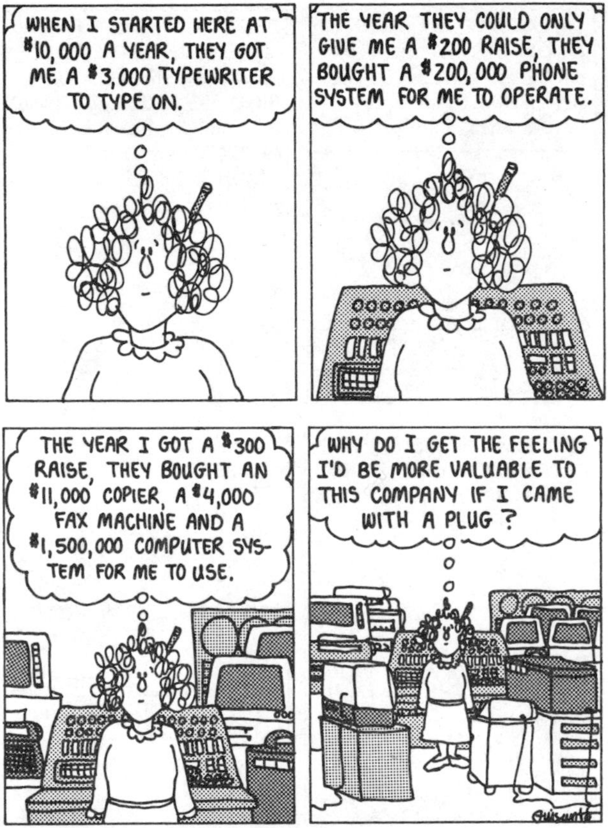
WHEN I STARTED HERE AT $10,000 A YEAR, THEY GOT ME A $3,000 TYPEWRITER TO TYPE ON.
THE YEAR THEY COULD ONLY GIVE ME A $200 RAISE, THEY BOUGHT A $200,000 PHONE SYSTEM FOR ME TO OPERATE.
THE YEAR I GOT A $300 RAISE, THEY BOUGHT AN $11,000 COPIER, A $4,000 FAX MACHINE AND A $1,500,000 COMPUTER SYSTEM FOR ME TO USE.
WHY DO I GET THE FEELING I'D BE MORE VALUABLE TO THIS COMPANY IF I CAME WITH A PLUG?
Guisewite

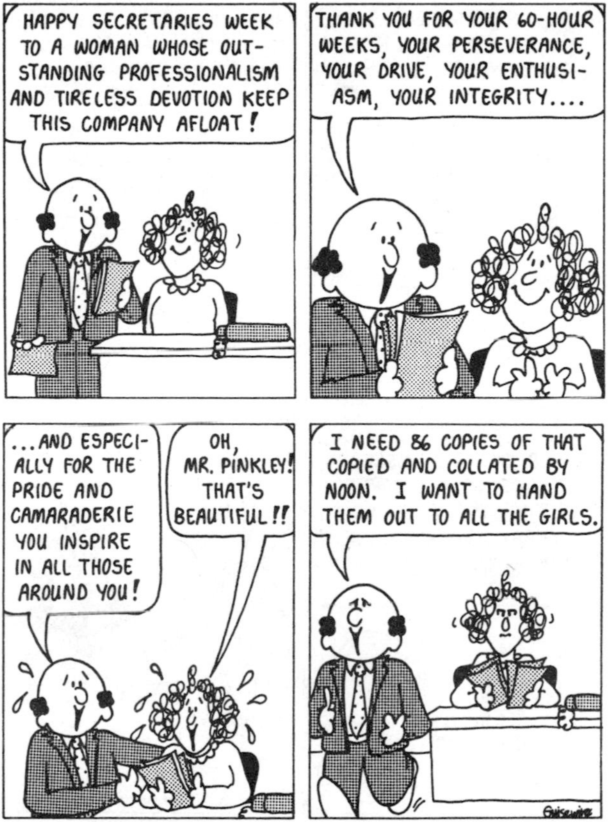
HAPPY SECRETARIES WEEK TO A WOMAN WHOSE OUT-STANDING PROFESSIONALISM AND TIRELESS DEVOTION KEEP THIS COMPANY AFLOAT!
THANK YOU FOR YOUR 60-HOUR WEEKS, YOUR PERSEVERANCE, YOUR DRIVE, YOUR ENTHUSI-ASM, YOUR INTEGRITY....
...AND ESPECI-ALLY FOR THE PRIDE AND CAMARADERIE YOU INSPIRE IN ALL THOSE AROUND YOU!
OH, MR. PINKLEY! THAT'S BEAUTIFUL!!
I NEED 86 COPIES OF THAT COPIED AND COLLATED BY NOON. I WANT TO HAND THEM OUT TO ALL THE GIRLS.
Guisewite

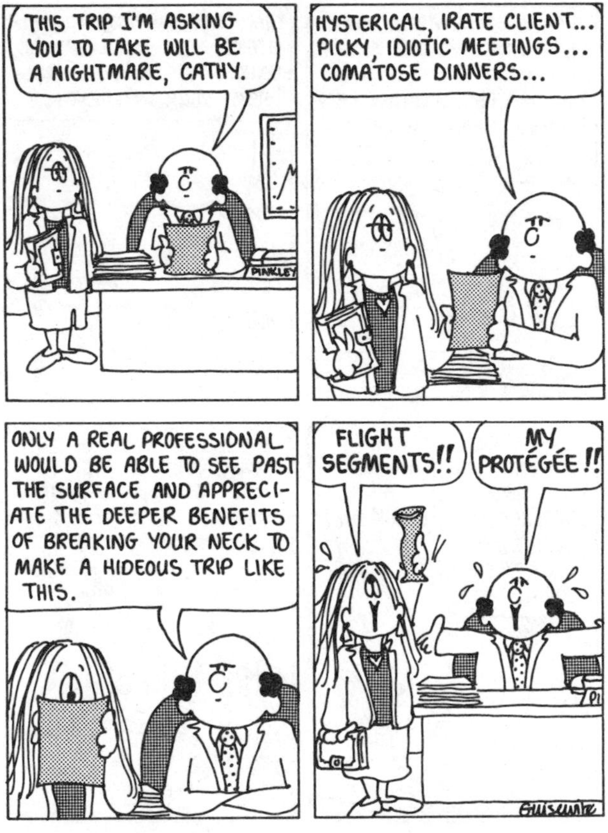
THIS TRIP I'M ASKING YOU TO TAKE WILL BE A NIGHTMARE, CATHY.
PINKLEY
HYSTERICAL, IRATE CLIENT... PICKY, IDIOTIC MEETINGS... COMATOSE DINNERS...
ONLY A REAL PROFESSIONAL WOULD BE ABLE TO SEE PAST THE SURFACE AND APPRECIATE THE DEEPER BENEFITS OF BREAKING YOUR NECK TO MAKE A HIDEOUS TRIP LIKE THIS.
FLIGHT SEGMENTS!!
MY PROTÉGÉE!!
Guisewite

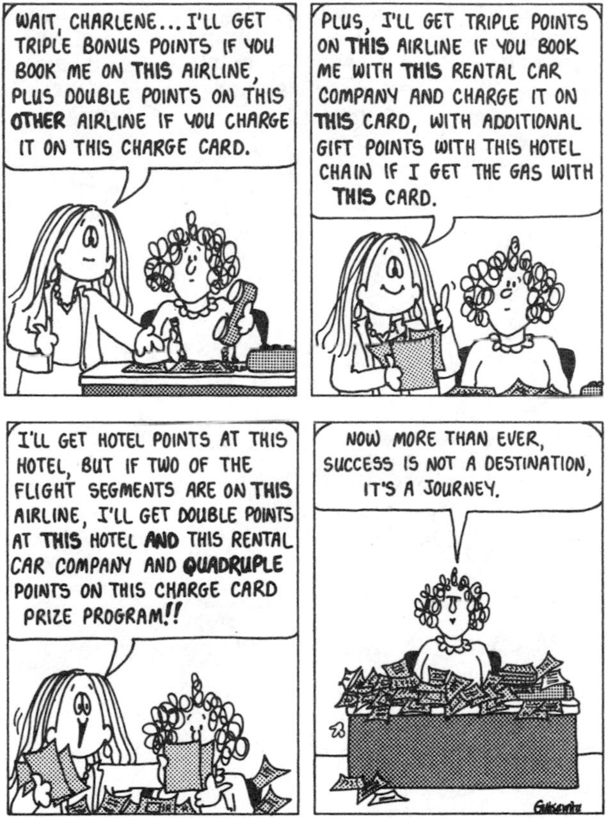
WAIT, CHARLENE... I'LL GET TRIPLE BONUS POINTS IF YOU BOOK ME ON THIS AIRLINE, PLUS DOUBLE POINTS ON THIS OTHER AIRLINE IF YOU CHARGE IT ON THIS CHARGE CARD.
PLUS, I'LL GET TRIPLE POINTS ON THIS AIRLINE IF YOU BOOK ME WITH THIS RENTAL CAR COMPANY AND CHARGE IT ON THIS CARD, WITH ADDITIONAL GIFT POINTS WITH THIS HOTEL CHAIN IF I GET THE GAS WITH THIS CARD.
I'LL GET HOTEL POINTS AT THIS HOTEL, BUT IF TWO OF THE FLIGHT SEGMENTS ARE ON THIS AIRLINE, I'LL GET DOUBLE POINTS AT THIS HOTEL AND THIS RENTAL CAR COMPANY AND QUADRUPLE POINTS ON THIS CHARGE CARD PRIZE PROGRAM!!
NOW MORE THAN EVER, SUCCESS IS NOT A DESTINATION, IT'S A JOURNEY.

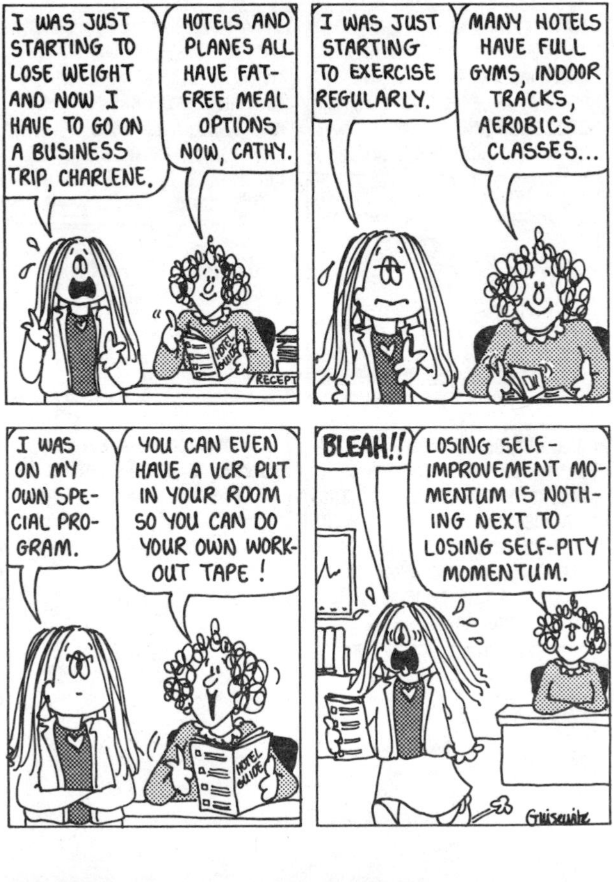
I WAS JUST STARTING TO LOSE WEIGHT AND NOW I HAVE TO GO ON A BUSINESS TRIP, CHARLENE.
HOTELS AND PLANES ALL HAVE FAT-FREE MEAL OPTIONS NOW, CATHY.
HOTEL GUIDE
RECEPT
I WAS JUST STARTING TO EXERCISE REGULARLY.
MANY HOTELS HAVE FULL GYMS, INDOOR TRACKS, AEROBICS CLASSES...
I WAS ON MY OWN SPECIAL PROGRAM.
YOU CAN EVEN HAVE A VCR PUT IN YOUR ROOM SO YOU CAN DO YOUR OWN WORKOUT TAPE!
HOTEL GUIDE
BLEAH!!
LOSING SELF-IMPROVEMENT MOMENTUM IS NOTHING NEXT TO LOSING SELF-PITY MOMENTUM.
Guisewite

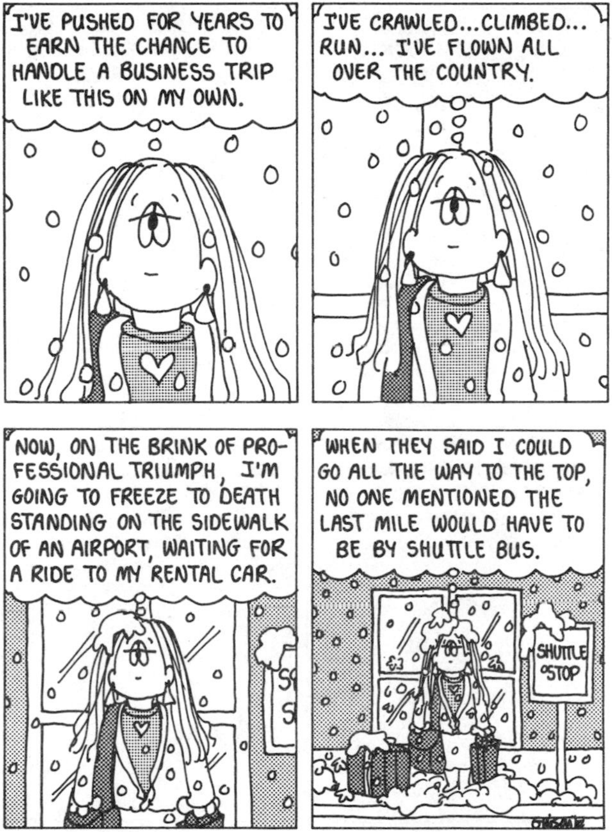
I'VE PUSHED FOR YEARS TO EARN THE CHANCE TO HANDLE A BUSINESS TRIP LIKE THIS ON MY OWN.
I'VE CRAWLED... CLIMBED... RUN... I'VE FLOWN ALL OVER THE COUNTRY.
NOW, ON THE BRINK OF PROFESSIONAL TRIUMPH, I'M GOING TO FREEZE TO DEATH STANDING ON THE SIDEWALK OF AN AIRPORT, WAITING FOR A RIDE TO MY RENTAL CAR.
WHEN THEY SAID I COULD GO ALL THE WAY TO THE TOP, NO ONE MENTIONED THE LAST MILE WOULD HAVE TO BE BY SHUTTLE BUS.
SHUTTLE STOP

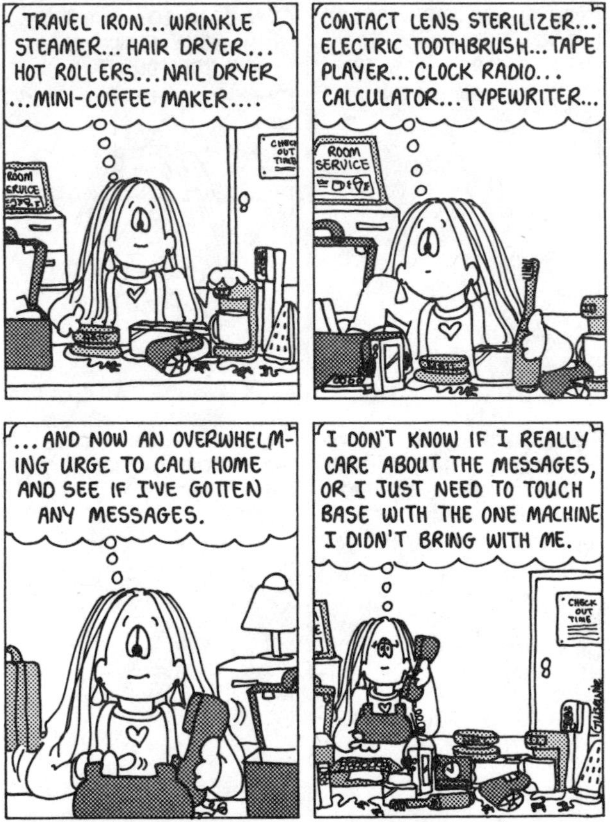
TRAVEL IRON... WRINKLE STEAMER... HAIR DRYER... HOT ROLLERS... NAIL DRYER ...MINI-COFFEE MAKER....
ROOM SERVICE
CHECK OUT TIME
CONTACT LENS STERILIZER... ELECTRIC TOOTHBRUSH... TAPE PLAYER... CLOCK RADIO... CALCULATOR... TYPEWRITER...
ROOM SERVICE
...AND NOW AN OVERWHELMING URGE TO CALL HOME AND SEE IF I'VE GOTTEN ANY MESSAGES.
I DON'T KNOW IF I REALLY CARE ABOUT THE MESSAGES, OR I JUST NEED TO TOUCH BASE WITH THE ONE MACHINE I DIDN'T BRING WITH ME.
CHECK OUT TIME

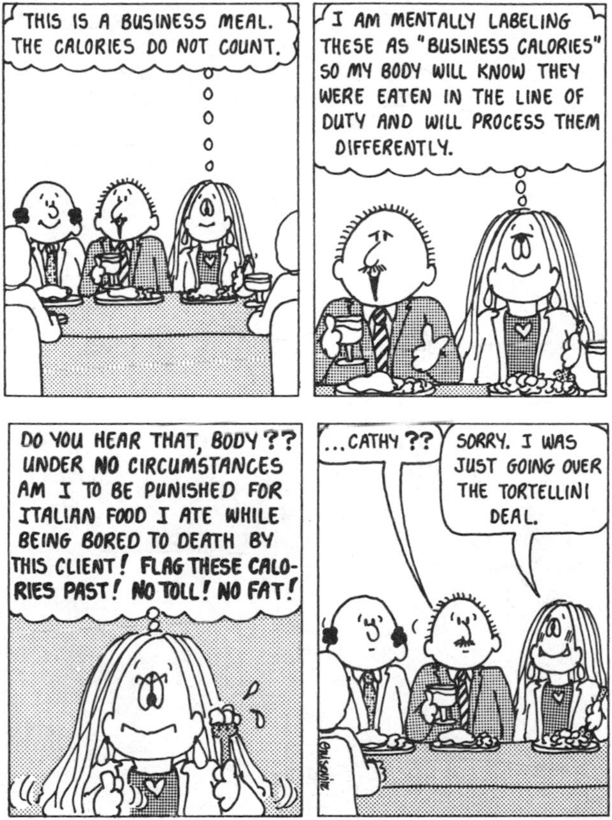

THIS IS A BUSINESS MEAL. THE CALORIES DO NOT COUNT.
I AM MENTALLY LABELING THESE AS "BUSINESS CALORIES" SO MY BODY WILL KNOW THEY WERE EATEN IN THE LINE OF DUTY AND WILL PROCESS THEM DIFFERENTLY.
DO YOU HEAR THAT, BODY?? UNDER NO CIRCUMSTANCES AM I TO BE PUNISHED FOR ITALIAN FOOD I ATE WHILE BEING BORED TO DEATH BY THIS CLIENT! FLAG THESE CALORIES PAST! NO TOLL! NO FAT!
...CATHY??
SORRY. I WAS JUST GOING OVER THE TORTELLINI DEAL.
©Guisewite

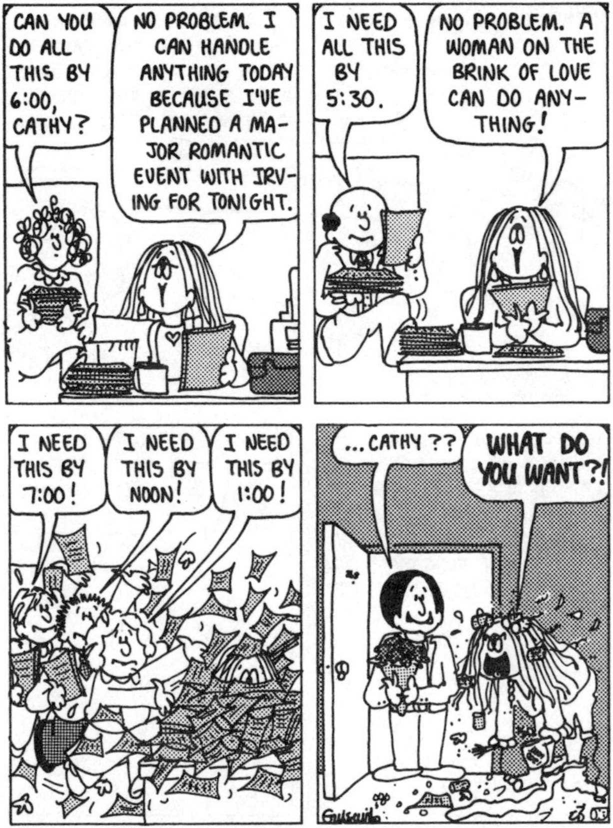
CAN YOU DO ALL THIS BY 6:00, CATHY?
NO PROBLEM. I CAN HANDLE ANYTHING TODAY BECAUSE I'VE PLANNED A MAJOR ROMANTIC EVENT WITH IRVING FOR TONIGHT.
I NEED ALL THIS BY 5:30.
NO PROBLEM. A WOMAN ON THE BRINK OF LOVE CAN DO ANYTHING!
I NEED THIS BY 7:00!
I NEED THIS BY NOON!
I NEED THIS BY 1:00!
...CATHY??
WHAT DO YOU WANT?!

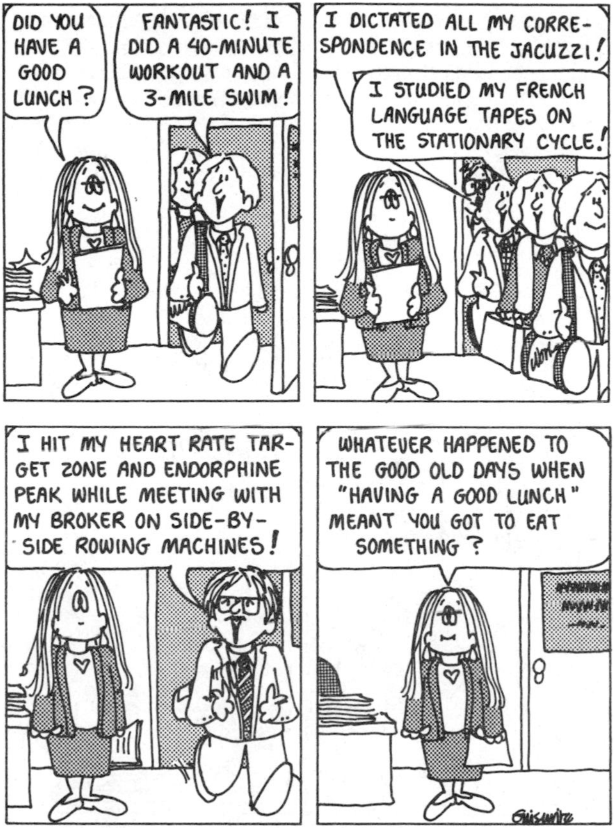
DID YOU HAVE A GOOD LUNCH?
FANTASTIC! I DID A 40-MINUTE WORKOUT AND A 3-MILE SWIM!
I DICTATED ALL MY CORRESPONDENCE IN THE JACUZZI!
I STUDIED MY FRENCH LANGUAGE TAPES ON THE STATIONARY CYCLE!
I HIT MY HEART RATE TARGET ZONE AND ENDORPHINE PEAK WHILE MEETING WITH MY BROKER ON SIDE-BY-SIDE ROWING MACHINES!
WHATEVER HAPPENED TO THE GOOD OLD DAYS WHEN "HAVING A GOOD LUNCH" MEANT YOU GOT TO EAT SOMETHING?
Guisewite

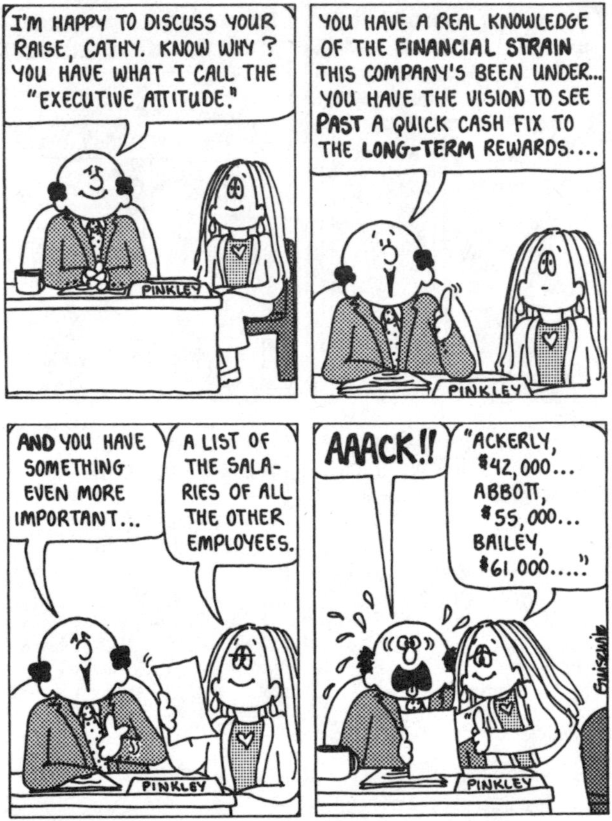
I'M HAPPY TO DISCUSS YOUR RAISE, CATHY. KNOW WHY? YOU HAVE WHAT I CALL THE "EXECUTIVE ATTITUDE."
PINKLEY
YOU HAVE A REAL KNOWLEDGE OF THE FINANCIAL STRAIN THIS COMPANY'S BEEN UNDER... YOU HAVE THE VISION TO SEE PAST A QUICK CASH FIX TO THE LONG-TERM REWARDS....
PINKLEY
AND YOU HAVE SOMETHING EVEN MORE IMPORTANT...
A LIST OF THE SALARIES OF ALL THE OTHER EMPLOYEES.
PINKLEY
AAACK!!
"ACKERLY, $42,000... ABBOTT, $55,000... BAILEY, $61,000...."
PINKLEY

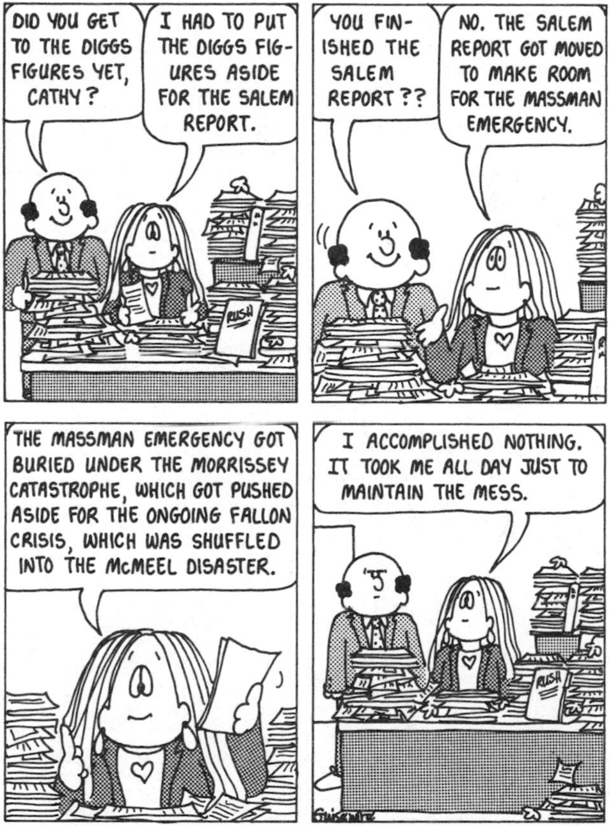
DID YOU GET TO THE DIGGS FIGURES YET, CATHY?
I HAD TO PUT THE DIGGS FIGURES ASIDE FOR THE SALEM REPORT.
RUSH
YOU FINISHED THE SALEM REPORT??
NO. THE SALEM REPORT GOT MOVED TO MAKE ROOM FOR THE MASSMAN EMERGENCY.
THE MASSMAN EMERGENCY GOT BURIED UNDER THE MORRISSEY CATASTROPHE, WHICH GOT PUSHED ASIDE FOR THE ONGOING FALLON CRISIS, WHICH WAS SHUFFLED INTO THE MCMEEL DISASTER.
I ACCOMPLISHED NOTHING. IT TOOK ME ALL DAY JUST TO MAINTAIN THE MESS.
RUSH
GUISEWITE

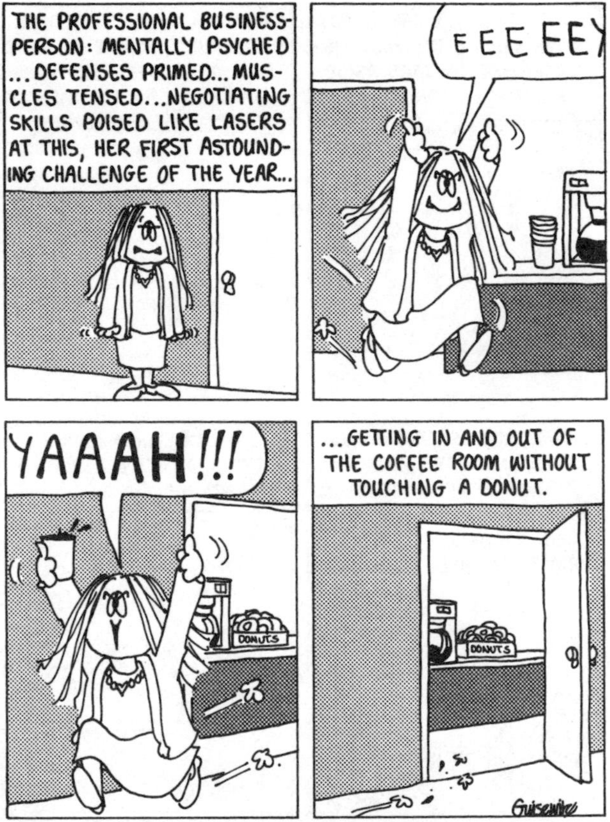
THE PROFESSIONAL BUSINESS-PERSON: MENTALLY PSYCHED ... DEFENSES PRIMED... MUSCLES TENSED... NEGOTIATING SKILLS POISED LIKE LASERS AT THIS, HER FIRST ASTOUNDING CHALLENGE OF THE YEAR...
EEEEEEY
YAAAH!!!
DONUTS
...GETTING IN AND OUT OF THE COFFEE ROOM WITHOUT TOUCHING A DONUT.
DONUTS
Guisewite

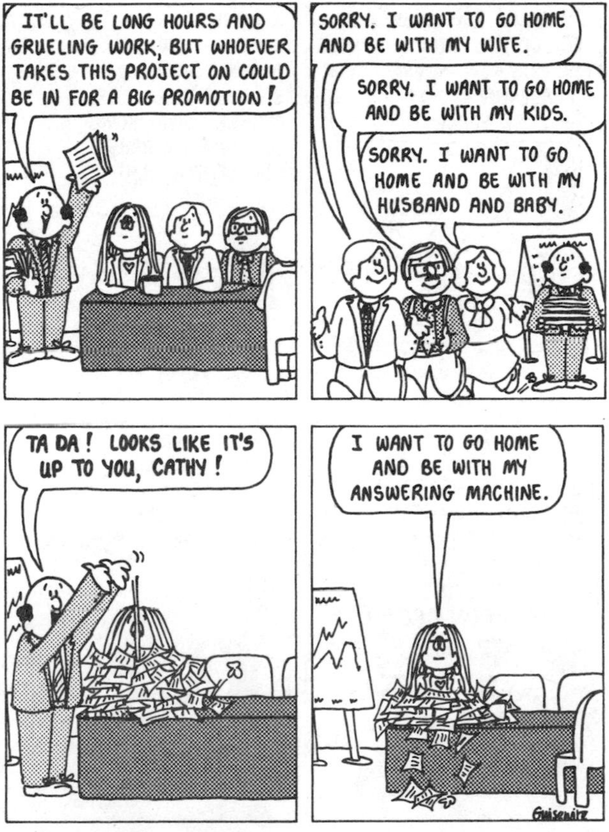
IT'LL BE LONG HOURS AND GRUELING WORK, BUT WHOEVER TAKES THIS PROJECT ON COULD BE IN FOR A BIG PROMOTION!
SORRY. I WANT TO GO HOME AND BE WITH MY WIFE.
SORRY. I WANT TO GO HOME AND BE WITH MY KIDS.
SORRY. I WANT TO GO HOME AND BE WITH MY HUSBAND AND BABY.
TA DA! LOOKS LIKE IT'S UP TO YOU, CATHY!
I WANT TO GO HOME AND BE WITH MY ANSWERING MACHINE.
GUISEWITE

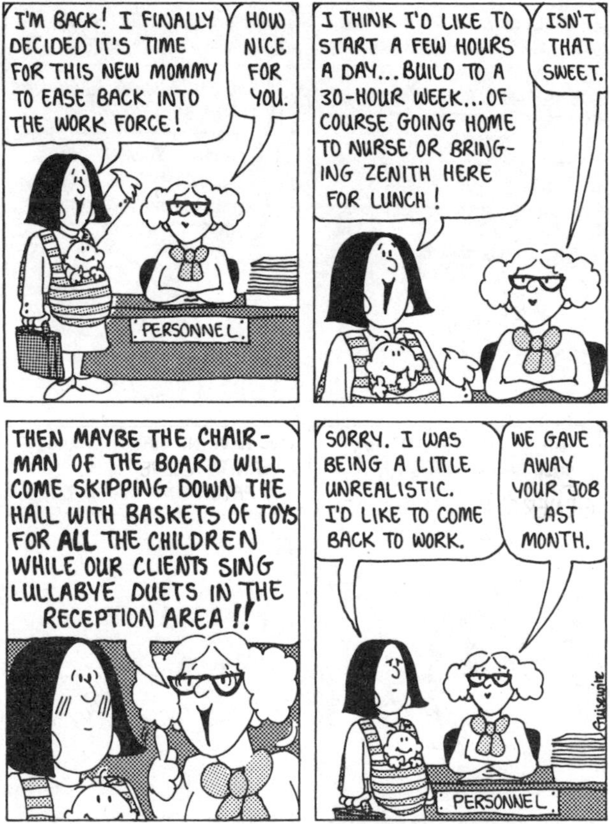
I'M BACK! I FINALLY DECIDED IT'S TIME FOR THIS NEW MOMMY TO EASE BACK INTO THE WORK FORCE!
HOW NICE FOR YOU.
PERSONNEL
I THINK I'D LIKE TO START A FEW HOURS A DAY... BUILD TO A 30-HOUR WEEK... OF COURSE GOING HOME TO NURSE OR BRINGING ZENITH HERE FOR LUNCH!
ISN'T THAT SWEET.
THEN MAYBE THE CHAIRMAN OF THE BOARD WILL COME SKIPPING DOWN THE HALL WITH BASKETS OF TOYS FOR **ALL** THE CHILDREN WHILE OUR CLIENTS SING LULLABYE DUETS IN THE RECEPTION AREA!!
SORRY. I WAS BEING A LITTLE UNREALISTIC. I'D LIKE TO COME BACK TO WORK.
WE GAVE AWAY YOUR JOB LAST MONTH.
GUISEWITE
PERSONNEL

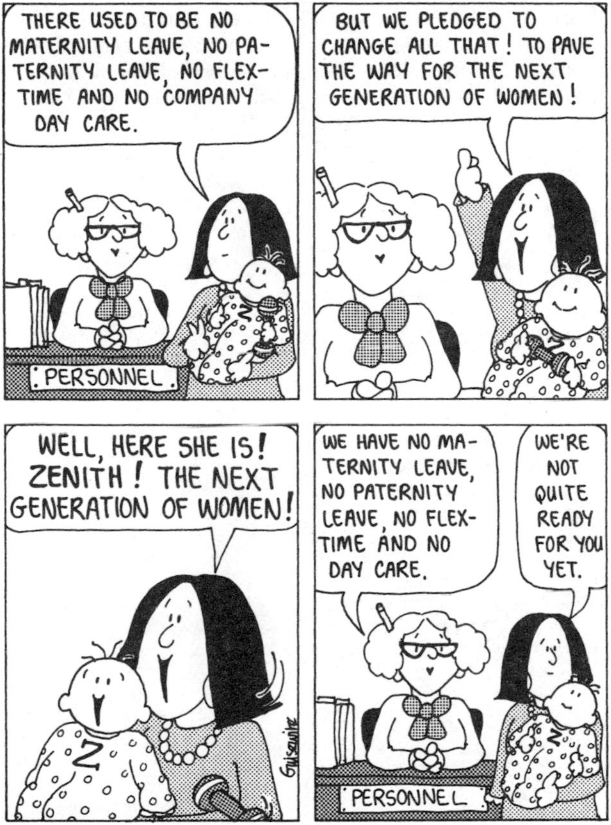
THERE USED TO BE NO MATERNITY LEAVE, NO PATERNITY LEAVE, NO FLEXTIME AND NO COMPANY DAY CARE.
PERSONNEL
BUT WE PLEDGED TO CHANGE ALL THAT! TO PAVE THE WAY FOR THE NEXT GENERATION OF WOMEN!
WELL, HERE SHE IS! ZENITH! THE NEXT GENERATION OF WOMEN!
WE HAVE NO MATERNITY LEAVE, NO PATERNITY LEAVE, NO FLEXTIME AND NO DAY CARE.
WE'RE NOT QUITE READY FOR YOU YET.
PERSONNEL

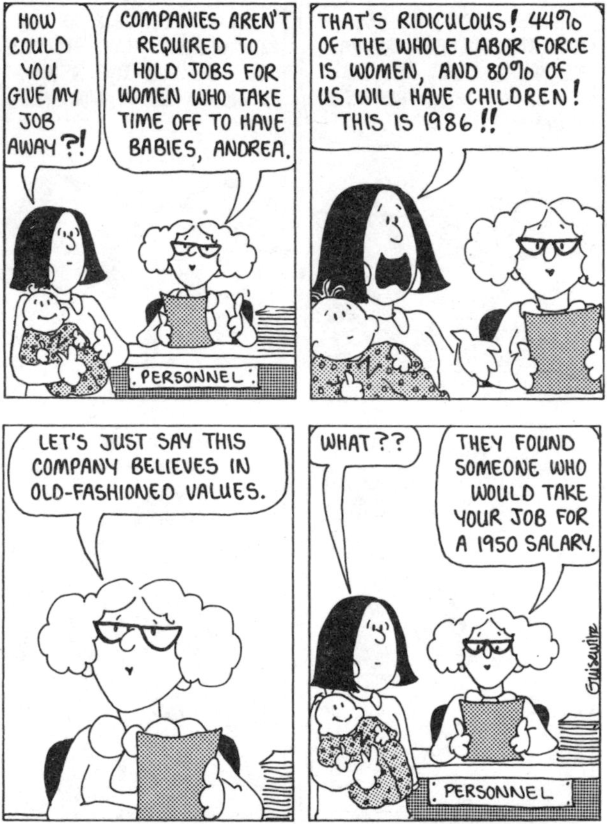
HOW COULD YOU GIVE MY JOB AWAY?!
COMPANIES AREN'T REQUIRED TO HOLD JOBS FOR WOMEN WHO TAKE TIME OFF TO HAVE BABIES, ANDREA.
PERSONNEL
THAT'S RIDICULOUS! 44% OF THE WHOLE LABOR FORCE IS WOMEN, AND 80% OF US WILL HAVE CHILDREN! THIS IS 1986!!
LET'S JUST SAY THIS COMPANY BELIEVES IN OLD-FASHIONED VALUES.
WHAT??
THEY FOUND SOMEONE WHO WOULD TAKE YOUR JOB FOR A 1950 SALARY.
GUISEWITE
PERSONNEL

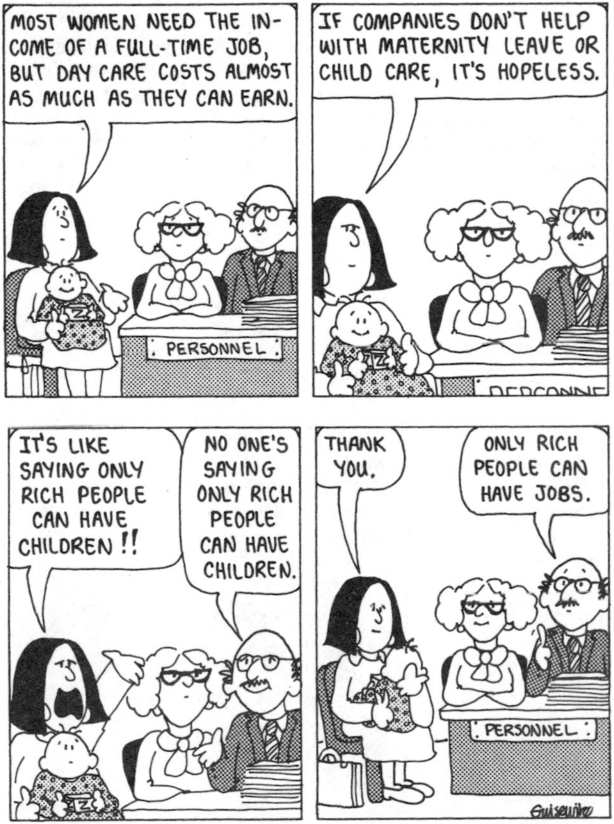
MOST WOMEN NEED THE INCOME OF A FULL-TIME JOB, BUT DAY CARE COSTS ALMOST AS MUCH AS THEY CAN EARN.
PERSONNEL
IF COMPANIES DON'T HELP WITH MATERNITY LEAVE OR CHILD CARE, IT'S HOPELESS.
IT'S LIKE SAYING ONLY RICH PEOPLE CAN HAVE CHILDREN!!
NO ONE'S SAYING ONLY RICH PEOPLE CAN HAVE CHILDREN.
THANK YOU.
ONLY RICH PEOPLE CAN HAVE JOBS.
PERSONNEL
Guisewite

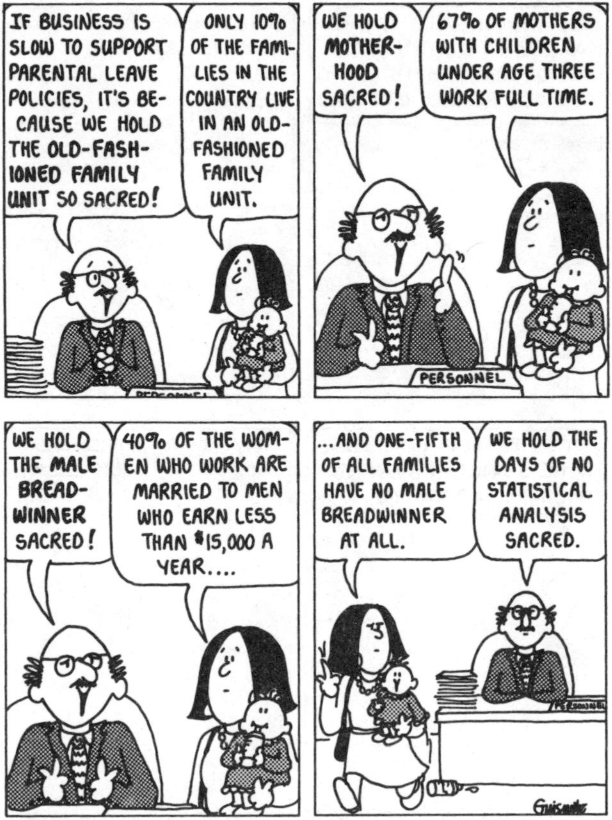

IF BUSINESS IS SLOW TO SUPPORT PARENTAL LEAVE POLICIES, IT'S BECAUSE WE HOLD THE OLD-FASHIONED FAMILY UNIT SO SACRED!
ONLY 10% OF THE FAMILIES IN THE COUNTRY LIVE IN AN OLD-FASHIONED FAMILY UNIT.
WE HOLD MOTHERHOOD SACRED!
67% OF MOTHERS WITH CHILDREN UNDER AGE THREE WORK FULL TIME.
PERSONNEL
WE HOLD THE MALE BREADWINNER SACRED!
40% OF THE WOMEN WHO WORK ARE MARRIED TO MEN WHO EARN LESS THAN $15,000 A YEAR....
...AND ONE-FIFTH OF ALL FAMILIES HAVE NO MALE BREADWINNER AT ALL.
WE HOLD THE DAYS OF NO STATISTICAL ANALYSIS SACRED.
Guisewite

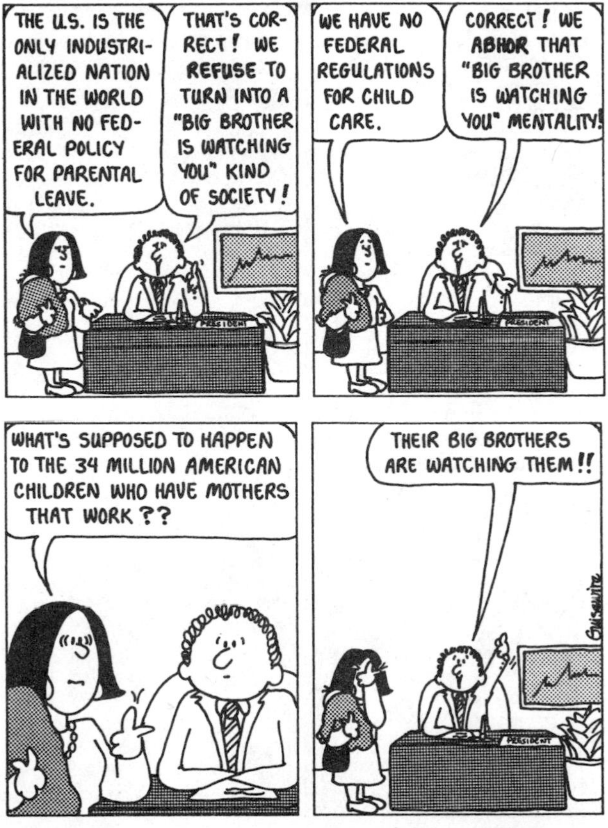
THE U.S. IS THE ONLY INDUSTRIALIZED NATION IN THE WORLD WITH NO FEDERAL POLICY FOR PARENTAL LEAVE.
THAT'S CORRECT! WE REFUSE TO TURN INTO A "BIG BROTHER IS WATCHING YOU" KIND OF SOCIETY!
PRESIDENT
WE HAVE NO FEDERAL REGULATIONS FOR CHILD CARE.
CORRECT! WE ABHOR THAT "BIG BROTHER IS WATCHING YOU" MENTALITY!
PRESIDENT
WHAT'S SUPPOSED TO HAPPEN TO THE 34 MILLION AMERICAN CHILDREN WHO HAVE MOTHERS THAT WORK??
THEIR BIG BROTHERS ARE WATCHING THEM!!
PRESIDENT
Guisewite

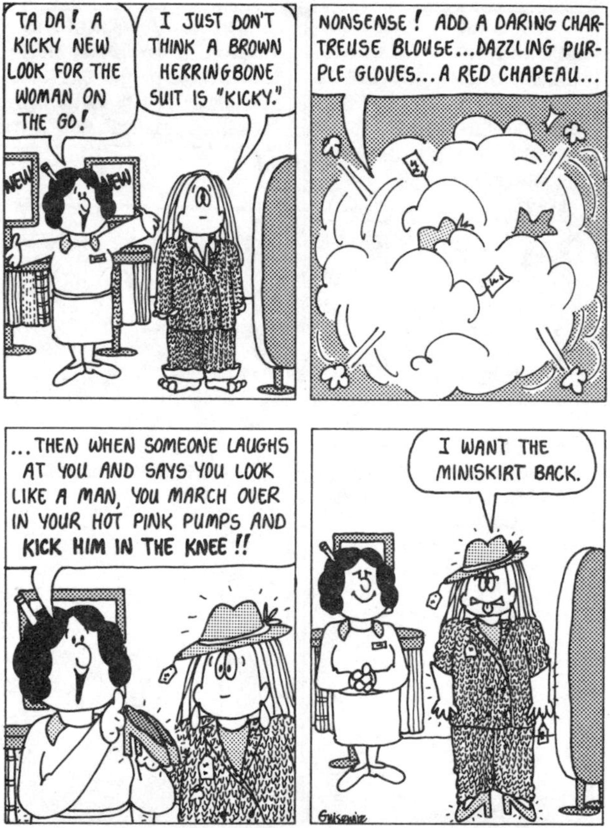
TA DA! A KICKY NEW LOOK FOR THE WOMAN ON THE GO!
I JUST DON'T THINK A BROWN HERRINGBONE SUIT IS "KICKY."
NEW
NEW
NONSENSE! ADD A DARING CHARTREUSE BLOUSE...DAZZLING PURPLE GLOVES...A RED CHAPEAU...
...THEN WHEN SOMEONE LAUGHS AT YOU AND SAYS YOU LOOK LIKE A MAN, YOU MARCH OVER IN YOUR HOT PINK PUMPS AND KICK HIM IN THE KNEE!!
I WANT THE MINISKIRT BACK.
GUISEWITE

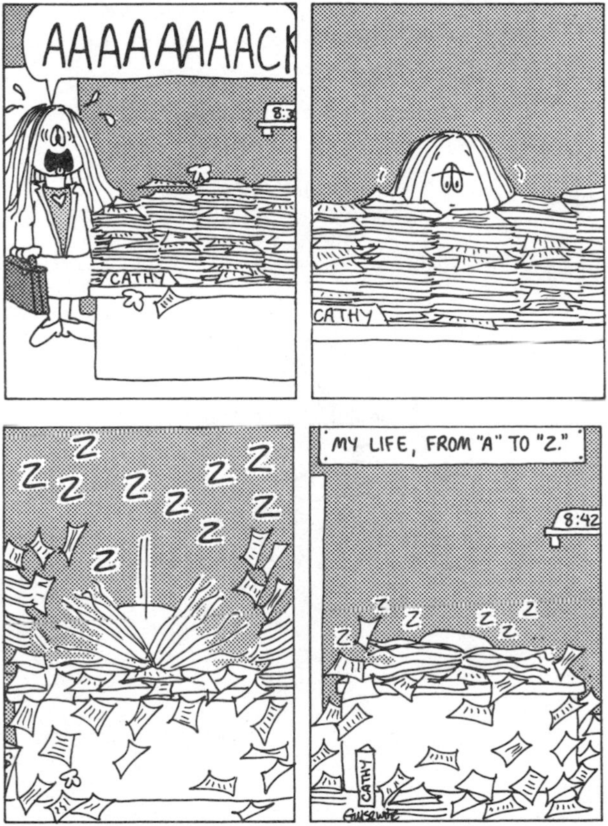
AAAAAAAACK
CATHY
CATHY
MY LIFE, FROM "A" TO "Z."
8:42
CATHY

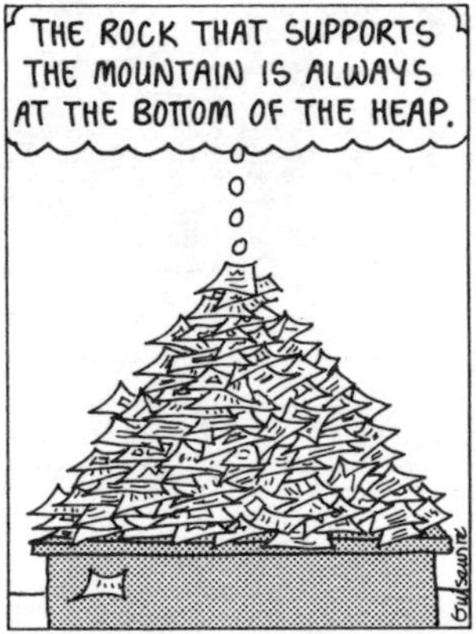
THE ROCK THAT SUPPORTS THE MOUNTAIN IS ALWAYS AT THE BOTTOM OF THE HEAP.
GUISEWITE

The Early '90s

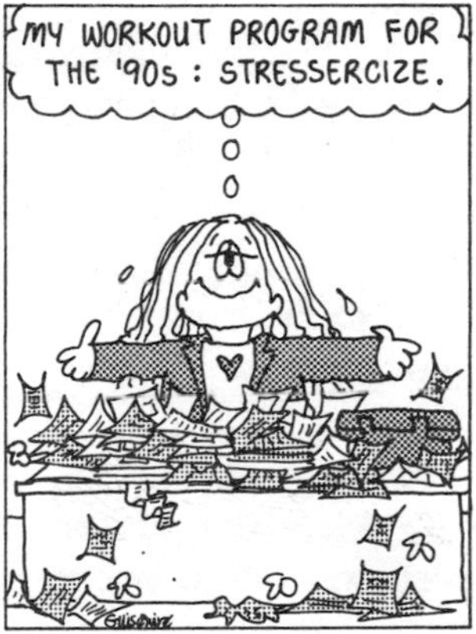
MY WORKOUT PROGRAM FOR THE '90s : STRESSERCIZE.

January 1, 1990:

7 A.M.—7:30 A.M.: Lay in bed trying to decide whether to leap up and run, power walk, do an aerobics tape, use the step machine, or go to the gym.

7:30 A.M. — 8 A.M.: Decided to clear my head with a shower. Faced a bathroom cupboard with six different nine-step hair and skin-care systems.

8 A.M. — 8:30 A.M.: Needed energy to cope with the shower decisions. Opened a cabinet and found 16 different boxes of cereal, all with "oat bran" in the name. Tried to figure out if any of them would be allowed on one of the 12 different "Food Programs for Life" that I had clipped and plastered to the front of the refrigerator and needed to decide upon before I could take bite number one out of the New Year.

8:30 A.M. — 9 A.M.: Was too overwhelmed by my kitchen to figure breakfast out. Drove to Starbucks, where I was immediately overwhelmed by coffee choices and intimidated by a shop full of perky clients who not only knew what they wanted, but were also asking for it in some foreign "coffee-speak" language, which no one had ever mentioned I was supposed to learn.

The rest of the day was spent in the electronics store, trying to choose the Time Management System that would restore order and efficiency to my life.

In retrospect, I see that somewhere during hour number three with salesperson number four of my Time Management System Search we experienced a cosmic event: the collision of the world-expanding "Options Era" with the universe shrinking "Oblivious Era."

With astonishing speed, we'd gone from a world where, when you needed a hammer, there was a little hardware store full of experts who could tell you everything about it, as well as teach you to use it . . . to a world of amazingly complex gadgets that came with instruction books no one could understand and which were sold in giant discount warehouses where no one knew anything about any of them except, sometimes, how to ring one up.

This was part of the anxiety that every single employee took to work in the early '90s.

A fake sense of community because of all the cars in the Electronics 'R' Us Superstore parking lot . . .

on top of a real sense of isolation caused by being in a 25,000-acre store where there was no one to ask who knew anything anymore . . .

on top of less and less time to do anything because all the time was getting used up trying to figure out which thing to do . . .

on top of a massive new sense of insecurity that—with 15 new sorts of dental hygiene systems available—we no longer were even making the right choices about brushing our teeth . . .

on top of a need to produce more to appease more demanding clients who were cranky and unreasonable for all the exact same reasons we were.

A person who worked late and tried to grab a "fast" meal on the way home suddenly faced a 30-foot-long aisle of thousands of microwaveable frozen food options. But the problem wasn't just that it took an hour to figure out which "three-minute" meal to buy. There weren't just too many options for every category of life, there were now categories of completely opposite options for each category.

The new $15 zillion workout industry was peaking at the exact same time as the new $15 zillion gourmet chocolate industry.

The organic, made-from-scratch cooking trend was happening at the exact same time people had completely run out of time to cook anything.

The "return to good, wholesome American family values" was happening at the exact same time as the booming new trashy lingerie industry. Offices full of people pored over their Victoria's Secret catalogs by day and argued over the Anita Hill-Clarence Thomas sexual harassment hearings by night.

Add all the unresolved issues from the '70s and '80s that we'd run out of time and energy to fix, and without knowing it, we were being prepared for the Internet era, where all the rest of our time would vanish into cyberspace.

What every office offered in the early '90s was the Stress Package.

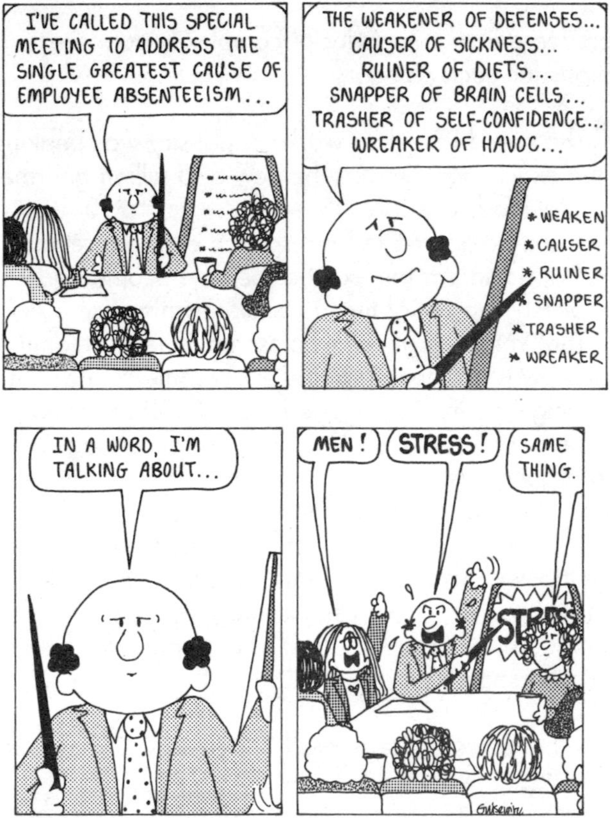
I'VE CALLED THIS SPECIAL MEETING TO ADDRESS THE SINGLE GREATEST CAUSE OF EMPLOYEE ABSENTEEISM...
THE WEAKENER OF DEFENSES... CAUSER OF SICKNESS... RUINER OF DIETS... SNAPPER OF BRAIN CELLS... TRASHER OF SELF-CONFIDENCE... WREAKER OF HAVOC...
* WEAKEN
* CAUSER
* RUINER
* SNAPPER
* TRASHER
* WREAKER
IN A WORD, I'M TALKING ABOUT...
MEN!
STRESS!
SAME THING.

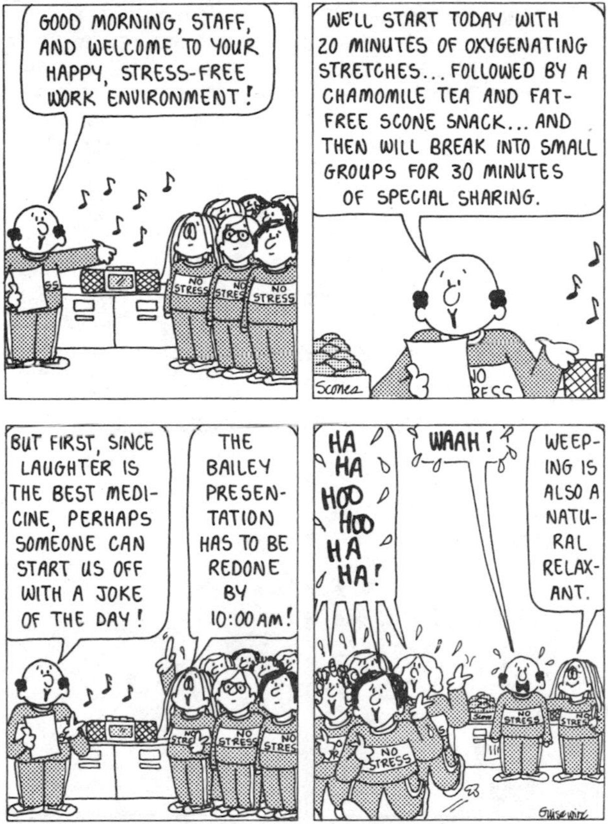
GOOD MORNING, STAFF, AND WELCOME TO YOUR HAPPY, STRESS-FREE WORK ENVIRONMENT!
NO STRESS
NO STRESS
NO STRESS
WE'LL START TODAY WITH 20 MINUTES OF OXYGENATING STRETCHES... FOLLOWED BY A CHAMOMILE TEA AND FAT-FREE SCONE SNACK... AND THEN WILL BREAK INTO SMALL GROUPS FOR 30 MINUTES OF SPECIAL SHARING.
Scones
BUT FIRST, SINCE LAUGHTER IS THE BEST MEDICINE, PERHAPS SOMEONE CAN START US OFF WITH A JOKE OF THE DAY!
THE BAILEY PRESENTATION HAS TO BE REDONE BY 10:00 AM!
HA HA HOO HOO HA HA!
WAAH!
WEEPING IS ALSO A NATURAL RELAXANT.
NO STRESS
NO STRESS

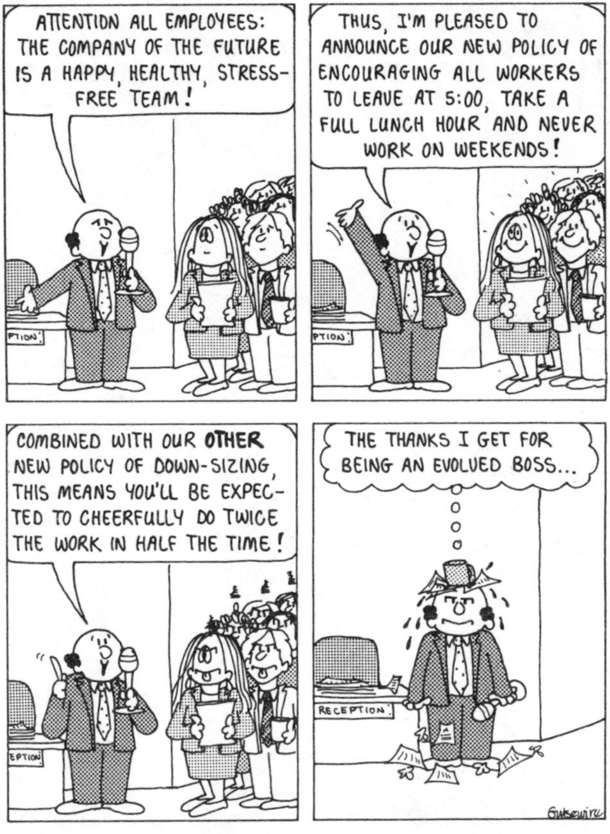
ATTENTION ALL EMPLOYEES: THE COMPANY OF THE FUTURE IS A HAPPY, HEALTHY, STRESS-FREE TEAM!
PTION
THUS, I'M PLEASED TO ANNOUNCE OUR NEW POLICY OF ENCOURAGING ALL WORKERS TO LEAVE AT 5:00, TAKE A FULL LUNCH HOUR AND NEVER WORK ON WEEKENDS!
PTION
COMBINED WITH OUR OTHER NEW POLICY OF DOWN-SIZING, THIS MEANS YOU'LL BE EXPECTED TO CHEERFULLY DO TWICE THE WORK IN HALF THE TIME!
EPTION
THE THANKS I GET FOR BEING AN EVOLVED BOSS...
RECEPTION
Guisewite

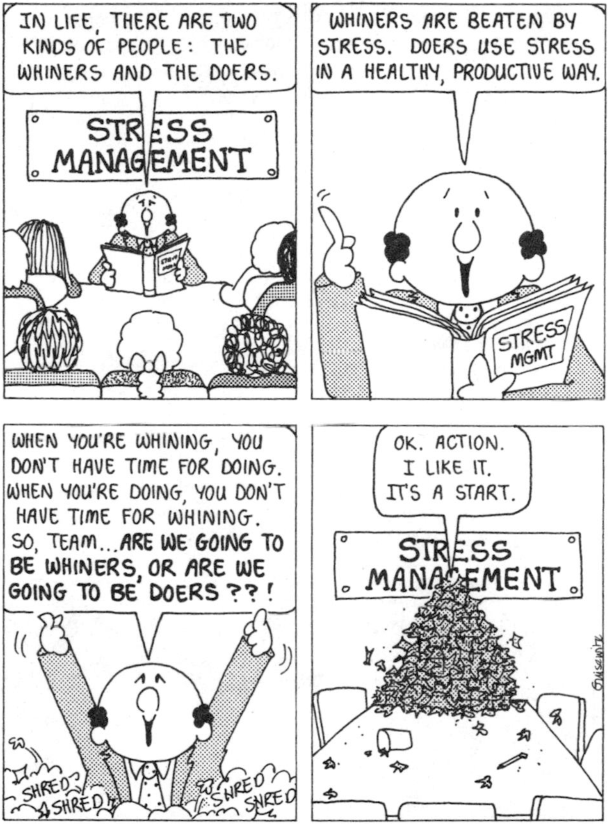
IN LIFE, THERE ARE TWO KINDS OF PEOPLE: THE WHINERS AND THE DOERS.
STRESS MANAGEMENT
STRESS MGMT
WHINERS ARE BEATEN BY STRESS. DOERS USE STRESS IN A HEALTHY, PRODUCTIVE WAY.
STRESS MGMT
WHEN YOU'RE WHINING, YOU DON'T HAVE TIME FOR DOING. WHEN YOU'RE DOING, YOU DON'T HAVE TIME FOR WHINING. SO, TEAM... ARE WE GOING TO BE WHINERS, OR ARE WE GOING TO BE DOERS??!
SHRED
SHRED
SHRED
SHRED
OK. ACTION. I LIKE IT. IT'S A START.
STRESS MANAGEMENT

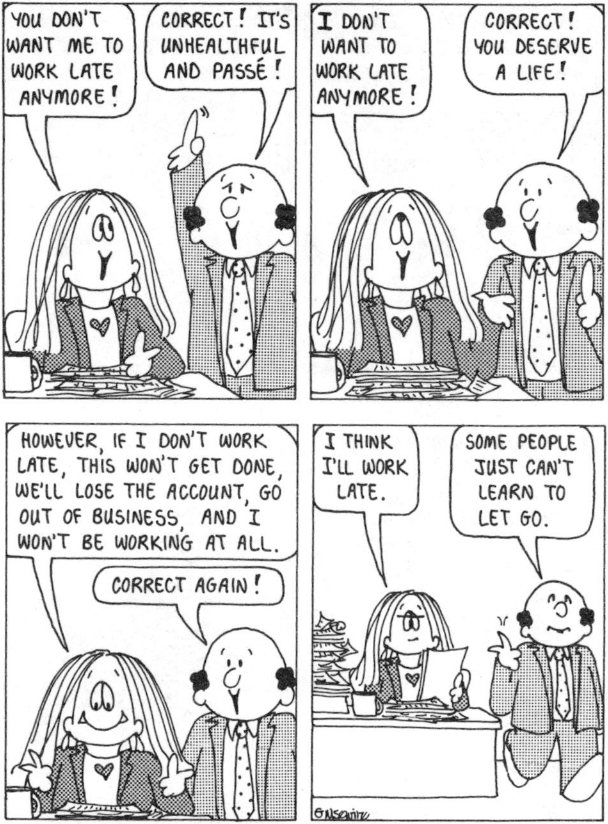
YOU DON'T WANT ME TO WORK LATE ANYMORE!
CORRECT! IT'S UNHEALTHFUL AND PASSÉ!
I DON'T WANT TO WORK LATE ANYMORE!
CORRECT! YOU DESERVE A LIFE!
HOWEVER, IF I DON'T WORK LATE, THIS WON'T GET DONE, WE'LL LOSE THE ACCOUNT, GO OUT OF BUSINESS, AND I WON'T BE WORKING AT ALL.
CORRECT AGAIN!
I THINK I'LL WORK LATE.
SOME PEOPLE JUST CAN'T LEARN TO LET GO.

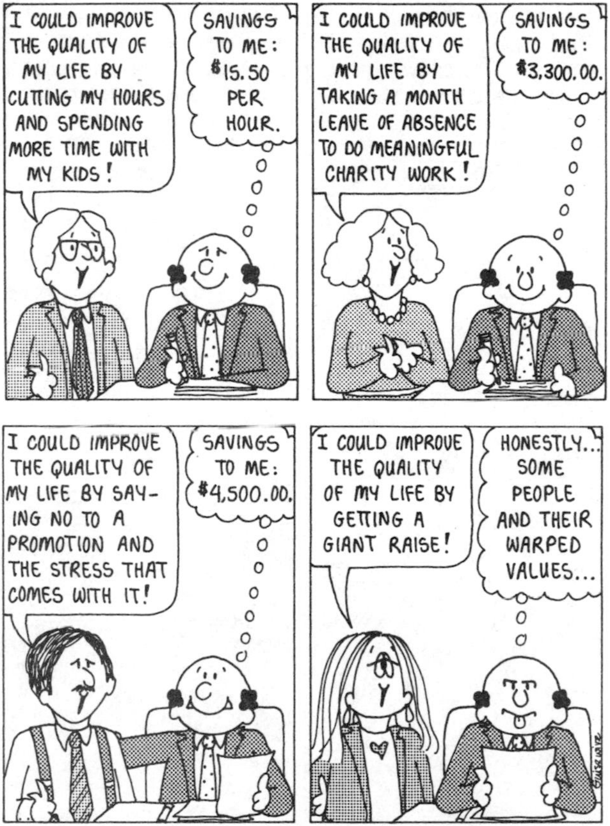
I COULD IMPROVE THE QUALITY OF MY LIFE BY CUTTING MY HOURS AND SPENDING MORE TIME WITH MY KIDS!
SAVINGS TO ME: $15.50 PER HOUR.
I COULD IMPROVE THE QUALITY OF MY LIFE BY TAKING A MONTH LEAVE OF ABSENCE TO DO MEANINGFUL CHARITY WORK!
SAVINGS TO ME: $3,300.00.
I COULD IMPROVE THE QUALITY OF MY LIFE BY SAYING NO TO A PROMOTION AND THE STRESS THAT COMES WITH IT!
SAVINGS TO ME: $4,500.00.
I COULD IMPROVE THE QUALITY OF MY LIFE BY GETTING A GIANT RAISE!
HONESTLY... SOME PEOPLE AND THEIR WARPED VALUES...

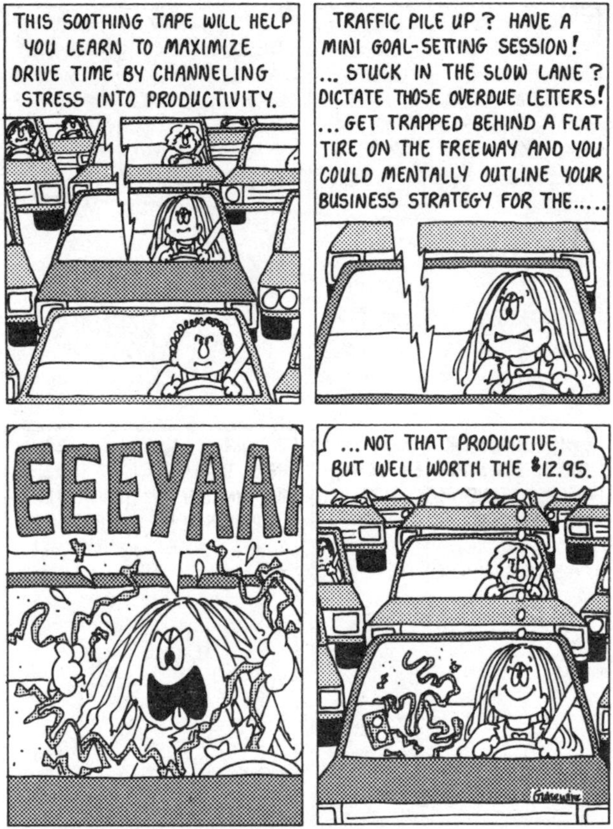
THIS SOOTHING TAPE WILL HELP YOU LEARN TO MAXIMIZE DRIVE TIME BY CHANNELING STRESS INTO PRODUCTIVITY.
TRAFFIC PILE UP? HAVE A MINI GOAL-SETTING SESSION! ... STUCK IN THE SLOW LANE? DICTATE THOSE OVERDUE LETTERS! ... GET TRAPPED BEHIND A FLAT TIRE ON THE FREEWAY AND YOU COULD MENTALLY OUTLINE YOUR BUSINESS STRATEGY FOR THE.....
EEEYAAA
...NOT THAT PRODUCTIVE, BUT WELL WORTH THE $12.95.

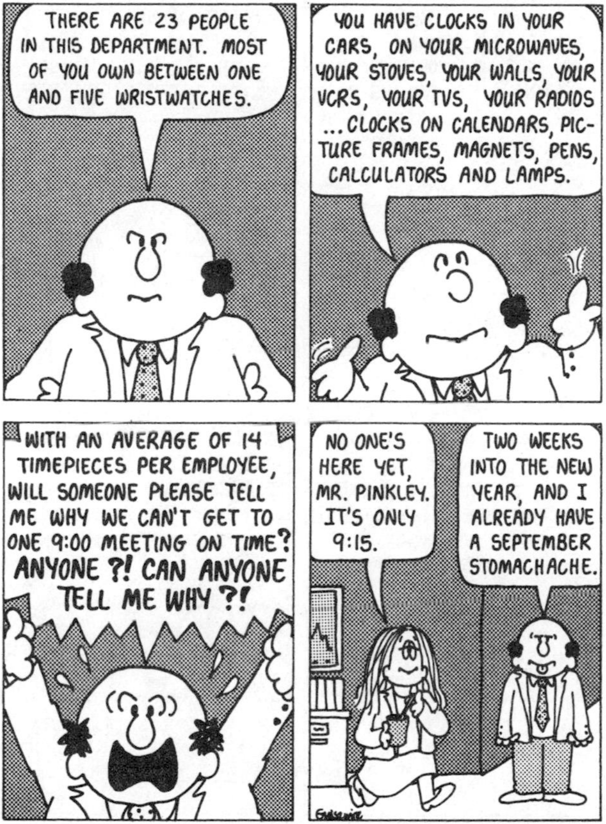
THERE ARE 23 PEOPLE IN THIS DEPARTMENT. MOST OF YOU OWN BETWEEN ONE AND FIVE WRISTWATCHES.
YOU HAVE CLOCKS IN YOUR CARS, ON YOUR MICROWAVES, YOUR STOVES, YOUR WALLS, YOUR VCRS, YOUR TVS, YOUR RADIOS ...CLOCKS ON CALENDARS, PICTURE FRAMES, MAGNETS, PENS, CALCULATORS AND LAMPS.
WITH AN AVERAGE OF 14 TIMEPIECES PER EMPLOYEE, WILL SOMEONE PLEASE TELL ME WHY WE CAN'T GET TO ONE 9:00 MEETING ON TIME? ANYONE ?! CAN ANYONE TELL ME WHY ?!
NO ONE'S HERE YET, MR. PINKLEY. IT'S ONLY 9:15.
TWO WEEKS INTO THE NEW YEAR, AND I ALREADY HAVE A SEPTEMBER STOMACHACHE.

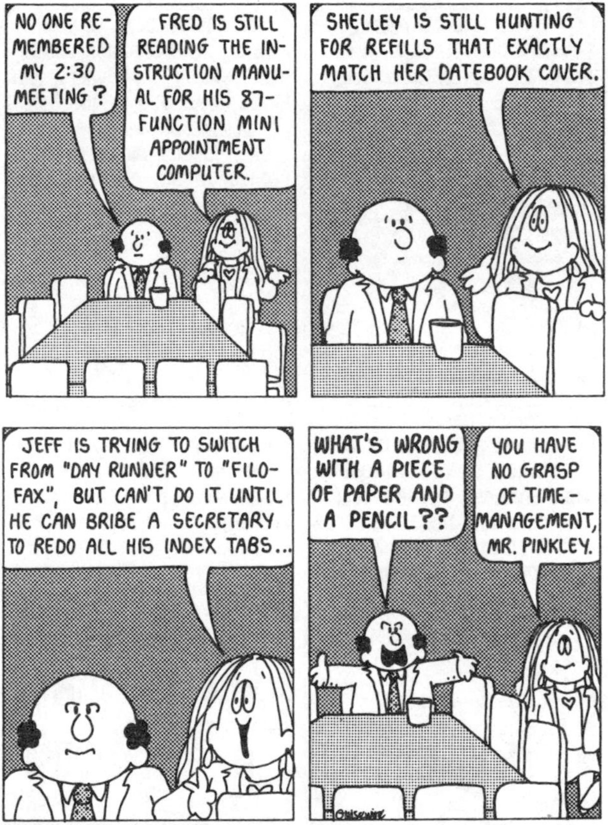
NO ONE RE-MEMBERED MY 2:30 MEETING?
FRED IS STILL READING THE IN-STRUCTION MANU-AL FOR HIS 87-FUNCTION MINI APPOINTMENT COMPUTER.
SHELLEY IS STILL HUNTING FOR REFILLS THAT EXACTLY MATCH HER DATEBOOK COVER.
JEFF IS TRYING TO SWITCH FROM "DAY RUNNER" TO "FILO-FAX", BUT CAN'T DO IT UNTIL HE CAN BRIBE A SECRETARY TO REDO ALL HIS INDEX TABS...
WHAT'S WRONG WITH A PIECE OF PAPER AND A PENCIL??
YOU HAVE NO GRASP OF TIME-MANAGEMENT, MR. PINKLEY.

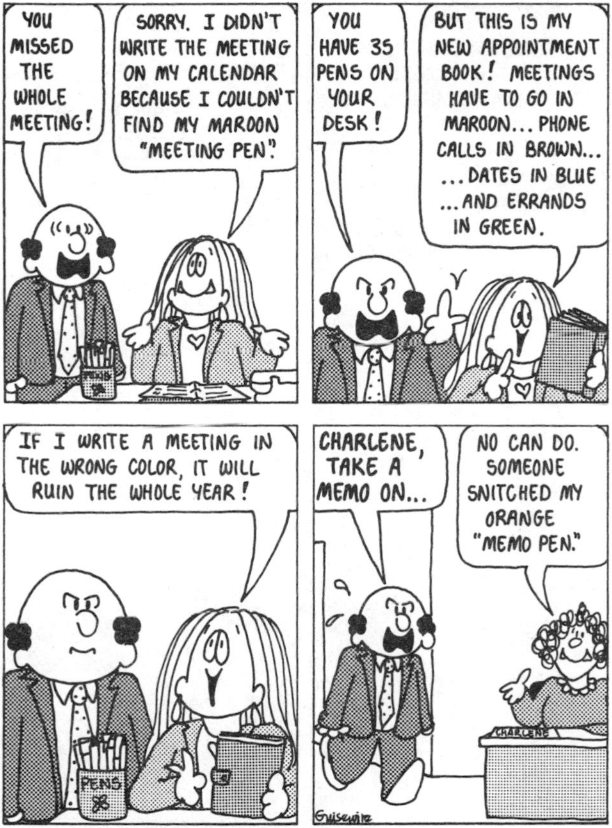
YOU MISSED THE WHOLE MEETING!
SORRY. I DIDN'T WRITE THE MEETING ON MY CALENDAR BECAUSE I COULDN'T FIND MY MAROON "MEETING PEN."
YOU HAVE 35 PENS ON YOUR DESK!
BUT THIS IS MY NEW APPOINTMENT BOOK! MEETINGS HAVE TO GO IN MAROON... PHONE CALLS IN BROWN... ...DATES IN BLUE ...AND ERRANDS IN GREEN.
IF I WRITE A MEETING IN THE WRONG COLOR, IT WILL RUIN THE WHOLE YEAR!
PENS
CHARLENE, TAKE A MEMO ON...
NO CAN DO. SOMEONE SNITCHED MY ORANGE "MEMO PEN."
CHARLENE
Guisewite

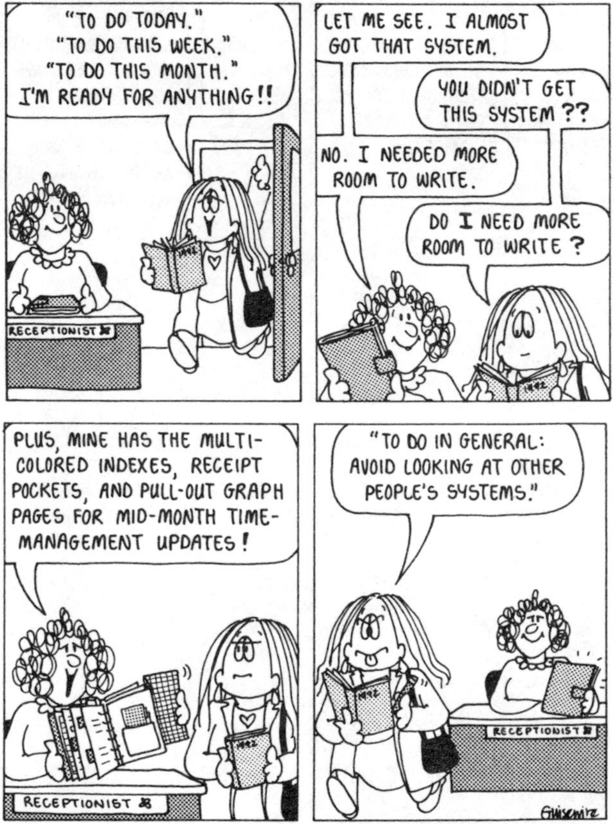
"TO DO TODAY."
"TO DO THIS WEEK."
"TO DO THIS MONTH."
I'M READY FOR ANYTHING!!
RECEPTIONIST
LET ME SEE. I ALMOST GOT THAT SYSTEM.
YOU DIDN'T GET THIS SYSTEM??
NO. I NEEDED MORE ROOM TO WRITE.
DO I NEED MORE ROOM TO WRITE?
PLUS, MINE HAS THE MULTI-COLORED INDEXES, RECEIPT POCKETS, AND PULL-OUT GRAPH PAGES FOR MID-MONTH TIME-MANAGEMENT UPDATES!
RECEPTIONIST
"TO DO IN GENERAL: AVOID LOOKING AT OTHER PEOPLE'S SYSTEMS."
RECEPTIONIST
Guisewite

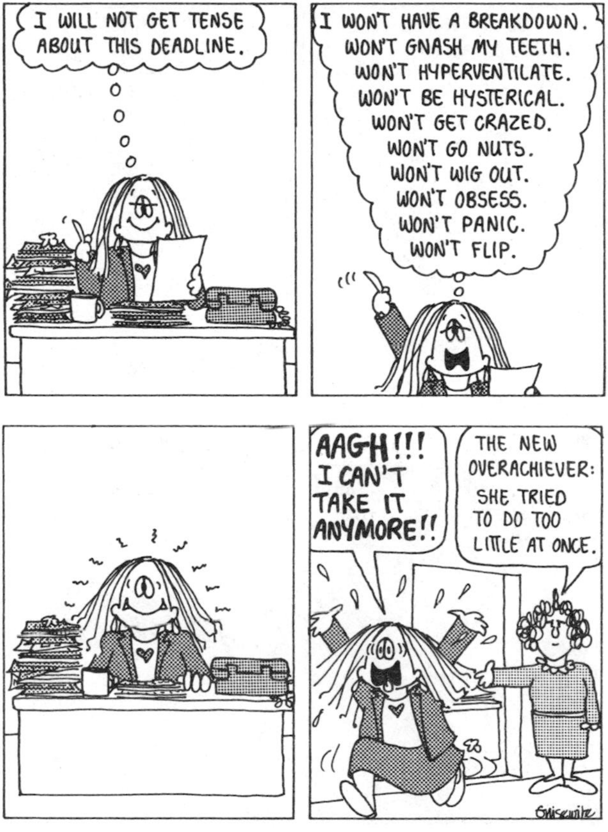
I WILL NOT GET TENSE ABOUT THIS DEADLINE.
I WON'T HAVE A BREAKDOWN. WON'T GNASH MY TEETH. WON'T HYPERVENTILATE. WON'T BE HYSTERICAL. WON'T GET CRAZED. WON'T GO NUTS. WON'T WIG OUT. WON'T OBSESS. WON'T PANIC. WON'T FLIP.
AAGH!!! I CAN'T TAKE IT ANYMORE!!
THE NEW OVERACHIEVER: SHE TRIED TO DO TOO LITTLE AT ONCE.
Guisewite

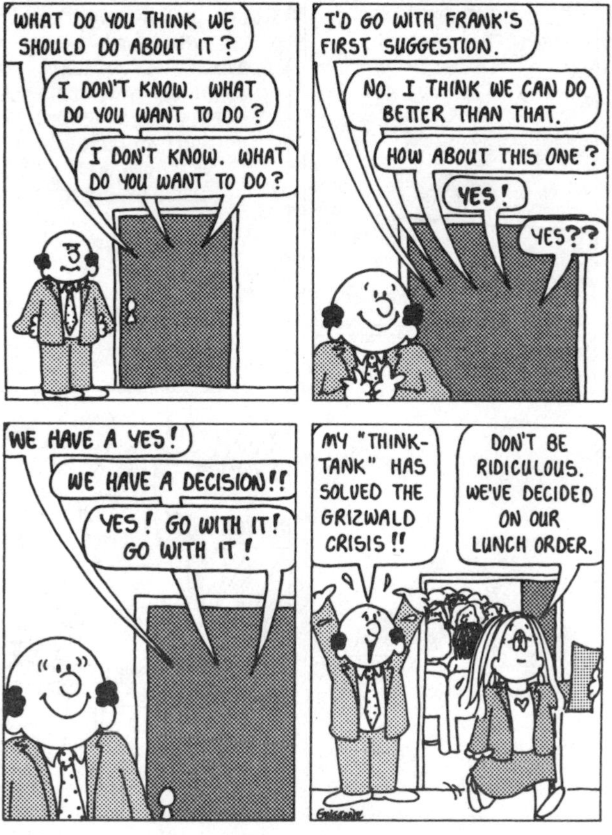
WHAT DO YOU THINK WE SHOULD DO ABOUT IT?
I DON'T KNOW. WHAT DO YOU WANT TO DO?
I DON'T KNOW. WHAT DO YOU WANT TO DO?
I'D GO WITH FRANK'S FIRST SUGGESTION.
NO. I THINK WE CAN DO BETTER THAN THAT.
HOW ABOUT THIS ONE?
YES!
YES??
WE HAVE A YES!
WE HAVE A DECISION!!
YES! GO WITH IT! GO WITH IT!
MY "THINK-TANK" HAS SOLVED THE GRIZWALD CRISIS!!
DON'T BE RIDICULOUS. WE'VE DECIDED ON OUR LUNCH ORDER.

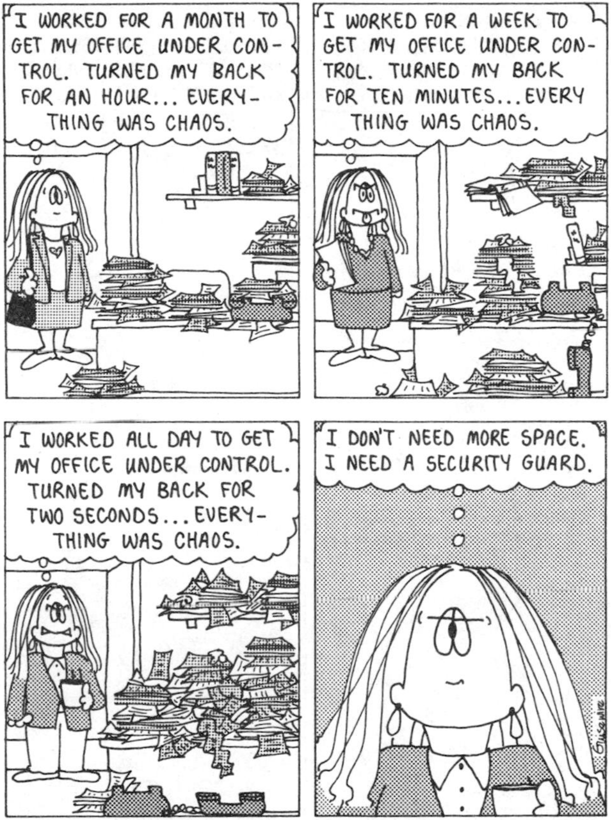
I WORKED FOR A MONTH TO GET MY OFFICE UNDER CON- TROL. TURNED MY BACK FOR AN HOUR... EVERY- THING WAS CHAOS.
I WORKED FOR A WEEK TO GET MY OFFICE UNDER CON- TROL. TURNED MY BACK FOR TEN MINUTES...EVERY THING WAS CHAOS.
I WORKED ALL DAY TO GET MY OFFICE UNDER CONTROL. TURNED MY BACK FOR TWO SECONDS... EVERY- THING WAS CHAOS.
I DON'T NEED MORE SPACE. I NEED A SECURITY GUARD.

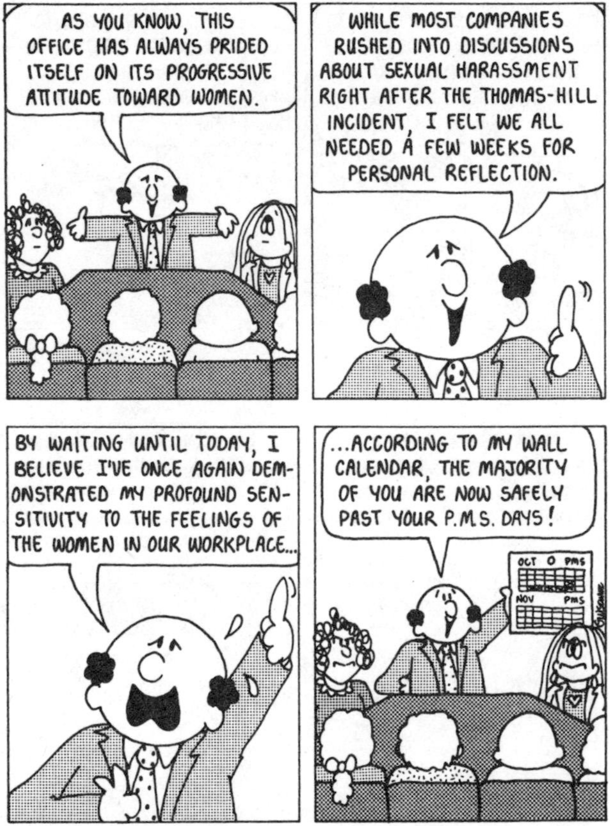
AS YOU KNOW, THIS OFFICE HAS ALWAYS PRIDED ITSELF ON ITS PROGRESSIVE ATTITUDE TOWARD WOMEN.
WHILE MOST COMPANIES RUSHED INTO DISCUSSIONS ABOUT SEXUAL HARASSMENT RIGHT AFTER THE THOMAS-HILL INCIDENT, I FELT WE ALL NEEDED A FEW WEEKS FOR PERSONAL REFLECTION.
BY WAITING UNTIL TODAY, I BELIEVE I'VE ONCE AGAIN DEMONSTRATED MY PROFOUND SENSITIVITY TO THE FEELINGS OF THE WOMEN IN OUR WORKPLACE...
...ACCORDING TO MY WALL CALENDAR, THE MAJORITY OF YOU ARE NOW SAFELY PAST YOUR P.M.S. DAYS!
OCT
PMS
NOV
PMS

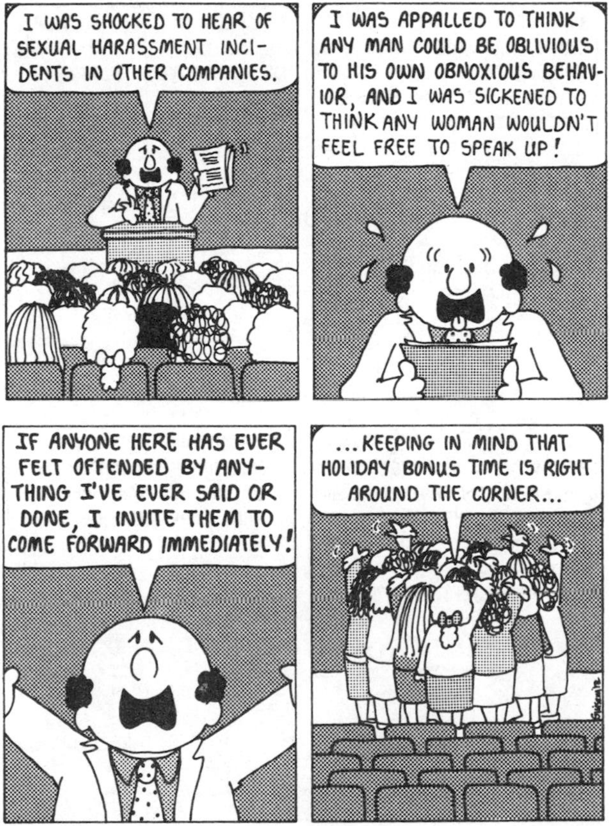
I WAS SHOCKED TO HEAR OF SEXUAL HARASSMENT INCIDENTS IN OTHER COMPANIES.
I WAS APPALLED TO THINK ANY MAN COULD BE OBLIVIOUS TO HIS OWN OBNOXIOUS BEHAVIOR, AND I WAS SICKENED TO THINK ANY WOMAN WOULDN'T FEEL FREE TO SPEAK UP!
IF ANYONE HERE HAS EVER FELT OFFENDED BY ANYTHING I'VE EVER SAID OR DONE, I INVITE THEM TO COME FORWARD IMMEDIATELY!
...KEEPING IN MIND THAT HOLIDAY BONUS TIME IS RIGHT AROUND THE CORNER...

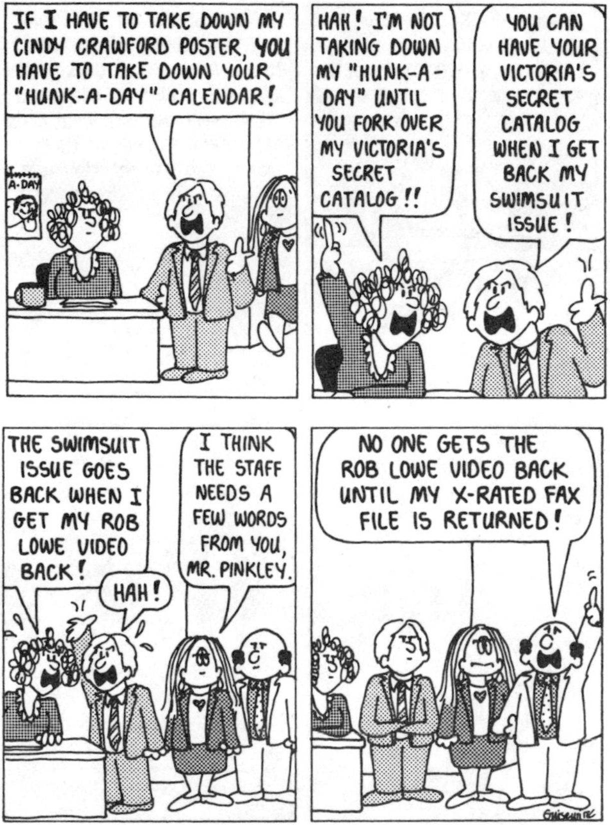
IF I HAVE TO TAKE DOWN MY CINDY CRAWFORD POSTER, YOU HAVE TO TAKE DOWN YOUR "HUNK-A-DAY" CALENDAR!
A-DAY
HAH! I'M NOT TAKING DOWN MY "HUNK-A-DAY" UNTIL YOU FORK OVER MY VICTORIA'S SECRET CATALOG!!
YOU CAN HAVE YOUR VICTORIA'S SECRET CATALOG WHEN I GET BACK MY SWIMSUIT ISSUE!
THE SWIMSUIT ISSUE GOES BACK WHEN I GET MY ROB LOWE VIDEO BACK!
HAH!
I THINK THE STAFF NEEDS A FEW WORDS FROM YOU, MR. PINKLEY.
NO ONE GETS THE ROB LOWE VIDEO BACK UNTIL MY X-RATED FAX FILE IS RETURNED!

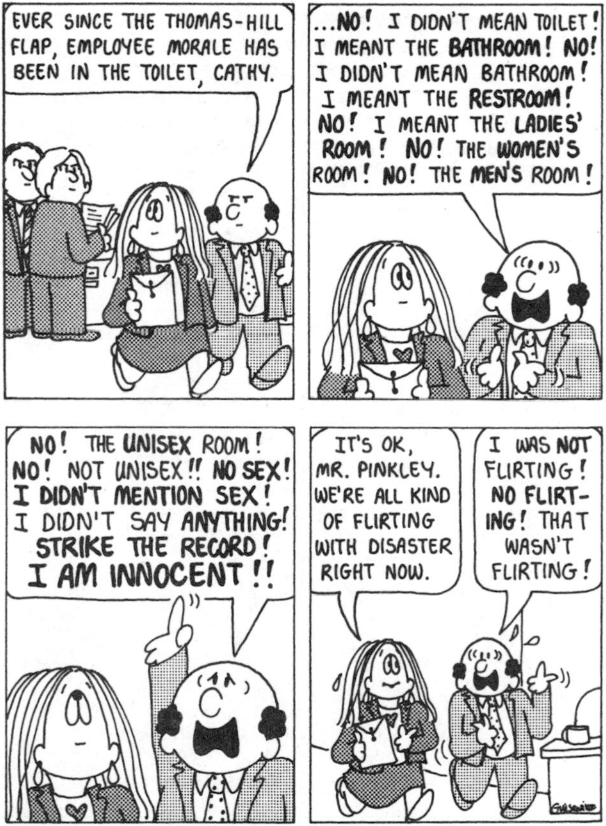
EVER SINCE THE THOMAS-HILL FLAP, EMPLOYEE MORALE HAS BEEN IN THE TOILET, CATHY.
...NO! I DIDN'T MEAN TOILET! I MEANT THE BATHROOM! NO! I DIDN'T MEAN BATHROOM! I MEANT THE RESTROOM! NO! I MEANT THE LADIES' ROOM! NO! THE WOMEN'S ROOM! NO! THE MEN'S ROOM!
NO! THE UNISEX ROOM! NO! NOT UNISEX!! NO SEX! I DIDN'T MENTION SEX! I DIDN'T SAY ANYTHING! STRIKE THE RECORD! I AM INNOCENT!!
IT'S OK, MR. PINKLEY. WE'RE ALL KIND OF FLIRTING WITH DISASTER RIGHT NOW.
I WAS NOT FLIRTING! NO FLIRTING! THAT WASN'T FLIRTING!

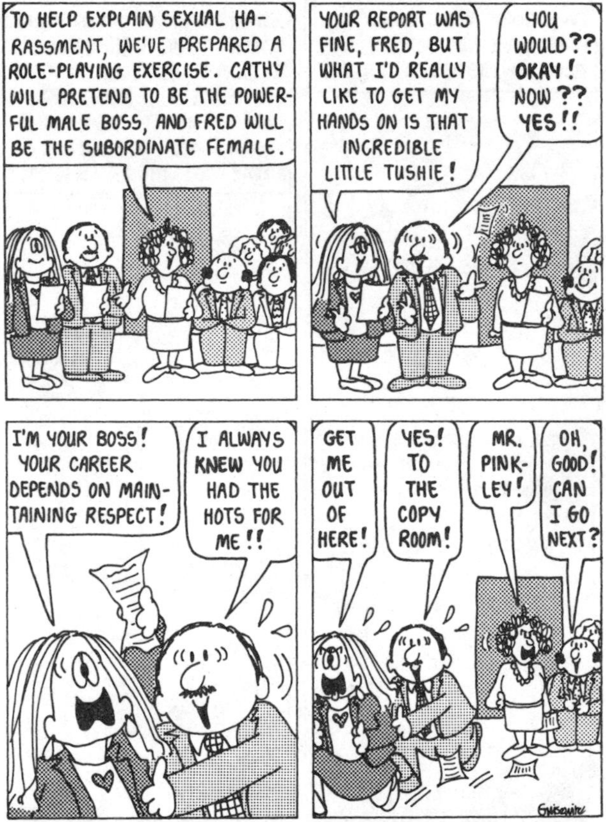
TO HELP EXPLAIN SEXUAL HARASSMENT, WE'VE PREPARED A ROLE-PLAYING EXERCISE. CATHY WILL PRETEND TO BE THE POWERFUL MALE BOSS, AND FRED WILL BE THE SUBORDINATE FEMALE.
YOUR REPORT WAS FINE, FRED, BUT WHAT I'D REALLY LIKE TO GET MY HANDS ON IS THAT INCREDIBLE LITTLE TUSHIE!
YOU WOULD?? OKAY! NOW?? YES!!
I'M YOUR BOSS! YOUR CAREER DEPENDS ON MAINTAINING RESPECT!
I ALWAYS KNEW YOU HAD THE HOTS FOR ME!!
GET ME OUT OF HERE!
YES! TO THE COPY ROOM!
MR. PINKLEY!
OH, GOOD! CAN I GO NEXT?
Guisewite

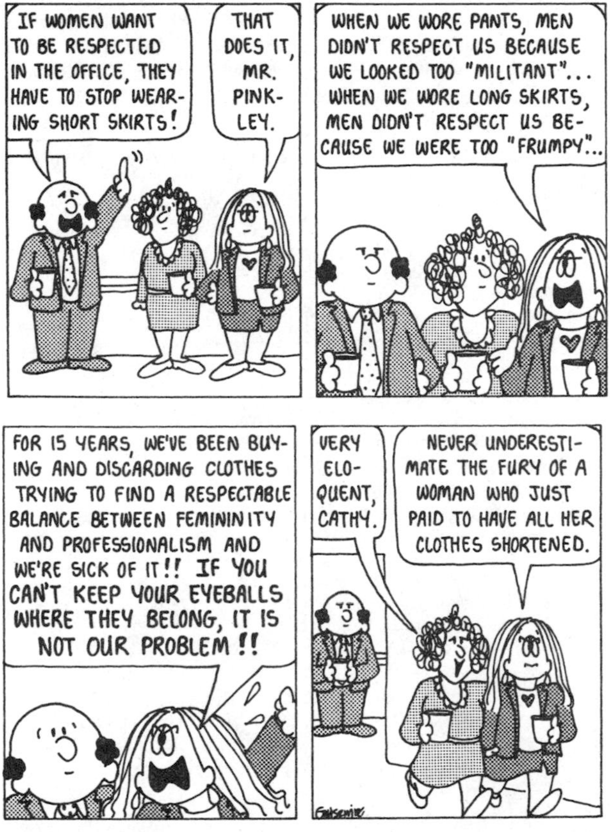
IF WOMEN WANT TO BE RESPECTED IN THE OFFICE, THEY HAVE TO STOP WEARING SHORT SKIRTS!
THAT DOES IT, MR. PINKLEY.
WHEN WE WORE PANTS, MEN DIDN'T RESPECT US BECAUSE WE LOOKED TOO "MILITANT"... WHEN WE WORE LONG SKIRTS, MEN DIDN'T RESPECT US BECAUSE WE WERE TOO "FRUMPY"...
FOR 15 YEARS, WE'VE BEEN BUYING AND DISCARDING CLOTHES TRYING TO FIND A RESPECTABLE BALANCE BETWEEN FEMININITY AND PROFESSIONALISM AND WE'RE SICK OF IT!! IF YOU CAN'T KEEP YOUR EYEBALLS WHERE THEY BELONG, IT IS NOT OUR PROBLEM!!
VERY ELOQUENT, CATHY.
NEVER UNDERESTIMATE THE FURY OF A WOMAN WHO JUST PAID TO HAVE ALL HER CLOTHES SHORTENED.

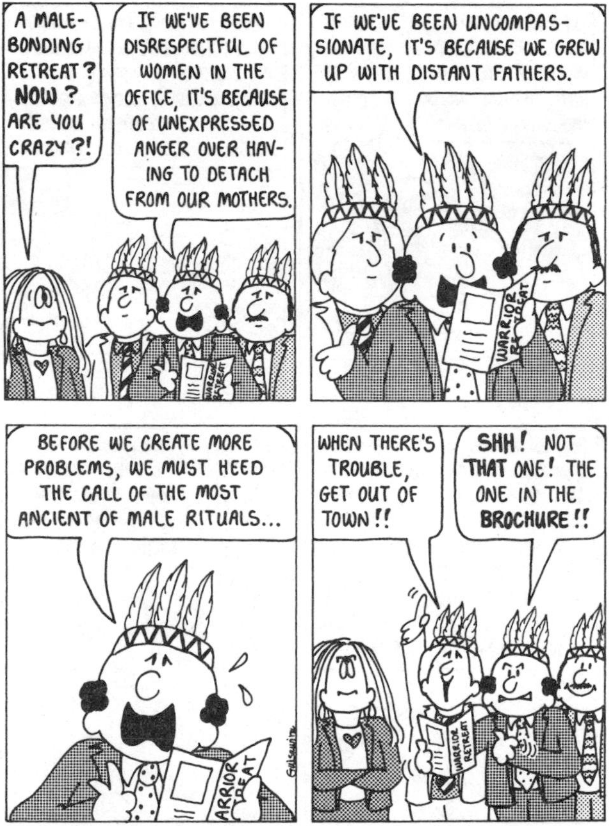
A MALE-BONDING RETREAT? NOW? ARE YOU CRAZY?!
IF WE'VE BEEN DISRESPECTFUL OF WOMEN IN THE OFFICE, IT'S BECAUSE OF UNEXPRESSED ANGER OVER HAVING TO DETACH FROM OUR MOTHERS.
IF WE'VE BEEN UNCOMPASSIONATE, IT'S BECAUSE WE GREW UP WITH DISTANT FATHERS.
WARRIOR RETREAT
BEFORE WE CREATE MORE PROBLEMS, WE MUST HEED THE CALL OF THE MOST ANCIENT OF MALE RITUALS...
WHEN THERE'S TROUBLE, GET OUT OF TOWN!!
SHH! NOT THAT ONE! THE ONE IN THE BROCHURE!!
WARRIOR RETREAT

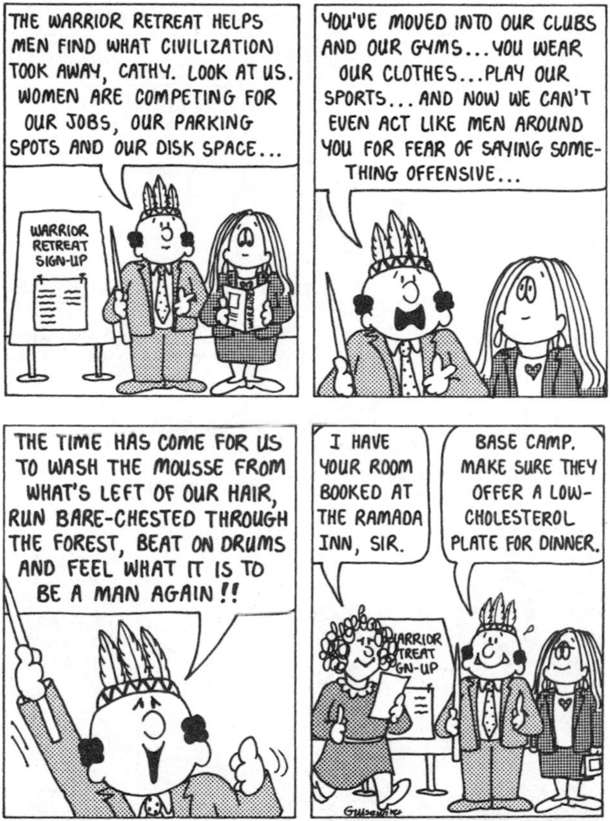
THE WARRIOR RETREAT HELPS MEN FIND WHAT CIVILIZATION TOOK AWAY, CATHY. LOOK AT US. WOMEN ARE COMPETING FOR OUR JOBS, OUR PARKING SPOTS AND OUR DISK SPACE...
WARRIOR RETREAT SIGN-UP
YOU'VE MOVED INTO OUR CLUBS AND OUR GYMS...YOU WEAR OUR CLOTHES...PLAY OUR SPORTS...AND NOW WE CAN'T EVEN ACT LIKE MEN AROUND YOU FOR FEAR OF SAYING SOMETHING OFFENSIVE...
THE TIME HAS COME FOR US TO WASH THE MOUSSE FROM WHAT'S LEFT OF OUR HAIR, RUN BARE-CHESTED THROUGH THE FOREST, BEAT ON DRUMS AND FEEL WHAT IT IS TO BE A MAN AGAIN!!
I HAVE YOUR ROOM BOOKED AT THE RAMADA INN, SIR.
BASE CAMP. MAKE SURE THEY OFFER A LOW-CHOLESTEROL PLATE FOR DINNER.

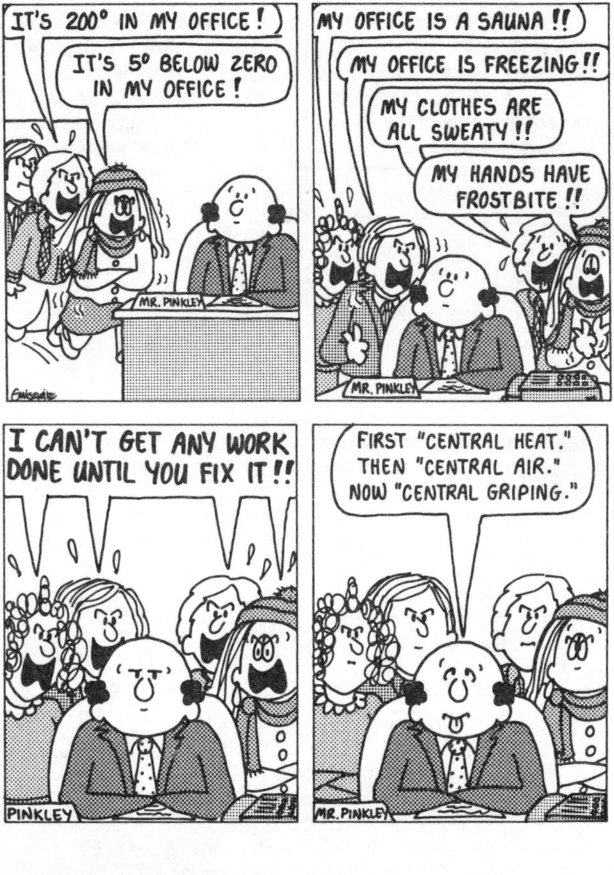
IT'S 200° IN MY OFFICE!
IT'S 5° BELOW ZERO IN MY OFFICE!
MR. PINKLEY
MY OFFICE IS A SAUNA!!
MY OFFICE IS FREEZING!!
MY CLOTHES ARE ALL SWEATY!!
MY HANDS HAVE FROSTBITE!!
MR. PINKLEY
I CAN'T GET ANY WORK DONE UNTIL YOU FIX IT!!
PINKLEY
FIRST "CENTRAL HEAT." THEN "CENTRAL AIR." NOW "CENTRAL GRIPING."
MR. PINKLEY

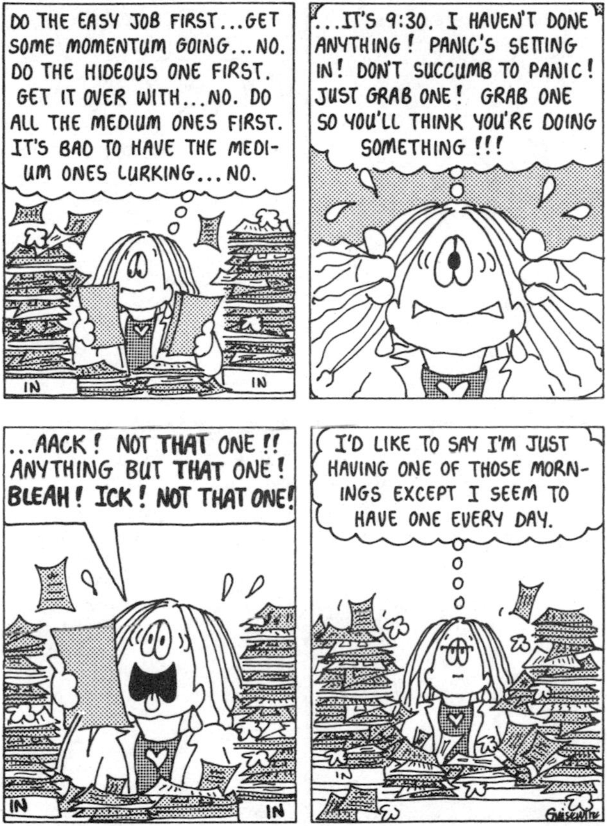
DO THE EASY JOB FIRST...GET SOME MOMENTUM GOING...NO. DO THE HIDEOUS ONE FIRST. GET IT OVER WITH...NO. DO ALL THE MEDIUM ONES FIRST. IT'S BAD TO HAVE THE MEDIUM ONES LURKING...NO.
IN
IN
...IT'S 9:30. I HAVEN'T DONE ANYTHING! PANIC'S SETTING IN! DON'T SUCCUMB TO PANIC! JUST GRAB ONE! GRAB ONE SO YOU'LL THINK YOU'RE DOING SOMETHING!!!
...AACK! NOT THAT ONE!! ANYTHING BUT THAT ONE! BLEAH! ICK! NOT THAT ONE!
IN
IN
I'D LIKE TO SAY I'M JUST HAVING ONE OF THOSE MORNINGS EXCEPT I SEEM TO HAVE ONE EVERY DAY.
IN
Guisewite

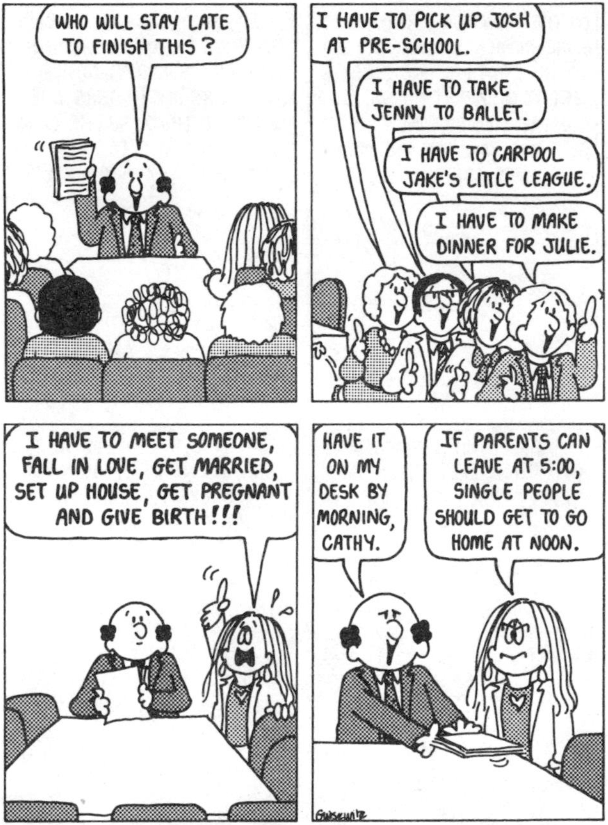
WHO WILL STAY LATE TO FINISH THIS?
I HAVE TO PICK UP JOSH AT PRE-SCHOOL.
I HAVE TO TAKE JENNY TO BALLET.
I HAVE TO CARPOOL JAKE'S LITTLE LEAGUE.
I HAVE TO MAKE DINNER FOR JULIE.
I HAVE TO MEET SOMEONE, FALL IN LOVE, GET MARRIED, SET UP HOUSE, GET PREGNANT AND GIVE BIRTH!!!
HAVE IT ON MY DESK BY MORNING, CATHY.
IF PARENTS CAN LEAVE AT 5:00, SINGLE PEOPLE SHOULD GET TO GO HOME AT NOON.
GUISEWITE

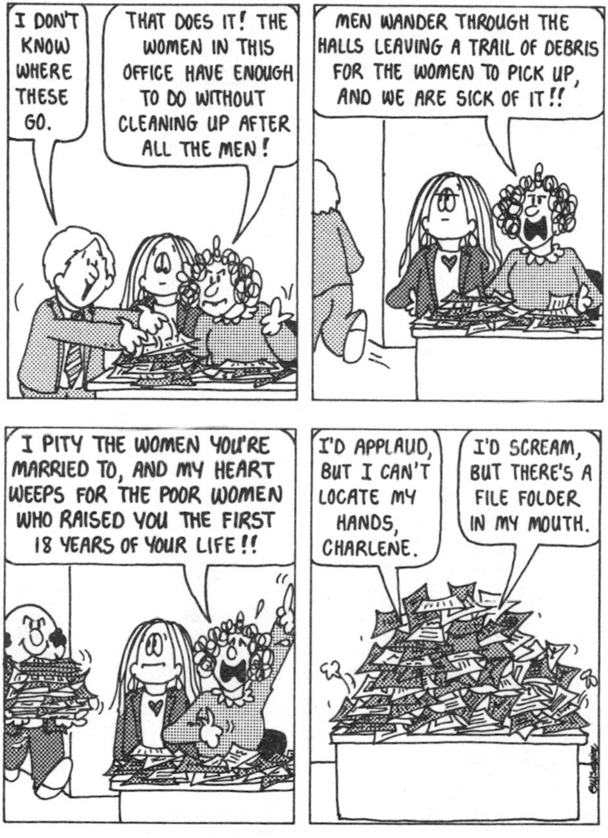

I DON'T KNOW WHERE THESE GO.
THAT DOES IT! THE WOMEN IN THIS OFFICE HAVE ENOUGH TO DO WITHOUT CLEANING UP AFTER ALL THE MEN!
MEN WANDER THROUGH THE HALLS LEAVING A TRAIL OF DEBRIS FOR THE WOMEN TO PICK UP, AND WE ARE SICK OF IT!!
I PITY THE WOMEN YOU'RE MARRIED TO, AND MY HEART WEEPS FOR THE POOR WOMEN WHO RAISED YOU THE FIRST 18 YEARS OF YOUR LIFE!!
I'D APPLAUD, BUT I CAN'T LOCATE MY HANDS, CHARLENE.
I'D SCREAM, BUT THERE'S A FILE FOLDER IN MY MOUTH.

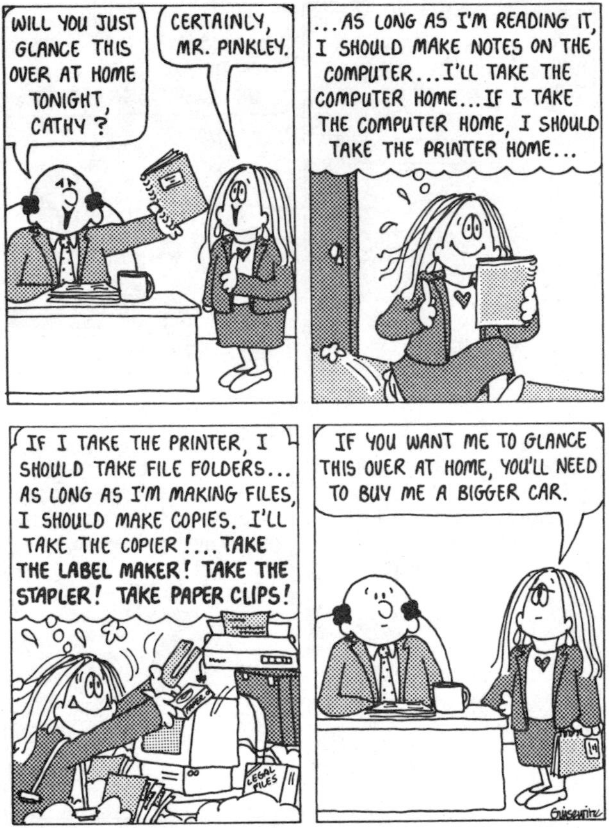
WILL YOU JUST GLANCE THIS OVER AT HOME TONIGHT, CATHY?
CERTAINLY, MR. PINKLEY.
...AS LONG AS I'M READING IT, I SHOULD MAKE NOTES ON THE COMPUTER...I'LL TAKE THE COMPUTER HOME...IF I TAKE THE COMPUTER HOME, I SHOULD TAKE THE PRINTER HOME...
IF I TAKE THE PRINTER, I SHOULD TAKE FILE FOLDERS... AS LONG AS I'M MAKING FILES, I SHOULD MAKE COPIES. I'LL TAKE THE COPIER!...TAKE THE LABEL MAKER! TAKE THE STAPLER! TAKE PAPER CLIPS!
LEGAL FILES
IF YOU WANT ME TO GLANCE THIS OVER AT HOME, YOU'LL NEED TO BUY ME A BIGGER CAR.
Guisewite

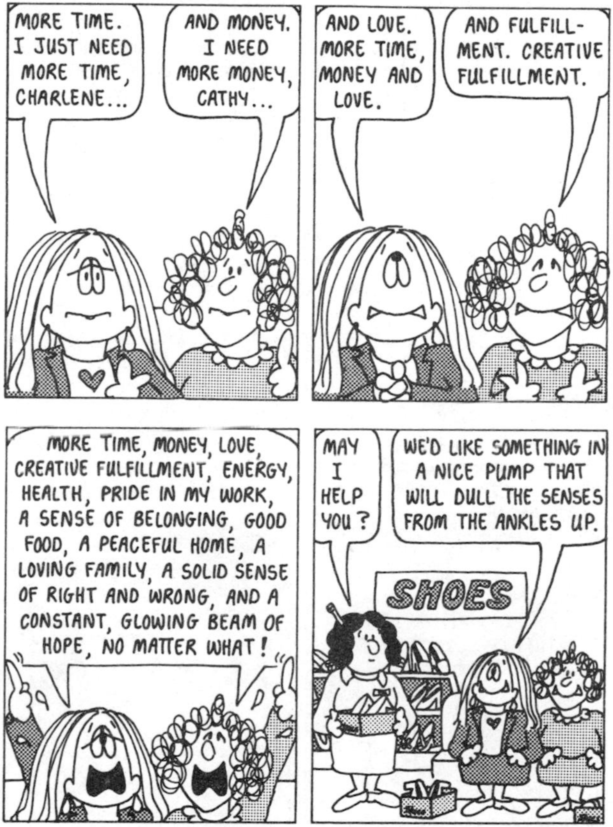
MORE TIME. I JUST NEED MORE TIME, CHARLENE...
AND MONEY. I NEED MORE MONEY, CATHY...
AND LOVE. MORE TIME, MONEY AND LOVE.
AND FULFILL-MENT. CREATIVE FULFILLMENT.
MORE TIME, MONEY, LOVE, CREATIVE FULFILLMENT, ENERGY, HEALTH, PRIDE IN MY WORK, A SENSE OF BELONGING, GOOD FOOD, A PEACEFUL HOME, A LOVING FAMILY, A SOLID SENSE OF RIGHT AND WRONG, AND A CONSTANT, GLOWING BEAM OF HOPE, NO MATTER WHAT!
MAY I HELP YOU?
WE'D LIKE SOMETHING IN A NICE PUMP THAT WILL DULL THE SENSES FROM THE ANKLES UP.
SHOES

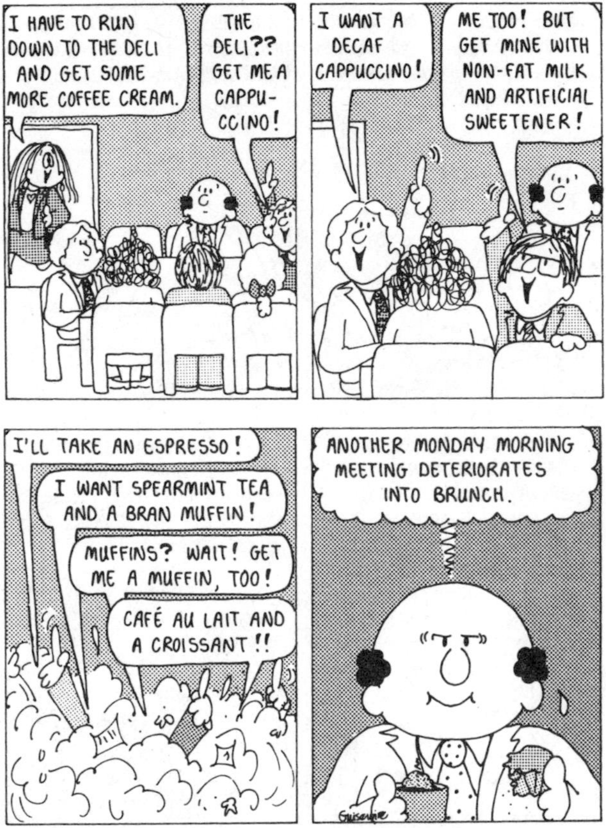
I HAVE TO RUN DOWN TO THE DELI AND GET SOME MORE COFFEE CREAM.
THE DELI?? GET ME A CAPPU-CCINO!
I WANT A DECAF CAPPUCCINO!
ME TOO! BUT GET MINE WITH NON-FAT MILK AND ARTIFICIAL SWEETENER!
I'LL TAKE AN ESPRESSO!
I WANT SPEARMINT TEA AND A BRAN MUFFIN!
MUFFINS? WAIT! GET ME A MUFFIN, TOO!
CAFÉ AU LAIT AND A CROISSANT!!
ANOTHER MONDAY MORNING MEETING DETERIORATES INTO BRUNCH.
Guisewite

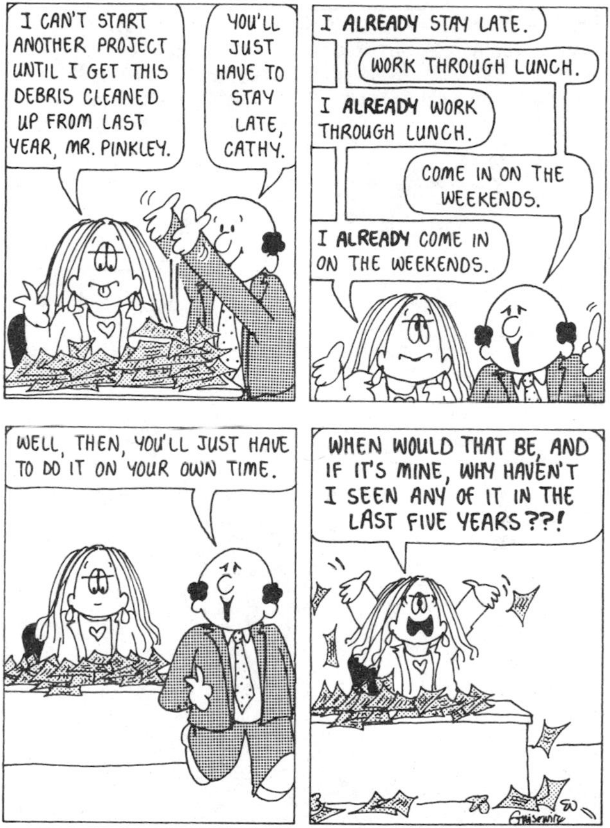

I CAN'T START ANOTHER PROJECT UNTIL I GET THIS DEBRIS CLEANED UP FROM LAST YEAR, MR. PINKLEY.
YOU'LL JUST HAVE TO STAY LATE, CATHY.
I ALREADY STAY LATE.
WORK THROUGH LUNCH.
I ALREADY WORK THROUGH LUNCH.
COME IN ON THE WEEKENDS.
I ALREADY COME IN ON THE WEEKENDS.
WELL, THEN, YOU'LL JUST HAVE TO DO IT ON YOUR OWN TIME.
WHEN WOULD THAT BE, AND IF IT'S MINE, WHY HAVEN'T I SEEN ANY OF IT IN THE LAST FIVE YEARS??!

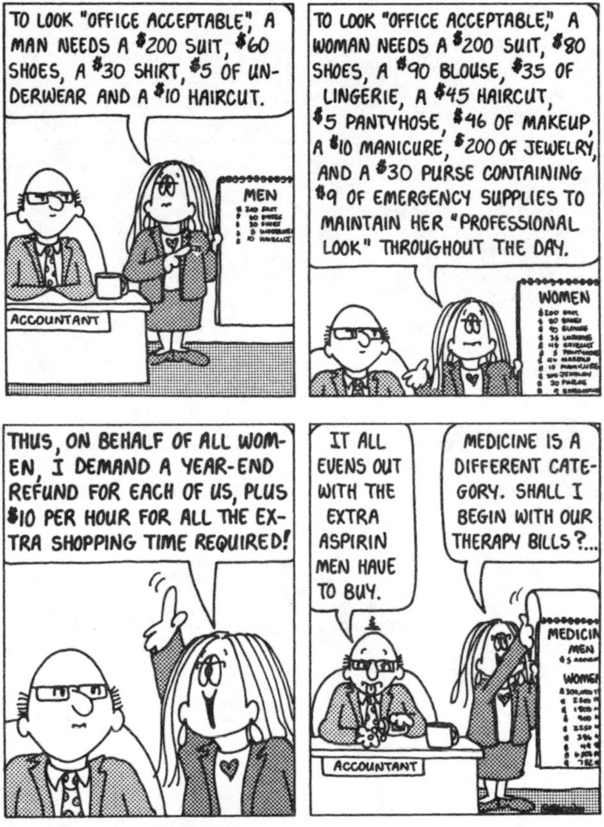
TO LOOK "OFFICE ACCEPTABLE," A MAN NEEDS A $200 SUIT, $60 SHOES, A $30 SHIRT, $5 OF UNDERWEAR AND A $10 HAIRCUT.
MEN
ACCOUNTANT
TO LOOK "OFFICE ACCEPTABLE," A WOMAN NEEDS A $200 SUIT, $80 SHOES, A $90 BLOUSE, $35 OF LINGERIE, A $45 HAIRCUT, $5 PANTYHOSE, $46 OF MAKEUP, A $10 MANICURE, $200 OF JEWELRY, AND A $30 PURSE CONTAINING $9 OF EMERGENCY SUPPLIES TO MAINTAIN HER "PROFESSIONAL LOOK" THROUGHOUT THE DAY.
WOMEN
THUS, ON BEHALF OF ALL WOMEN, I DEMAND A YEAR-END REFUND FOR EACH OF US, PLUS $10 PER HOUR FOR ALL THE EXTRA SHOPPING TIME REQUIRED!
IT ALL EVENS OUT WITH THE EXTRA ASPIRIN MEN HAVE TO BUY.
MEDICINE IS A DIFFERENT CATEGORY. SHALL I BEGIN WITH OUR THERAPY BILLS?...
MEDICIN
MEN
WOMEN
ACCOUNTANT

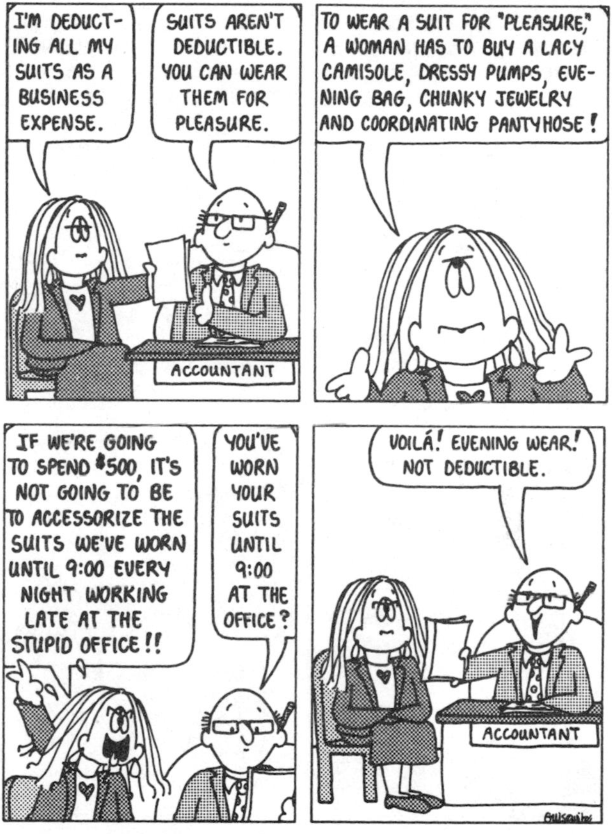
I'M DEDUCTING ALL MY SUITS AS A BUSINESS EXPENSE.
SUITS AREN'T DEDUCTIBLE. YOU CAN WEAR THEM FOR PLEASURE.
ACCOUNTANT
TO WEAR A SUIT FOR "PLEASURE," A WOMAN HAS TO BUY A LACY CAMISOLE, DRESSY PUMPS, EVENING BAG, CHUNKY JEWELRY AND COORDINATING PANTYHOSE!
IF WE'RE GOING TO SPEND $500, IT'S NOT GOING TO BE TO ACCESSORIZE THE SUITS WE'VE WORN UNTIL 9:00 EVERY NIGHT WORKING LATE AT THE STUPID OFFICE!!
YOU'VE WORN YOUR SUITS UNTIL 9:00 AT THE OFFICE?
VOILÁ! EVENING WEAR! NOT DEDUCTIBLE.
ACCOUNTANT

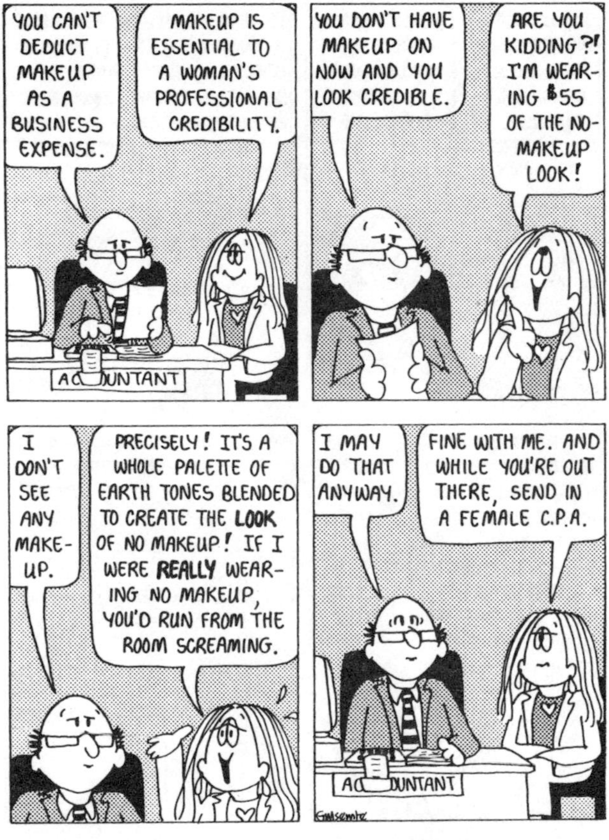
YOU CAN'T DEDUCT MAKEUP AS A BUSINESS EXPENSE.
MAKEUP IS ESSENTIAL TO A WOMAN'S PROFESSIONAL CREDIBILITY.
ACCOUNTANT
YOU DON'T HAVE MAKEUP ON NOW AND YOU LOOK CREDIBLE.
ARE YOU KIDDING?! I'M WEARING $55 OF THE NO-MAKEUP LOOK!
I DON'T SEE ANY MAKEUP.
PRECISELY! IT'S A WHOLE PALETTE OF EARTH TONES BLENDED TO CREATE THE LOOK OF NO MAKEUP! IF I WERE REALLY WEARING NO MAKEUP, YOU'D RUN FROM THE ROOM SCREAMING.
I MAY DO THAT ANYWAY.
FINE WITH ME. AND WHILE YOU'RE OUT THERE, SEND IN A FEMALE C.P.A.
ACCOUNTANT
Guisewite

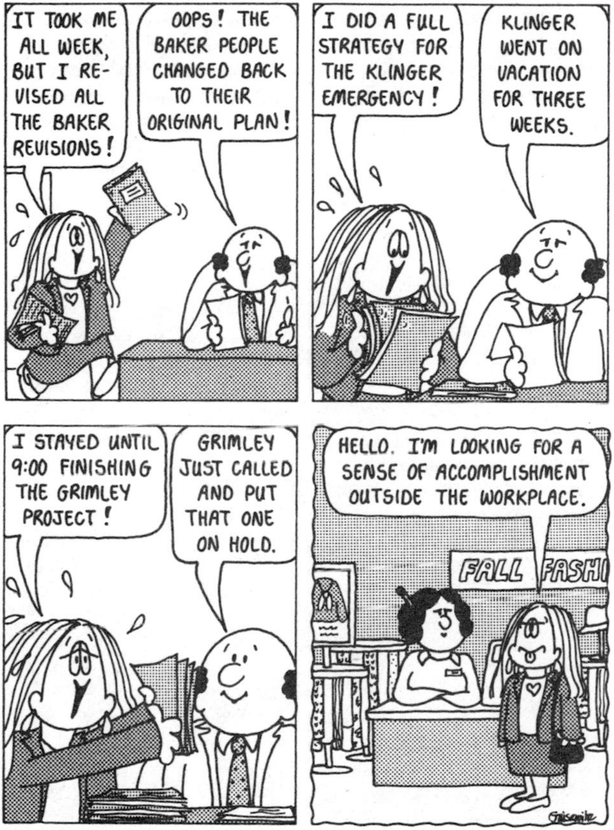
IT TOOK ME ALL WEEK, BUT I REVISED ALL THE BAKER REVISIONS!
OOPS! THE BAKER PEOPLE CHANGED BACK TO THEIR ORIGINAL PLAN!
I DID A FULL STRATEGY FOR THE KLINGER EMERGENCY!
KLINGER WENT ON VACATION FOR THREE WEEKS.
I STAYED UNTIL 9:00 FINISHING THE GRIMLEY PROJECT!
GRIMLEY JUST CALLED AND PUT THAT ONE ON HOLD.
HELLO. I'M LOOKING FOR A SENSE OF ACCOMPLISHMENT OUTSIDE THE WORKPLACE.
FALL FASHI
Guisewite

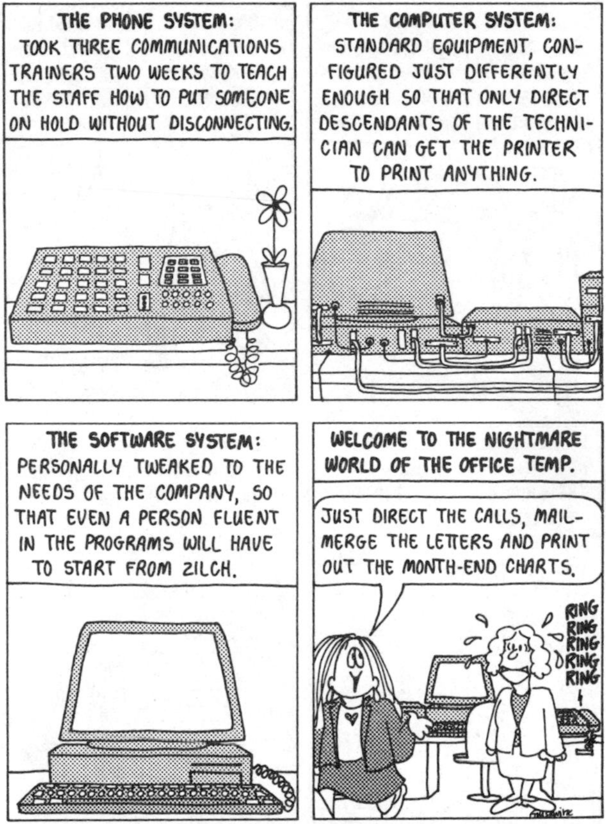
THE PHONE SYSTEM:
TOOK THREE COMMUNICATIONS TRAINERS TWO WEEKS TO TEACH THE STAFF HOW TO PUT SOMEONE ON HOLD WITHOUT DISCONNECTING.
THE COMPUTER SYSTEM:
STANDARD EQUIPMENT, CONFIGURED JUST DIFFERENTLY ENOUGH SO THAT ONLY DIRECT DESCENDANTS OF THE TECHNICIAN CAN GET THE PRINTER TO PRINT ANYTHING.
THE SOFTWARE SYSTEM:
PERSONALLY TWEAKED TO THE NEEDS OF THE COMPANY, SO THAT EVEN A PERSON FLUENT IN THE PROGRAMS WILL HAVE TO START FROM ZILCH.
WELCOME TO THE NIGHTMARE WORLD OF THE OFFICE TEMP.
JUST DIRECT THE CALLS, MAIL-MERGE THE LETTERS AND PRINT OUT THE MONTH-END CHARTS.
RING RING RING RING RING

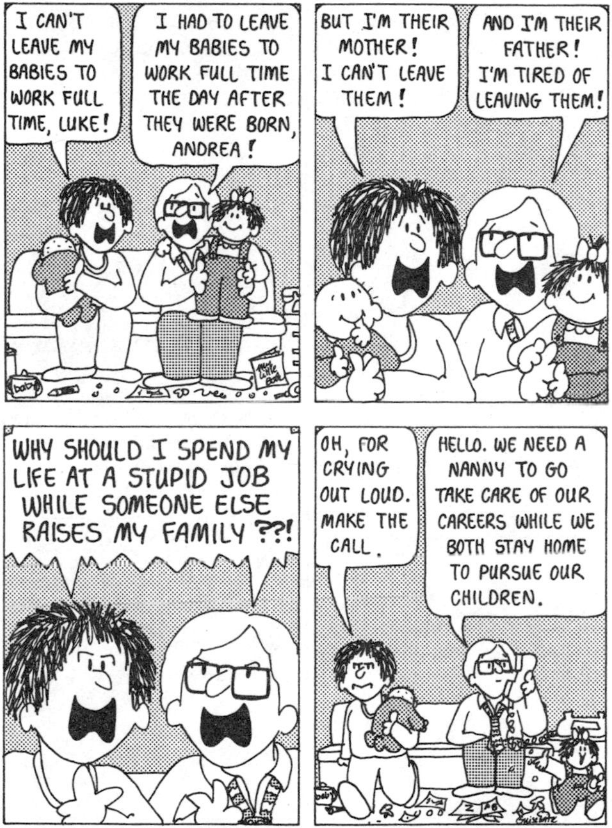
I CAN'T LEAVE MY BABIES TO WORK FULL TIME, LUKE!
I HAD TO LEAVE MY BABIES TO WORK FULL TIME THE DAY AFTER THEY WERE BORN, ANDREA!
BUT I'M THEIR MOTHER! I CAN'T LEAVE THEM!
AND I'M THEIR FATHER! I'M TIRED OF LEAVING THEM!
WHY SHOULD I SPEND MY LIFE AT A STUPID JOB WHILE SOMEONE ELSE RAISES MY FAMILY ??!
OH, FOR CRYING OUT LOUD. MAKE THE CALL.
HELLO. WE NEED A NANNY TO GO TAKE CARE OF OUR CAREERS WHILE WE BOTH STAY HOME TO PURSUE OUR CHILDREN.

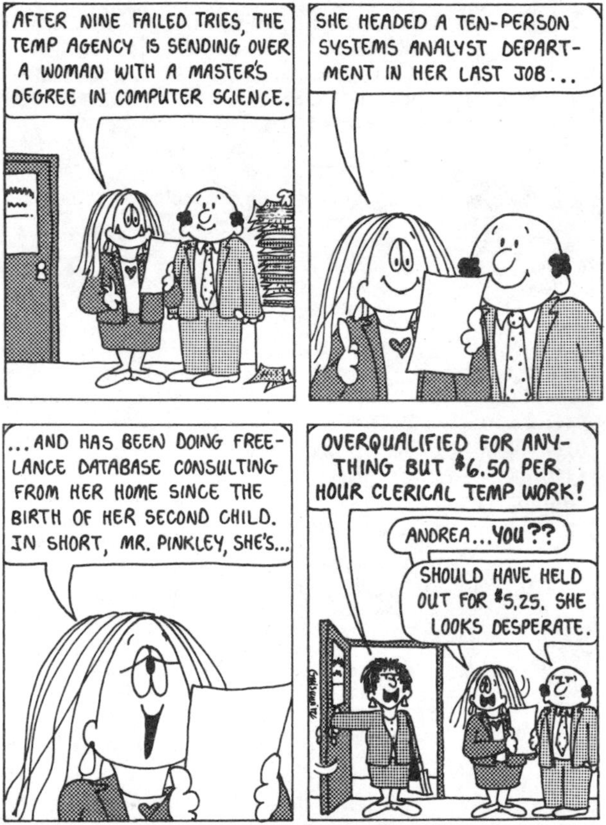
AFTER NINE FAILED TRIES, THE TEMP AGENCY IS SENDING OVER A WOMAN WITH A MASTER'S DEGREE IN COMPUTER SCIENCE.
SHE HEADED A TEN-PERSON SYSTEMS ANALYST DEPARTMENT IN HER LAST JOB...
...AND HAS BEEN DOING FREE-LANCE DATABASE CONSULTING FROM HER HOME SINCE THE BIRTH OF HER SECOND CHILD. IN SHORT, MR. PINKLEY, SHE'S...
OVERQUALIFIED FOR ANYTHING BUT $6.50 PER HOUR CLERICAL TEMP WORK!
ANDREA...YOU??
SHOULD HAVE HELD OUT FOR $5.25. SHE LOOKS DESPERATE.

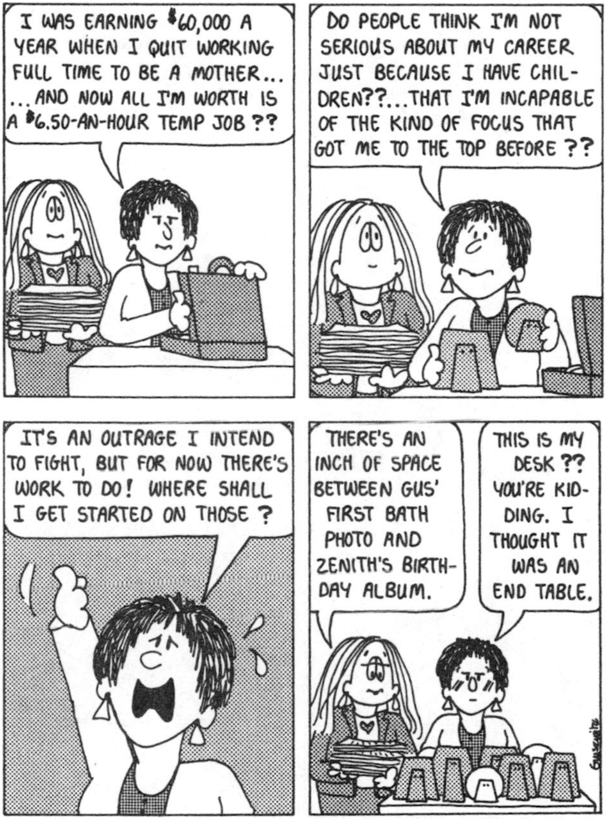
I WAS EARNING $60,000 A YEAR WHEN I QUIT WORKING FULL TIME TO BE A MOTHER... ...AND NOW ALL I'M WORTH IS A $6.50-AN-HOUR TEMP JOB??
DO PEOPLE THINK I'M NOT SERIOUS ABOUT MY CAREER JUST BECAUSE I HAVE CHIL-DREN??...THAT I'M INCAPABLE OF THE KIND OF FOCUS THAT GOT ME TO THE TOP BEFORE??
IT'S AN OUTRAGE I INTEND TO FIGHT, BUT FOR NOW THERE'S WORK TO DO! WHERE SHALL I GET STARTED ON THOSE?
THERE'S AN INCH OF SPACE BETWEEN GUS' FIRST BATH PHOTO AND ZENITH'S BIRTH-DAY ALBUM.
THIS IS MY DESK?? YOU'RE KID-DING. I THOUGHT IT WAS AN END TABLE.
GUISEWITE

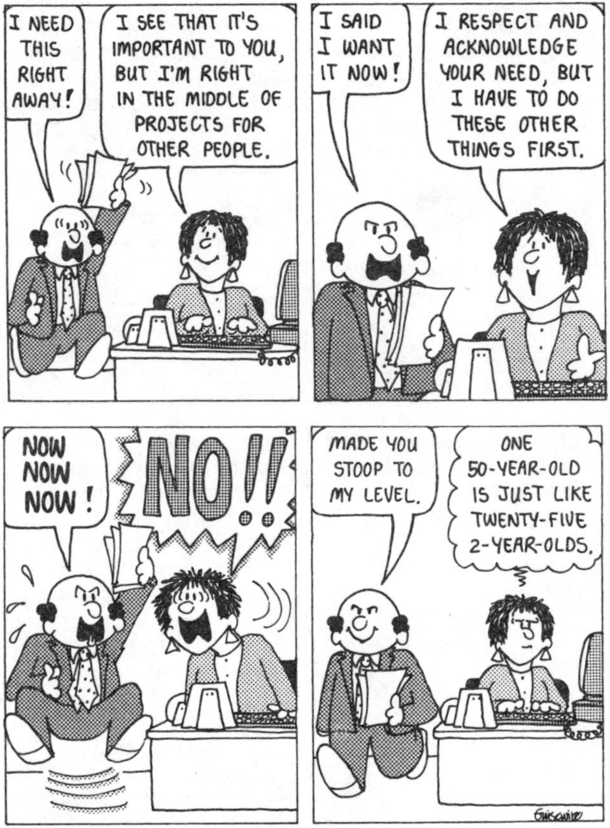
I NEED THIS RIGHT AWAY!
I SEE THAT IT'S IMPORTANT TO YOU, BUT I'M RIGHT IN THE MIDDLE OF PROJECTS FOR OTHER PEOPLE.
I SAID I WANT IT NOW!
I RESPECT AND ACKNOWLEDGE YOUR NEED, BUT I HAVE TO DO THESE OTHER THINGS FIRST.
NOW NOW NOW!
NO!!
MADE YOU STOOP TO MY LEVEL.
ONE 50-YEAR-OLD IS JUST LIKE TWENTY-FIVE 2-YEAR-OLDS.

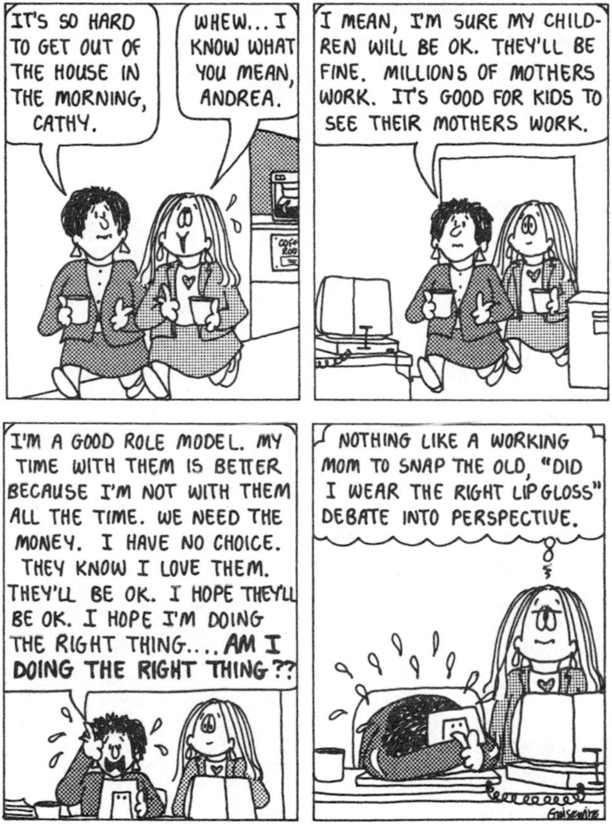
IT'S SO HARD TO GET OUT OF THE HOUSE IN THE MORNING, CATHY.
WHEW... I KNOW WHAT YOU MEAN, ANDREA.
I MEAN, I'M SURE MY CHILDREN WILL BE OK. THEY'LL BE FINE. MILLIONS OF MOTHERS WORK. IT'S GOOD FOR KIDS TO SEE THEIR MOTHERS WORK.
I'M A GOOD ROLE MODEL. MY TIME WITH THEM IS BETTER BECAUSE I'M NOT WITH THEM ALL THE TIME. WE NEED THE MONEY. I HAVE NO CHOICE. THEY KNOW I LOVE THEM. THEY'LL BE OK. I HOPE THEY'LL BE OK. I HOPE I'M DOING THE RIGHT THING.... AM I DOING THE RIGHT THING??
NOTHING LIKE A WORKING MOM TO SNAP THE OLD, "DID I WEAR THE RIGHT LIPGLOSS" DEBATE INTO PERSPECTIVE.
Guisewite

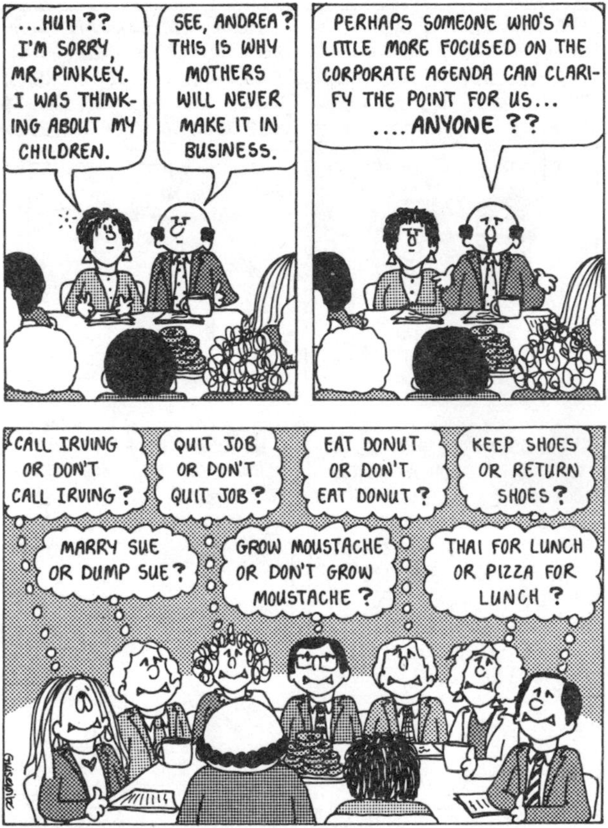
...HUH ?? I'M SORRY, MR. PINKLEY. I WAS THINKING ABOUT MY CHILDREN.
SEE, ANDREA? THIS IS WHY MOTHERS WILL NEVER MAKE IT IN BUSINESS.
PERHAPS SOMEONE WHO'S A LITTLE MORE FOCUSED ON THE CORPORATE AGENDA CAN CLARIFY THE POINT FOR US... ....ANYONE ??
CALL IRVING OR DON'T CALL IRVING?
QUIT JOB OR DON'T QUIT JOB?
EAT DONUT OR DON'T EAT DONUT?
KEEP SHOES OR RETURN SHOES?
MARRY SUE OR DUMP SUE?
GROW MOUSTACHE OR DON'T GROW MOUSTACHE?
THAI FOR LUNCH OR PIZZA FOR LUNCH?
GUISEWITE

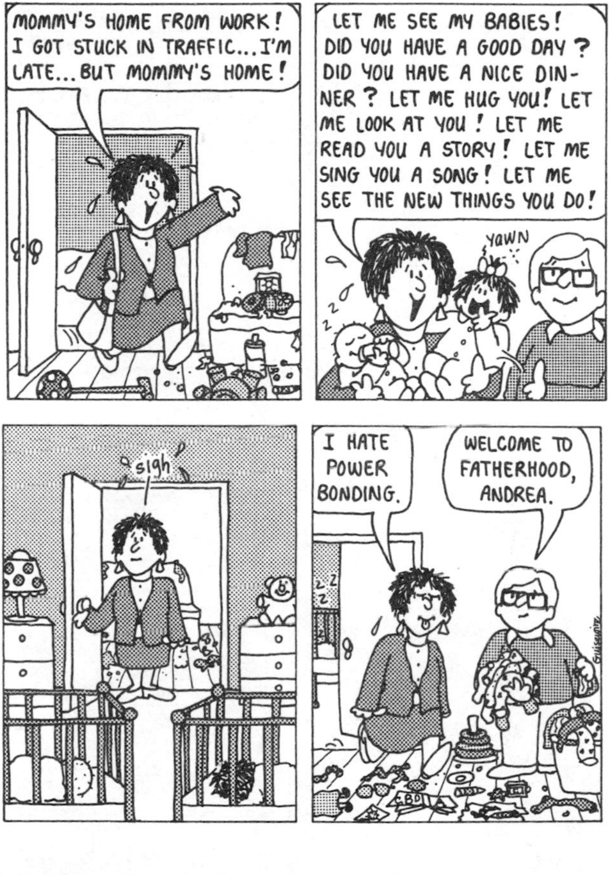
MOMMY'S HOME FROM WORK! I GOT STUCK IN TRAFFIC... I'M LATE... BUT MOMMY'S HOME!
LET ME SEE MY BABIES! DID YOU HAVE A GOOD DAY? DID YOU HAVE A NICE DINNER? LET ME HUG YOU! LET ME LOOK AT YOU! LET ME READ YOU A STORY! LET ME SING YOU A SONG! LET ME SEE THE NEW THINGS YOU DO!
YAWN
sigh
I HATE POWER BONDING.
WELCOME TO FATHERHOOD, ANDREA.

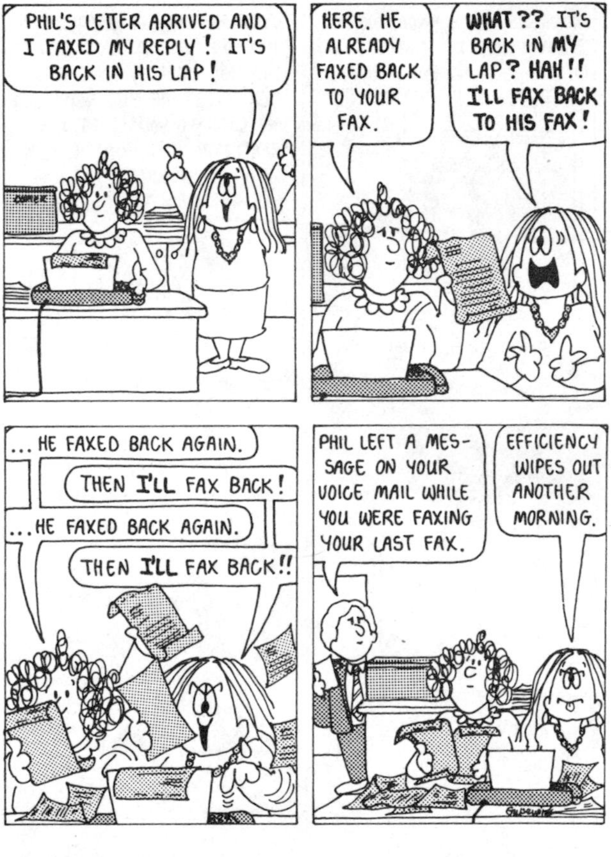
PHIL'S LETTER ARRIVED AND I FAXED MY REPLY! IT'S BACK IN HIS LAP!
HERE. HE ALREADY FAXED BACK TO YOUR FAX.
WHAT?? IT'S BACK IN MY LAP? HAH!! I'LL FAX BACK TO HIS FAX!
... HE FAXED BACK AGAIN.
THEN I'LL FAX BACK!
... HE FAXED BACK AGAIN.
THEN I'LL FAX BACK!!
PHIL LEFT A MES-SAGE ON YOUR VOICE MAIL WHILE YOU WERE FAXING YOUR LAST FAX.
EFFICIENCY WIPES OUT ANOTHER MORNING.

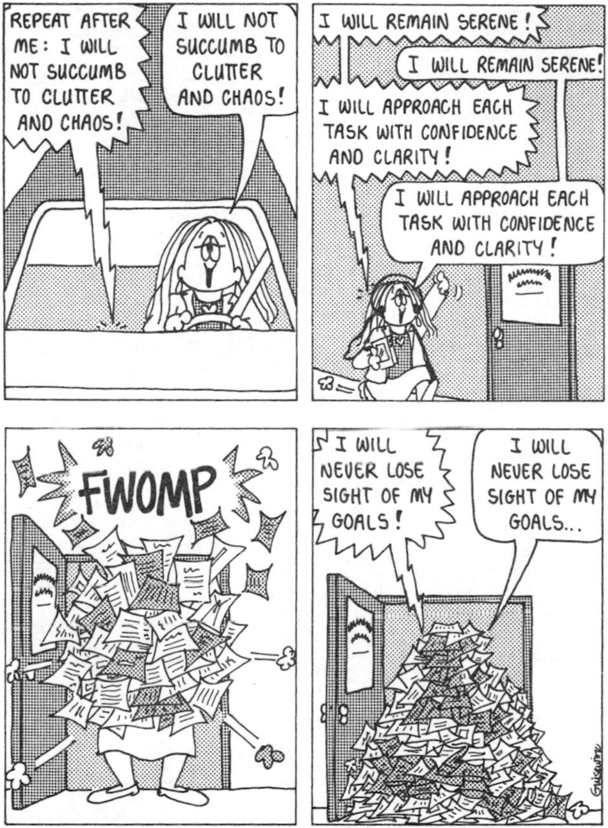
REPEAT AFTER ME: I WILL NOT SUCCUMB TO CLUTTER AND CHAOS!
I WILL NOT SUCCUMB TO CLUTTER AND CHAOS!
I WILL REMAIN SERENE!
I WILL REMAIN SERENE!
I WILL APPROACH EACH TASK WITH CONFIDENCE AND CLARITY!
I WILL APPROACH EACH TASK WITH CONFIDENCE AND CLARITY!
FWOMP
I WILL NEVER LOSE SIGHT OF MY GOALS!
I WILL NEVER LOSE SIGHT OF MY GOALS...

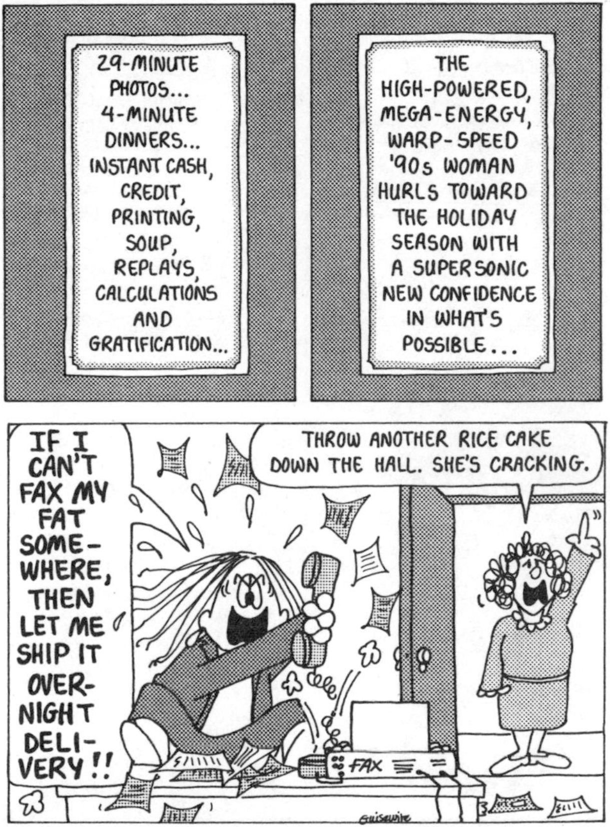
29-MINUTE PHOTOS... 4-MINUTE DINNERS... INSTANT CASH, CREDIT, PRINTING, SOUP, REPLAYS, CALCULATIONS AND GRATIFICATION...
THE HIGH-POWERED, MEGA-ENERGY, WARP-SPEED '90s WOMAN HURLS TOWARD THE HOLIDAY SEASON WITH A SUPERSONIC NEW CONFIDENCE IN WHAT'S POSSIBLE...
IF I CAN'T FAX MY FAT SOMEWHERE, THEN LET ME SHIP IT OVERNIGHT DELIVERY!!
THROW ANOTHER RICE CAKE DOWN THE HALL. SHE'S CRACKING.
FAX
Guisewite

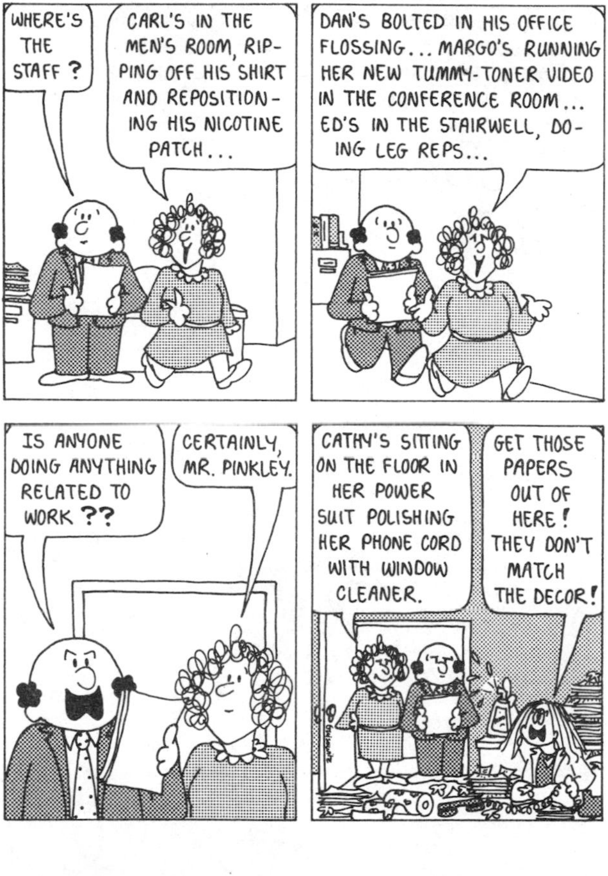
WHERE'S THE STAFF ?
CARL'S IN THE MEN'S ROOM, RIPPING OFF HIS SHIRT AND REPOSITIONING HIS NICOTINE PATCH...
DAN'S BOLTED IN HIS OFFICE FLOSSING... MARGO'S RUNNING HER NEW TUMMY-TONER VIDEO IN THE CONFERENCE ROOM... ED'S IN THE STAIRWELL, DOING LEG REPS...
IS ANYONE DOING ANYTHING RELATED TO WORK ??
CERTAINLY, MR. PINKLEY.
CATHY'S SITTING ON THE FLOOR IN HER POWER SUIT POLISHING HER PHONE CORD WITH WINDOW CLEANER.
GET THOSE PAPERS OUT OF HERE! THEY DON'T MATCH THE DECOR!

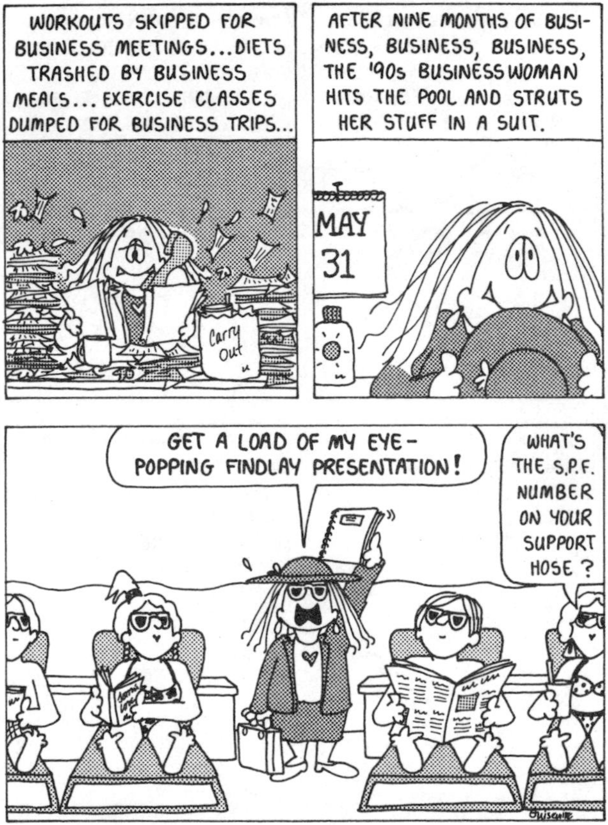
WORKOUTS SKIPPED FOR BUSINESS MEETINGS...DIETS TRASHED BY BUSINESS MEALS... EXERCISE CLASSES DUMPED FOR BUSINESS TRIPS...
Carry Out
AFTER NINE MONTHS OF BUSINESS, BUSINESS, BUSINESS, THE '90s BUSINESSWOMAN HITS THE POOL AND STRUTS HER STUFF IN A SUIT.
MAY
31
GET A LOAD OF MY EYE-POPPING FINDLAY PRESENTATION!
WHAT'S THE S.P.F. NUMBER ON YOUR SUPPORT HOSE?

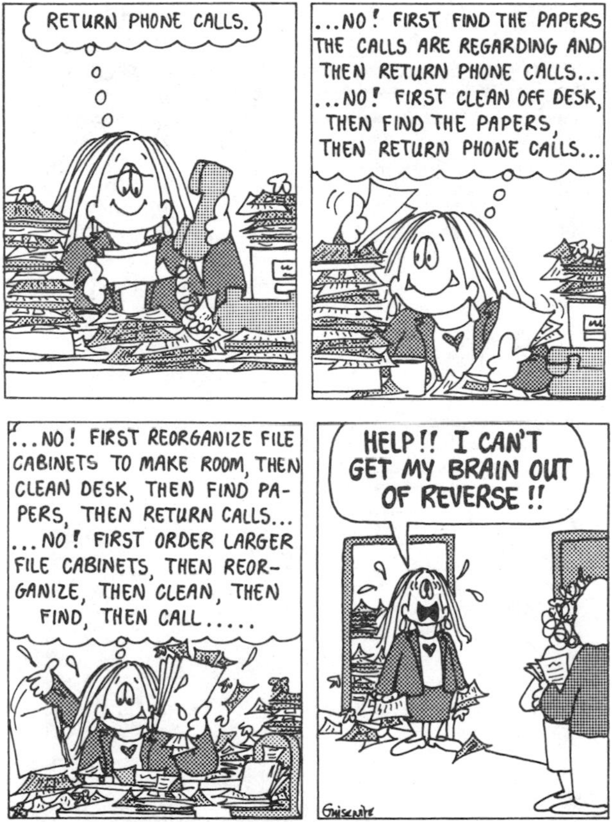
RETURN PHONE CALLS.
...NO! FIRST FIND THE PAPERS THE CALLS ARE REGARDING AND THEN RETURN PHONE CALLS... ...NO! FIRST CLEAN OFF DESK, THEN FIND THE PAPERS, THEN RETURN PHONE CALLS...
...NO! FIRST REORGANIZE FILE CABINETS TO MAKE ROOM, THEN CLEAN DESK, THEN FIND PAPERS, THEN RETURN CALLS... ...NO! FIRST ORDER LARGER FILE CABINETS, THEN REORGANIZE, THEN CLEAN, THEN FIND, THEN CALL.....
HELP!! I CAN'T GET MY BRAIN OUT OF REVERSE!!
GUISEWITE

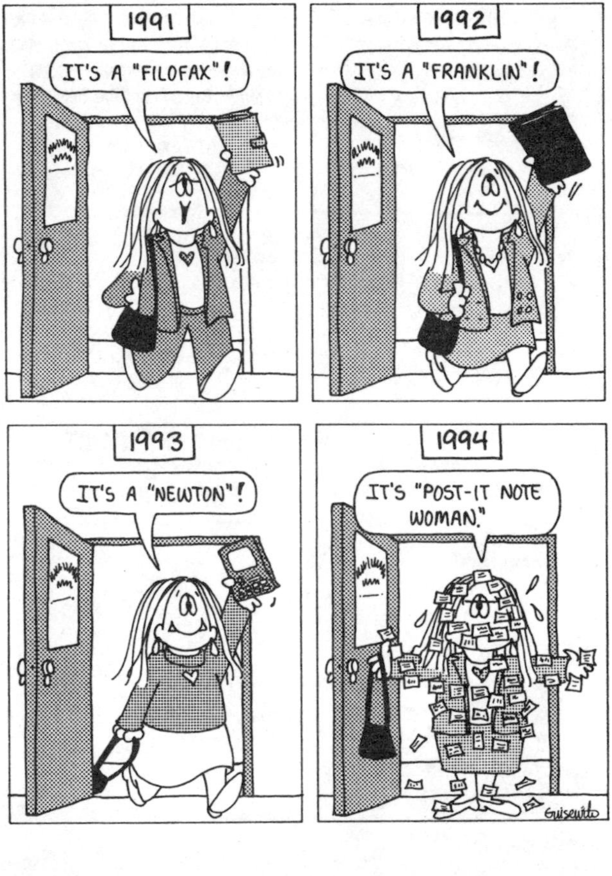
1991
IT'S A "FILOFAX"!
1992
IT'S A "FRANKLIN"!
1993
IT'S A "NEWTON"!
1994
IT'S "POST-IT NOTE WOMAN."
Guisewite

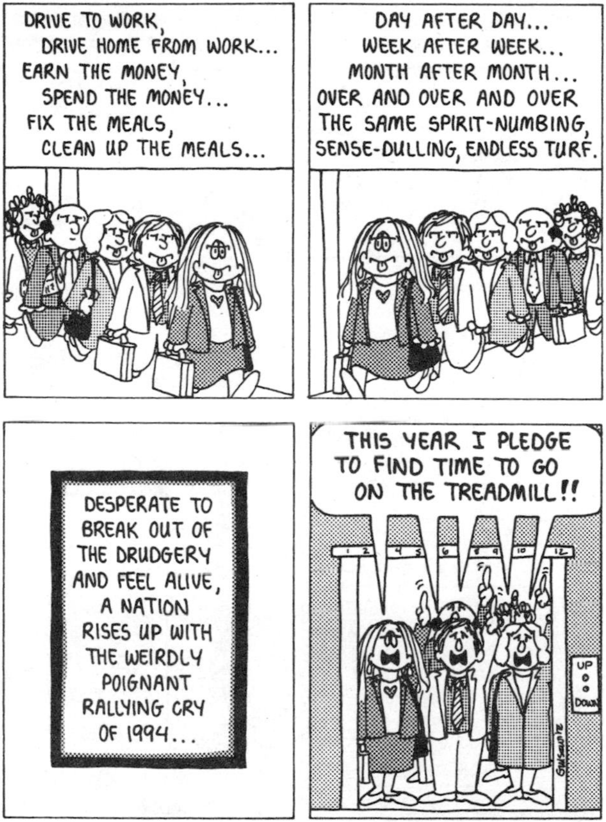
DRIVE TO WORK,
DRIVE HOME FROM WORK...
EARN THE MONEY,
SPEND THE MONEY...
FIX THE MEALS,
CLEAN UP THE MEALS...
DAY AFTER DAY...
WEEK AFTER WEEK...
MONTH AFTER MONTH...
OVER AND OVER AND OVER
THE SAME SPIRIT-NUMBING,
SENSE-DULLING, ENDLESS TURF.
DESPERATE TO BREAK OUT OF THE DRUDGERY AND FEEL ALIVE, A NATION RISES UP WITH THE WEIRDLY POIGNANT RALLYING CRY OF 1994...
THIS YEAR I PLEDGE TO FIND TIME TO GO ON THE TREADMILL!!
UP
DOWN

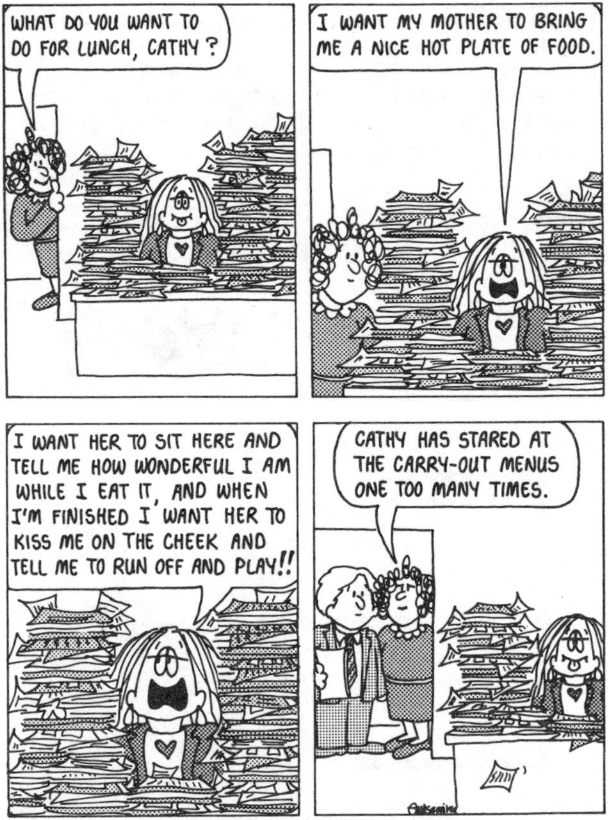
WHAT DO YOU WANT TO DO FOR LUNCH, CATHY?
I WANT MY MOTHER TO BRING ME A NICE HOT PLATE OF FOOD.
I WANT HER TO SIT HERE AND TELL ME HOW WONDERFUL I AM WHILE I EAT IT, AND WHEN I'M FINISHED I WANT HER TO KISS ME ON THE CHEEK AND TELL ME TO RUN OFF AND PLAY!!
CATHY HAS STARED AT THE CARRY-OUT MENUS ONE TOO MANY TIMES.

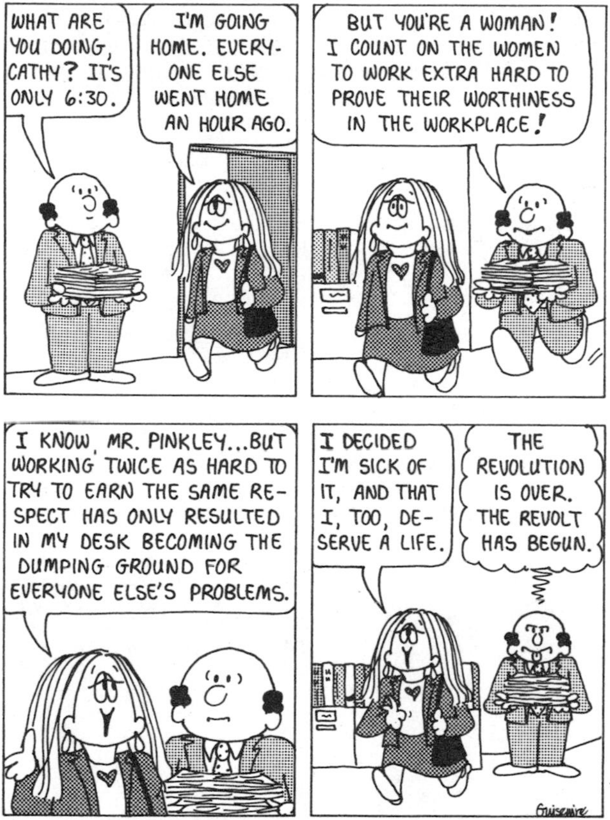
WHAT ARE YOU DOING, CATHY? IT'S ONLY 6:30.
I'M GOING HOME. EVERY-ONE ELSE WENT HOME AN HOUR AGO.
BUT YOU'RE A WOMAN! I COUNT ON THE WOMEN TO WORK EXTRA HARD TO PROVE THEIR WORTHINESS IN THE WORKPLACE!
I KNOW, MR. PINKLEY...BUT WORKING TWICE AS HARD TO TRY TO EARN THE SAME RE-SPECT HAS ONLY RESULTED IN MY DESK BECOMING THE DUMPING GROUND FOR EVERYONE ELSE'S PROBLEMS.
I DECIDED I'M SICK OF IT, AND THAT I, TOO, DE-SERVE A LIFE.
THE REVOLUTION IS OVER. THE REVOLT HAS BEGUN.
Guisewite

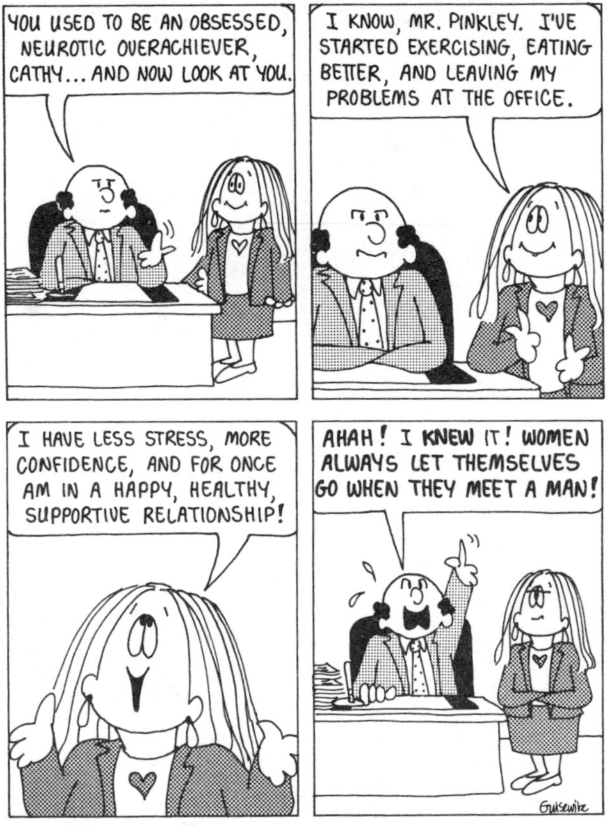
YOU USED TO BE AN OBSESSED, NEUROTIC OVERACHIEVER, CATHY... AND NOW LOOK AT YOU.
I KNOW, MR. PINKLEY. I'VE STARTED EXERCISING, EATING BETTER, AND LEAVING MY PROBLEMS AT THE OFFICE.
I HAVE LESS STRESS, MORE CONFIDENCE, AND FOR ONCE AM IN A HAPPY, HEALTHY, SUPPORTIVE RELATIONSHIP!
AHAH! I KNEW IT! WOMEN ALWAYS LET THEMSELVES GO WHEN THEY MEET A MAN!
Guisewite

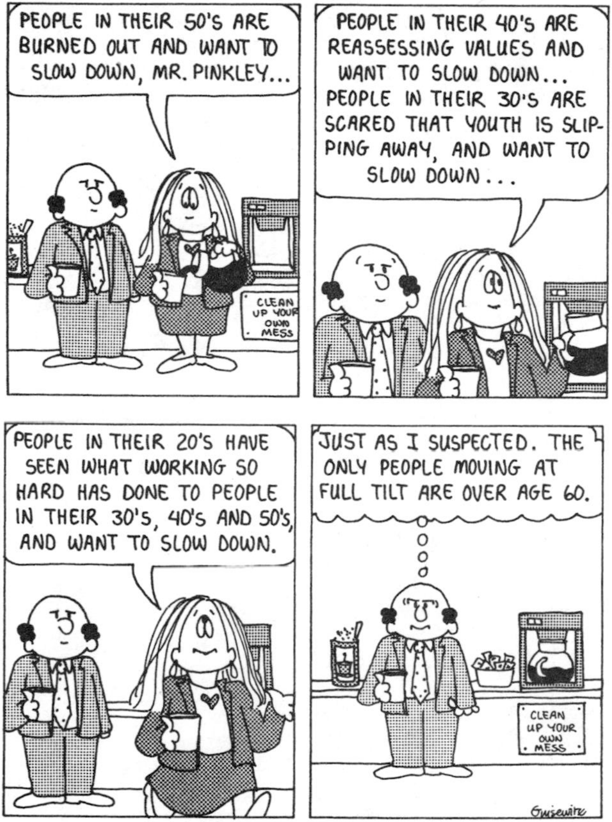
PEOPLE IN THEIR 50'S ARE BURNED OUT AND WANT TO SLOW DOWN, MR. PINKLEY...
CLEAN UP YOUR OWN MESS
PEOPLE IN THEIR 40'S ARE REASSESSING VALUES AND WANT TO SLOW DOWN... PEOPLE IN THEIR 30'S ARE SCARED THAT YOUTH IS SLIPPING AWAY, AND WANT TO SLOW DOWN...
PEOPLE IN THEIR 20'S HAVE SEEN WHAT WORKING SO HARD HAS DONE TO PEOPLE IN THEIR 30'S, 40'S AND 50'S, AND WANT TO SLOW DOWN.
JUST AS I SUSPECTED. THE ONLY PEOPLE MOVING AT FULL TILT ARE OVER AGE 60.
CLEAN UP YOUR OWN MESS
Guisewite

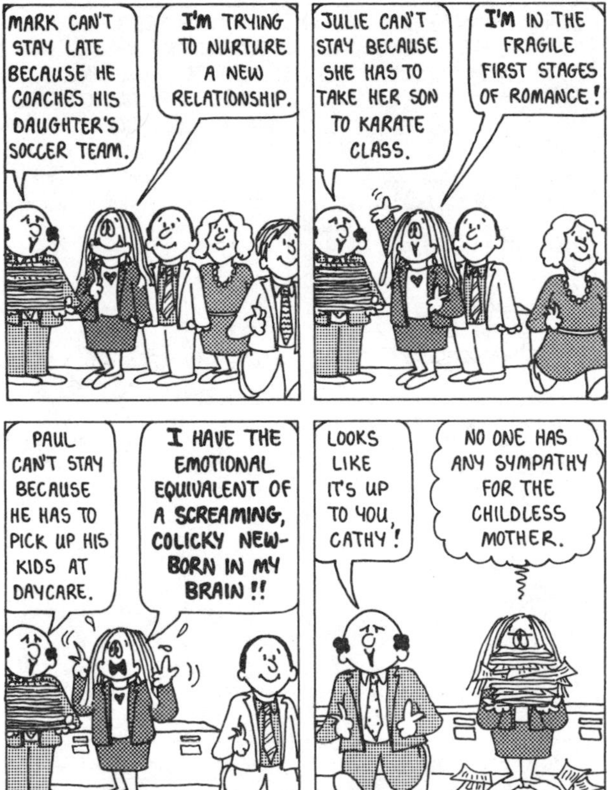
MARK CAN'T STAY LATE BECAUSE HE COACHES HIS DAUGHTER'S SOCCER TEAM.
I'M TRYING TO NURTURE A NEW RELATIONSHIP.
JULIE CAN'T STAY BECAUSE SHE HAS TO TAKE HER SON TO KARATE CLASS.
I'M IN THE FRAGILE FIRST STAGES OF ROMANCE!
PAUL CAN'T STAY BECAUSE HE HAS TO PICK UP HIS KIDS AT DAYCARE.
I HAVE THE EMOTIONAL EQUIVALENT OF A SCREAMING, COLICKY NEW-BORN IN MY BRAIN!!
LOOKS LIKE IT'S UP TO YOU, CATHY!
NO ONE HAS ANY SYMPATHY FOR THE CHILDLESS MOTHER.
Guisewite

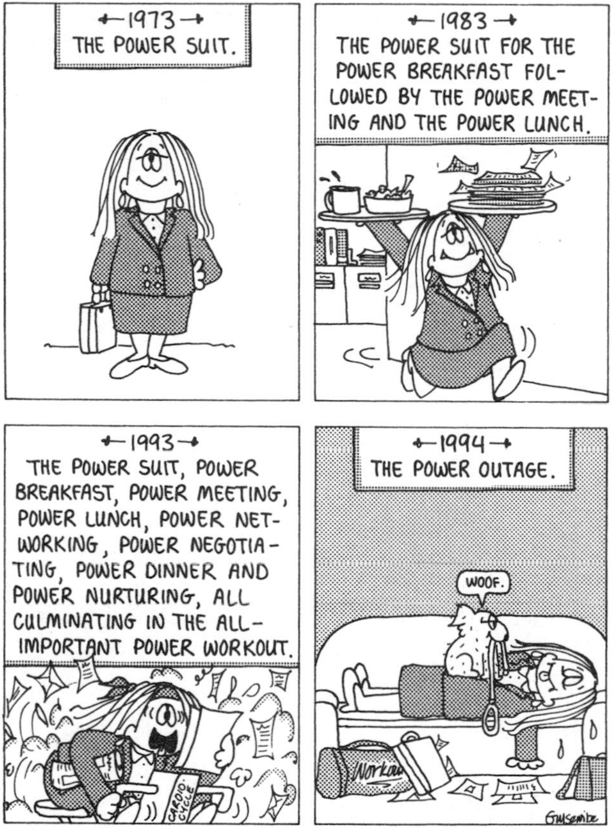
1973
THE POWER SUIT.
1983
THE POWER SUIT FOR THE POWER BREAKFAST FOLLOWED BY THE POWER MEETING AND THE POWER LUNCH.
1993
THE POWER SUIT, POWER BREAKFAST, POWER MEETING, POWER LUNCH, POWER NETWORKING, POWER NEGOTIATING, POWER DINNER AND POWER NURTURING, ALL CULMINATING IN THE ALL-IMPORTANT POWER WORKOUT.
CARDIO CYCLE
1994
THE POWER OUTAGE.
WOOF.
Workout
Guisewite

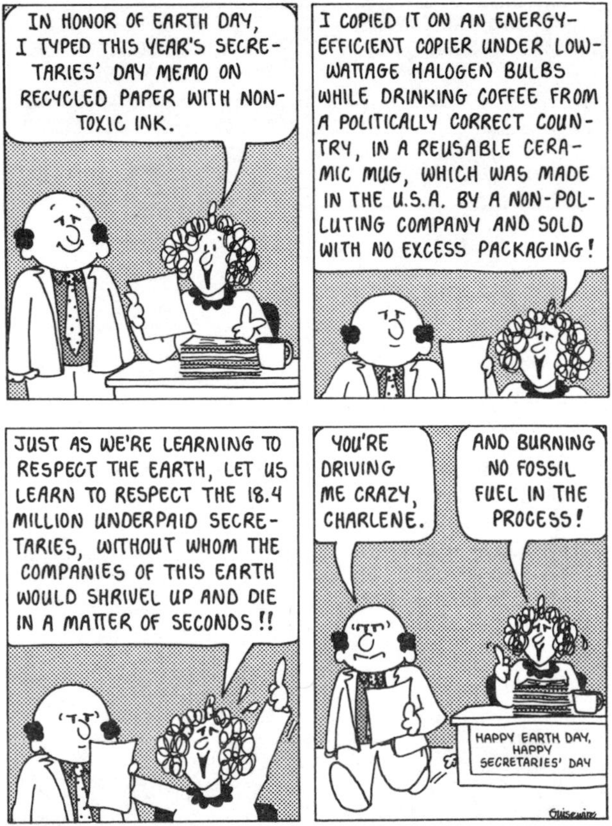
IN HONOR OF EARTH DAY, I TYPED THIS YEAR'S SECRETARIES' DAY MEMO ON RECYCLED PAPER WITH NON-TOXIC INK.
I COPIED IT ON AN ENERGY-EFFICIENT COPIER UNDER LOW-WATTAGE HALOGEN BULBS WHILE DRINKING COFFEE FROM A POLITICALLY CORRECT COUNTRY, IN A REUSABLE CERAMIC MUG, WHICH WAS MADE IN THE U.S.A. BY A NON-POLLUTING COMPANY AND SOLD WITH NO EXCESS PACKAGING!
JUST AS WE'RE LEARNING TO RESPECT THE EARTH, LET US LEARN TO RESPECT THE 18.4 MILLION UNDERPAID SECRETARIES, WITHOUT WHOM THE COMPANIES OF THIS EARTH WOULD SHRIVEL UP AND DIE IN A MATTER OF SECONDS!!
YOU'RE DRIVING ME CRAZY, CHARLENE.
AND BURNING NO FOSSIL FUEL IN THE PROCESS!
HAPPY EARTH DAY, HAPPY SECRETARIES' DAY
Guisewite

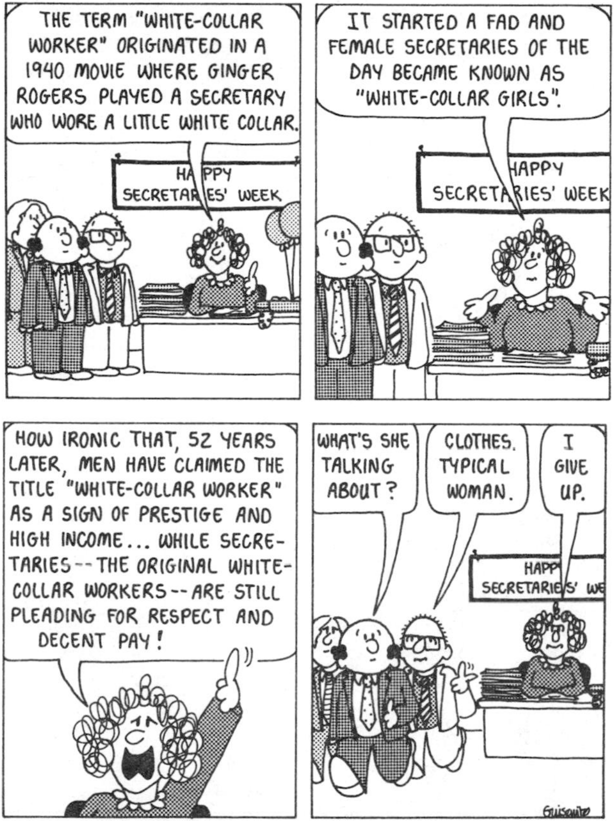
THE TERM "WHITE-COLLAR WORKER" ORIGINATED IN A 1940 MOVIE WHERE GINGER ROGERS PLAYED A SECRETARY WHO WORE A LITTLE WHITE COLLAR.
HAPPY SECRETARIES' WEEK
IT STARTED A FAD AND FEMALE SECRETARIES OF THE DAY BECAME KNOWN AS "WHITE-COLLAR GIRLS".
HAPPY SECRETARIES' WEEK
HOW IRONIC THAT, 52 YEARS LATER, MEN HAVE CLAIMED THE TITLE "WHITE-COLLAR WORKER" AS A SIGN OF PRESTIGE AND HIGH INCOME... WHILE SECRETARIES--THE ORIGINAL WHITE-COLLAR WORKERS--ARE STILL PLEADING FOR RESPECT AND DECENT PAY!
WHAT'S SHE TALKING ABOUT?
CLOTHES. TYPICAL WOMAN.
I GIVE UP.
GUISEWITE

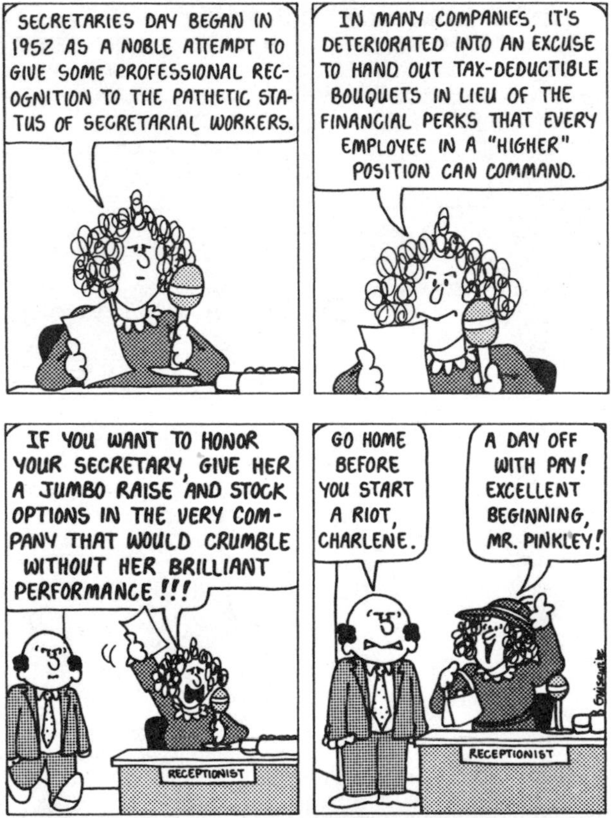
SECRETARIES DAY BEGAN IN 1952 AS A NOBLE ATTEMPT TO GIVE SOME PROFESSIONAL RECOGNITION TO THE PATHETIC STATUS OF SECRETARIAL WORKERS.
IN MANY COMPANIES, IT'S DETERIORATED INTO AN EXCUSE TO HAND OUT TAX-DEDUCTIBLE BOUQUETS IN LIEU OF THE FINANCIAL PERKS THAT EVERY EMPLOYEE IN A "HIGHER" POSITION CAN COMMAND.
IF YOU WANT TO HONOR YOUR SECRETARY, GIVE HER A JUMBO RAISE AND STOCK OPTIONS IN THE VERY COMPANY THAT WOULD CRUMBLE WITHOUT HER BRILLIANT PERFORMANCE!!!
RECEPTIONIST
GO HOME BEFORE YOU START A RIOT, CHARLENE.
A DAY OFF WITH PAY! EXCELLENT BEGINNING, MR. PINKLEY!
RECEPTIONIST

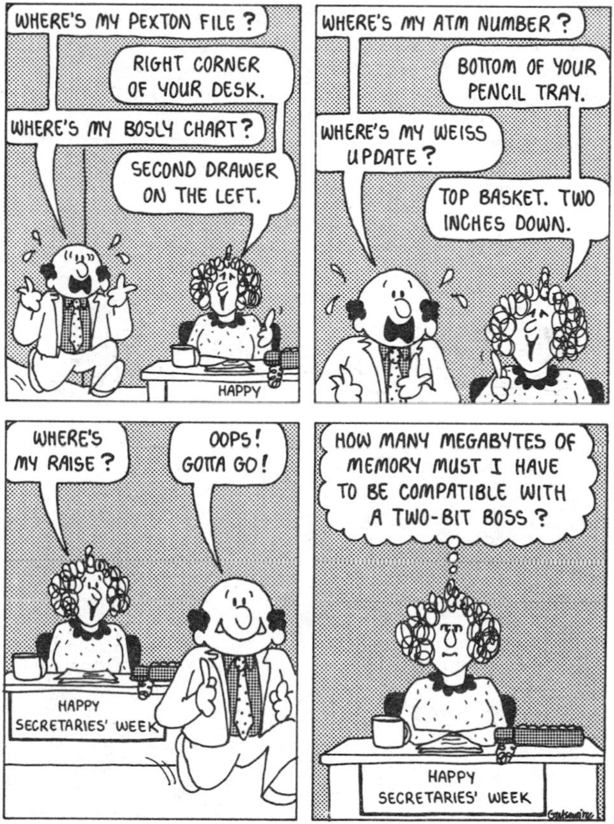

WHERE'S MY PEXTON FILE?
RIGHT CORNER OF YOUR DESK.
WHERE'S MY BOSLY CHART?
SECOND DRAWER ON THE LEFT.
HAPPY
WHERE'S MY ATM NUMBER?
BOTTOM OF YOUR PENCIL TRAY.
WHERE'S MY WEISS UPDATE?
TOP BASKET. TWO INCHES DOWN.
WHERE'S MY RAISE?
OOPS! GOTTA GO!
HAPPY SECRETARIES' WEEK
HOW MANY MEGABYTES OF MEMORY MUST I HAVE TO BE COMPATIBLE WITH A TWO-BIT BOSS?
HAPPY SECRETARIES' WEEK
Guisewite

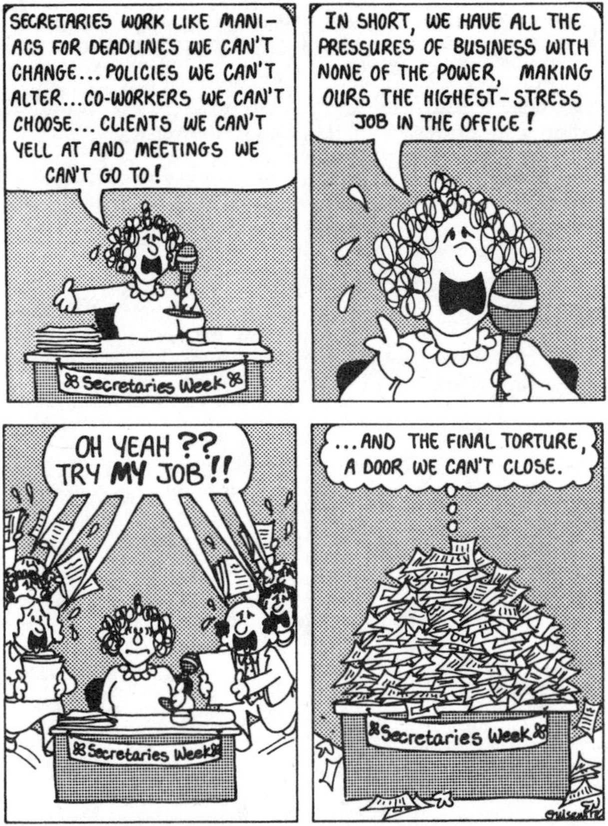
SECRETARIES WORK LIKE MANIACS FOR DEADLINES WE CAN'T CHANGE... POLICIES WE CAN'T ALTER...CO-WORKERS WE CAN'T CHOOSE... CLIENTS WE CAN'T YELL AT AND MEETINGS WE CAN'T GO TO!
Secretaries Week
IN SHORT, WE HAVE ALL THE PRESSURES OF BUSINESS WITH NONE OF THE POWER, MAKING OURS THE HIGHEST-STRESS JOB IN THE OFFICE!
OH YEAH?? TRY MY JOB!!
Secretaries Week
...AND THE FINAL TORTURE, A DOOR WE CAN'T CLOSE.
Secretaries Week

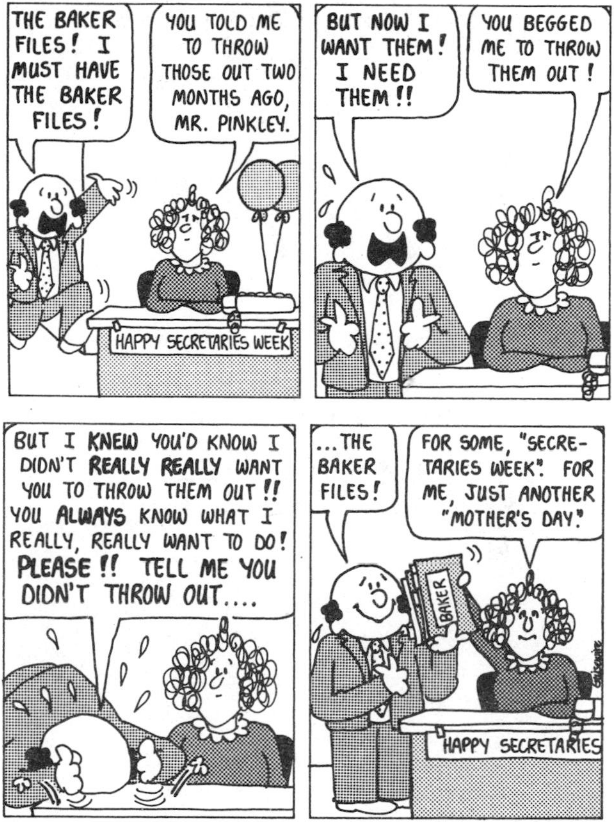
THE BAKER FILES! I MUST HAVE THE BAKER FILES!
YOU TOLD ME TO THROW THOSE OUT TWO MONTHS AGO, MR. PINKLEY.
HAPPY SECRETARIES WEEK
BUT NOW I WANT THEM! I NEED THEM!!
YOU BEGGED ME TO THROW THEM OUT!
BUT I KNEW YOU'D KNOW I DIDN'T REALLY REALLY WANT YOU TO THROW THEM OUT!! YOU ALWAYS KNOW WHAT I REALLY, REALLY WANT TO DO! PLEASE!! TELL ME YOU DIDN'T THROW OUT....
...THE BAKER FILES!
FOR SOME, "SECRETARIES WEEK". FOR ME, JUST ANOTHER "MOTHER'S DAY."
BAKER
HAPPY SECRETARIES

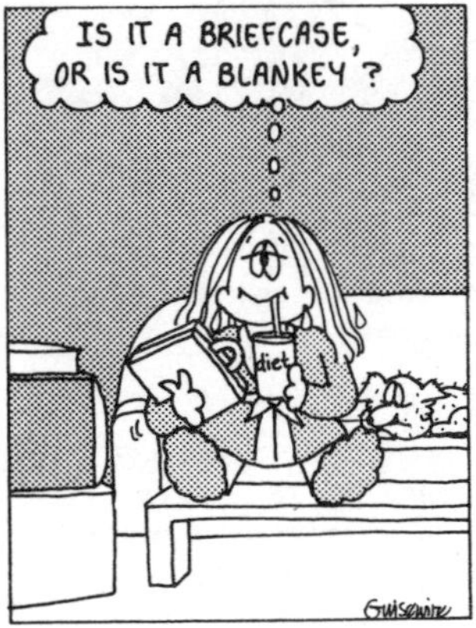
IS IT A BRIEFCASE, OR IS IT A BLANKEY ?
diet

The Late '90s

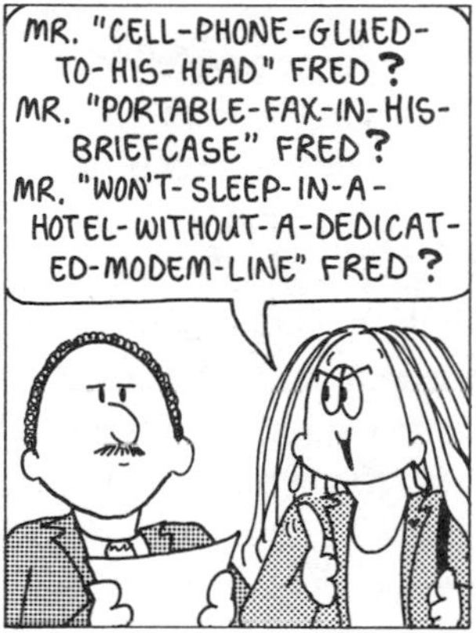
MR. "CELL-PHONE-GLUED-TO-HIS-HEAD" FRED? MR. "PORTABLE-FAX-IN-HIS-BRIEFCASE" FRED? MR. "WON'T-SLEEP-IN-A-HOTEL-WITHOUT-A-DEDICATED-MODEM-LINE" FRED?

The day I had wireless Internet access from the ladies' room, I knew life was changed forever.

Computer, scanner, printer, fax, copy machine, shredder, filing system. What was once the office became the home office and, by the late '90s, was quickly on its way to becoming the purse office.

The office, which we alternately dreamed of quitting and feared being fired from, was everywhere. Grandma had a fax machine. Grandpa did e-mail. Great Uncle Bill had a charge account at Staples.

The office supply superstore expanded its open hours to 24 a day. Apparently, the former 12 hours weren't nearly enough to accommodate all the traffic. Perfectly normal people were going out into the night to buy reams of legal pads at 1 A.M., crates of mailing envelopes at 2 A.M., 500-count tape dispensers at 4:30 A.M..

By the late '90s, in real life, I had a husband, daughter, and stepson, and a whole new sense of who I was. However, I could no longer tell where I was.

The offices I visited started being so homey: Ping-Pong tables, snack bars, meditation gardens, TV rooms, juice bars, gyms, espresso machines.

The homes I visited started being so office-y: "Look! I downloaded the specs and faxed them to Shelly, who scanned in photos and clip art, e-mailed a rendering of the prototype to ebay, and had $4 million in orders by the time little Louis was up from his nap!"

While I struggled to write a thank-you note from last Christmas on my kitchen counter, every time I opened a paper, someone had launched another million-dollar dot-com from hers.

For working moms, this added one more pressure: Not only was it impossible to find enough hours to go to the office, it was impossible to be home and feel like we weren't wasting some grand opportunity if we just plopped down and had a cup of tea.

The late '90s were one grand role reversal. The office was home. The home was office. It all became a blur.

People started eating breakfast, lunch, and dinner at work. People started buying swimwear online from their desks.

The coffee room counter started looking like Mom's medicine cabinet. Mom's kitchen counter looked like a shipping department. People launched million-dollar Web sites from their back porches, and made stock killings from canoes.

There was enough RAM on the bedside table to run a small country.

"Taking work home from the office" became sort of redundant. The office was everywhere, and so were the worries that went with it.

Will I be let go?

Will I be replaced by a person half my age for half my salary?

Will the entire management team know what size underwear I wear if I buy it online during my lunch hour?

No one wanted the Y2K disaster. But many of us wouldn't have minded if someone had just flipped all the fuses for a few days.

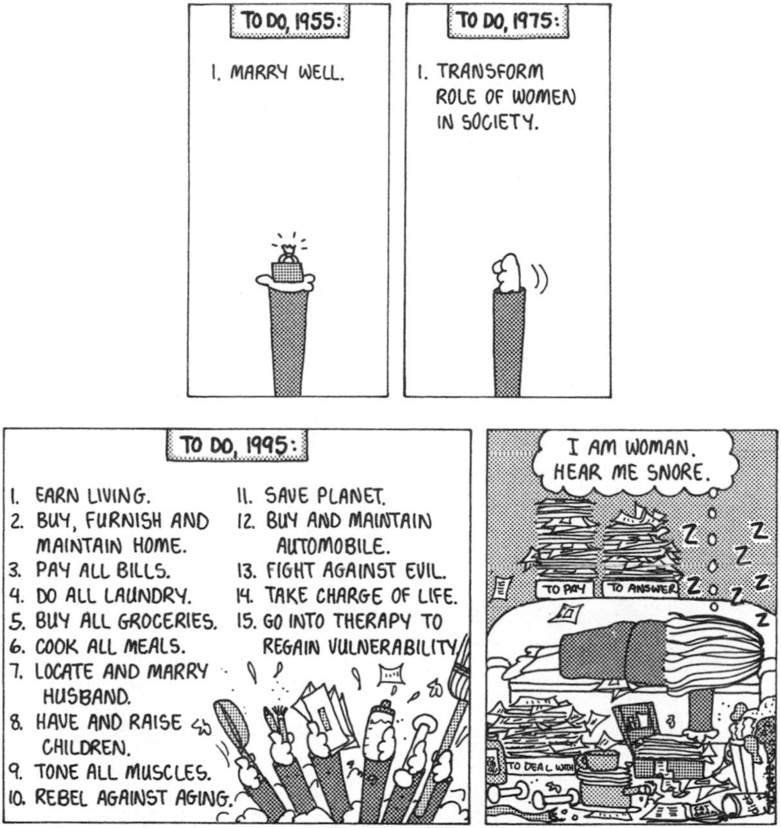
TO DO, 1955:
1. MARRY WELL.
TO DO, 1975:
1. TRANSFORM ROLE OF WOMEN IN SOCIETY.
TO DO, 1995:
1. EARN LIVING.
2. BUY, FURNISH AND MAINTAIN HOME.
3. PAY ALL BILLS.
4. DO ALL LAUNDRY.
5. BUY ALL GROCERIES.
6. COOK ALL MEALS.
7. LOCATE AND MARRY HUSBAND.
8. HAVE AND RAISE CHILDREN.
9. TONE ALL MUSCLES.
10. REBEL AGAINST AGING.
11. SAVE PLANET.
12. BUY AND MAINTAIN AUTOMOBILE.
13. FIGHT AGAINST EVIL.
14. TAKE CHARGE OF LIFE.
15. GO INTO THERAPY TO REGAIN VULNERABILITY.
I AM WOMAN. HEAR ME SNORE.
TO PAY
TO ANSWER
TO DEAL WITH
Z Z Z Z Z Z

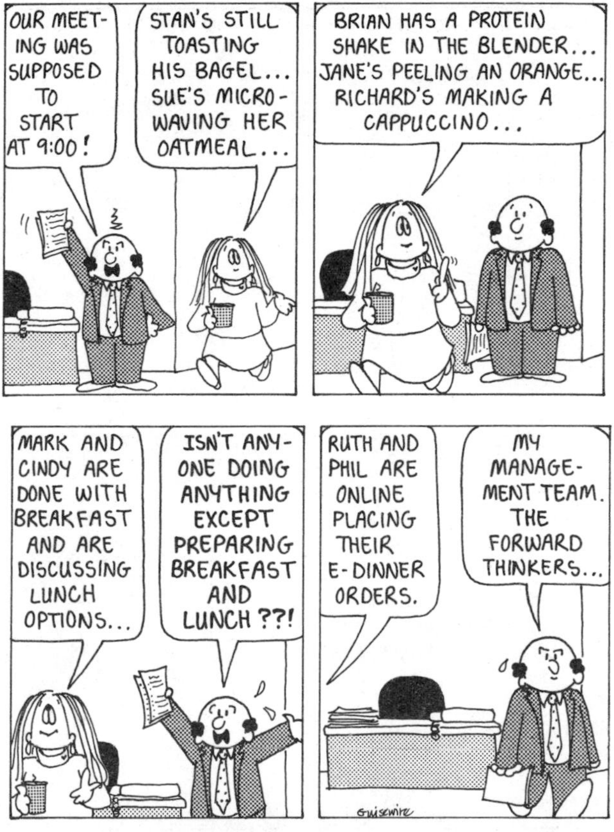
OUR MEETING WAS SUPPOSED TO START AT 9:00!
STAN'S STILL TOASTING HIS BAGEL... SUE'S MICROWAVING HER OATMEAL...
BRIAN HAS A PROTEIN SHAKE IN THE BLENDER... JANE'S PEELING AN ORANGE... RICHARD'S MAKING A CAPPUCCINO...
MARK AND CINDY ARE DONE WITH BREAKFAST AND ARE DISCUSSING LUNCH OPTIONS...
ISN'T ANYONE DOING ANYTHING EXCEPT PREPARING BREAKFAST AND LUNCH??!
RUTH AND PHIL ARE ONLINE PLACING THEIR E-DINNER ORDERS.
MY MANAGEMENT TEAM. THE FORWARD THINKERS...
Guisewite

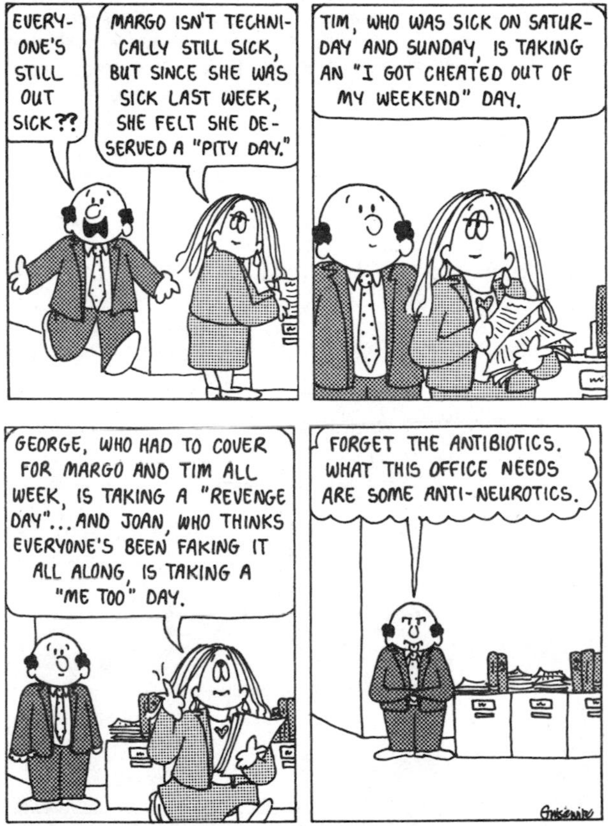
EVERYONE'S STILL OUT SICK??
MARGO ISN'T TECHNICALLY STILL SICK, BUT SINCE SHE WAS SICK LAST WEEK, SHE FELT SHE DESERVED A "PITY DAY."
TIM, WHO WAS SICK ON SATURDAY AND SUNDAY, IS TAKING AN "I GOT CHEATED OUT OF MY WEEKEND" DAY.
GEORGE, WHO HAD TO COVER FOR MARGO AND TIM ALL WEEK, IS TAKING A "REVENGE DAY"... AND JOAN, WHO THINKS EVERYONE'S BEEN FAKING IT ALL ALONG, IS TAKING A "ME TOO" DAY.
FORGET THE ANTIBIOTICS. WHAT THIS OFFICE NEEDS ARE SOME ANTI-NEUROTICS.

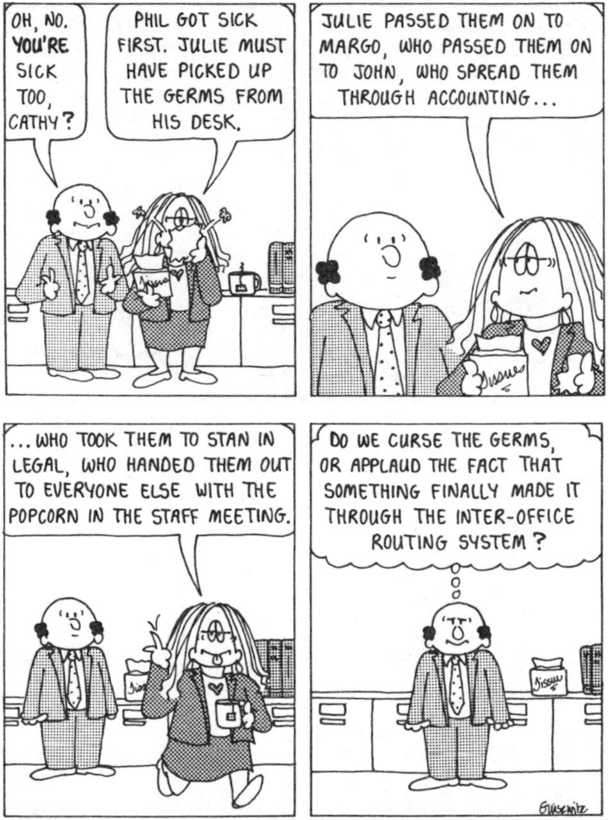
OH, NO. YOU'RE SICK TOO, CATHY?
PHIL GOT SICK FIRST. JULIE MUST HAVE PICKED UP THE GERMS FROM HIS DESK.
JULIE PASSED THEM ON TO MARGO, WHO PASSED THEM ON TO JOHN, WHO SPREAD THEM THROUGH ACCOUNTING...
...WHO TOOK THEM TO STAN IN LEGAL, WHO HANDED THEM OUT TO EVERYONE ELSE WITH THE POPCORN IN THE STAFF MEETING.
DO WE CURSE THE GERMS, OR APPLAUD THE FACT THAT SOMETHING FINALLY MADE IT THROUGH THE INTER-OFFICE ROUTING SYSTEM?

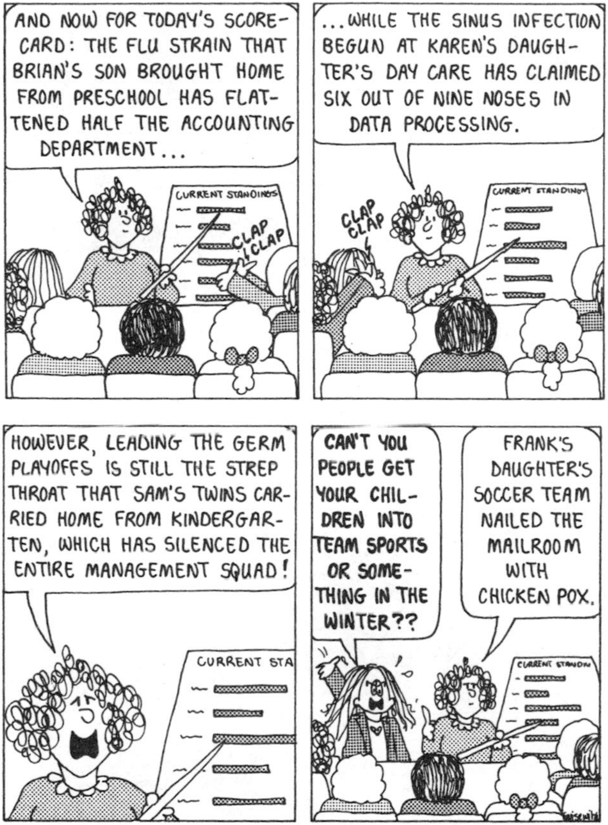
AND NOW FOR TODAY'S SCORE-CARD: THE FLU STRAIN THAT BRIAN'S SON BROUGHT HOME FROM PRESCHOOL HAS FLATTENED HALF THE ACCOUNTING DEPARTMENT...
CURRENT STANDINGS
CLAP CLAP
...WHILE THE SINUS INFECTION BEGUN AT KAREN'S DAUGHTER'S DAY CARE HAS CLAIMED SIX OUT OF NINE NOSES IN DATA PROCESSING.
CLAP CLAP
HOWEVER, LEADING THE GERM PLAYOFFS IS STILL THE STREP THROAT THAT SAM'S TWINS CARRIED HOME FROM KINDERGARTEN, WHICH HAS SILENCED THE ENTIRE MANAGEMENT SQUAD!
CURRENT STA
CAN'T YOU PEOPLE GET YOUR CHILDREN INTO TEAM SPORTS OR SOMETHING IN THE WINTER??
FRANK'S DAUGHTER'S SOCCER TEAM NAILED THE MAILROOM WITH CHICKEN POX.

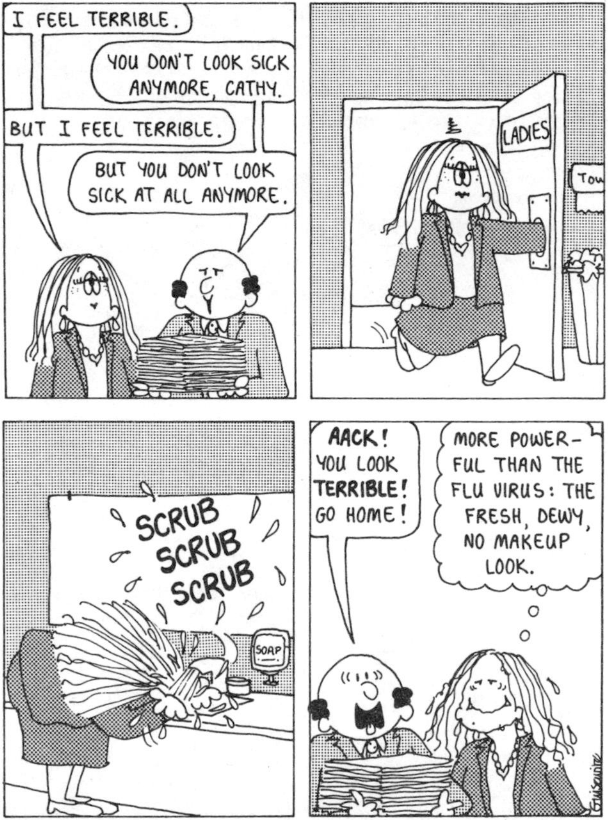
I FEEL TERRIBLE.
YOU DON'T LOOK SICK ANYMORE, CATHY.
BUT I FEEL TERRIBLE.
BUT YOU DON'T LOOK SICK AT ALL ANYMORE.
LADIES
SCRUB SCRUB SCRUB
SOAP
AACK! YOU LOOK TERRIBLE! GO HOME!
MORE POWERFUL THAN THE FLU VIRUS: THE FRESH, DEWY, NO MAKEUP LOOK.

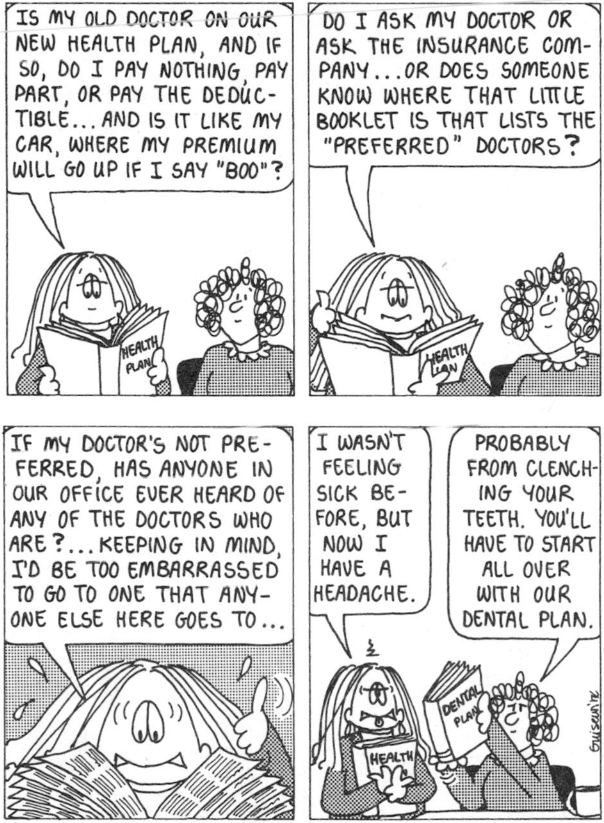
IS MY OLD DOCTOR ON OUR NEW HEALTH PLAN, AND IF SO, DO I PAY NOTHING, PAY PART, OR PAY THE DEDUCTIBLE... AND IS IT LIKE MY CAR, WHERE MY PREMIUM WILL GO UP IF I SAY "BOO"?
HEALTH PLAN
DO I ASK MY DOCTOR OR ASK THE INSURANCE COMPANY...OR DOES SOMEONE KNOW WHERE THAT LITTLE BOOKLET IS THAT LISTS THE "PREFERRED" DOCTORS?
HEALTH PLAN
IF MY DOCTOR'S NOT PREFERRED, HAS ANYONE IN OUR OFFICE EVER HEARD OF ANY OF THE DOCTORS WHO ARE?... KEEPING IN MIND, I'D BE TOO EMBARRASSED TO GO TO ONE THAT ANYONE ELSE HERE GOES TO...
I WASN'T FEELING SICK BEFORE, BUT NOW I HAVE A HEADACHE.
PROBABLY FROM CLENCHING YOUR TEETH. YOU'LL HAVE TO START ALL OVER WITH OUR DENTAL PLAN.
HEALTH
DENTAL PLAN
GUISEWITE

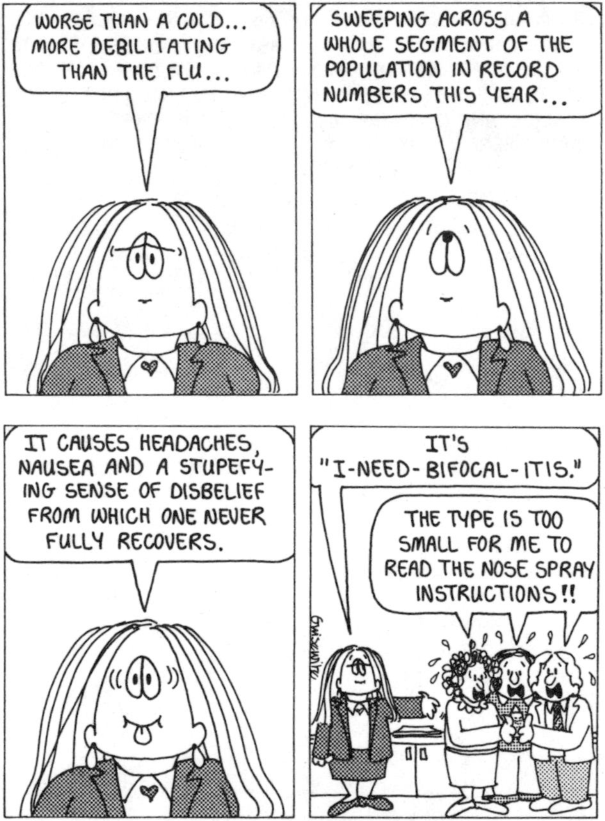
WORSE THAN A COLD... MORE DEBILITATING THAN THE FLU...
SWEEPING ACROSS A WHOLE SEGMENT OF THE POPULATION IN RECORD NUMBERS THIS YEAR...
IT CAUSES HEADACHES, NAUSEA AND A STUPEFYING SENSE OF DISBELIEF FROM WHICH ONE NEVER FULLY RECOVERS.
IT'S "I-NEED-BIFOCAL-ITIS."
THE TYPE IS TOO SMALL FOR ME TO READ THE NOSE SPRAY INSTRUCTIONS!!
GUISEWITE

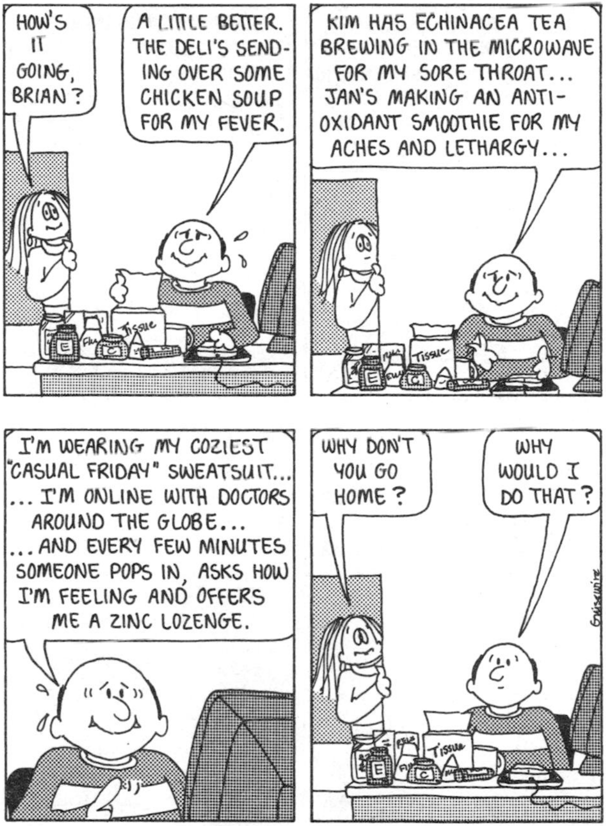
HOW'S IT GOING, BRIAN?
A LITTLE BETTER. THE DELI'S SENDING OVER SOME CHICKEN SOUP FOR MY FEVER.
KIM HAS ECHINACEA TEA BREWING IN THE MICROWAVE FOR MY SORE THROAT... JAN'S MAKING AN ANTI-OXIDANT SMOOTHIE FOR MY ACHES AND LETHARGY...
I'M WEARING MY COZIEST "CASUAL FRIDAY" SWEATSUIT... ... I'M ONLINE WITH DOCTORS AROUND THE GLOBE... ... AND EVERY FEW MINUTES SOMEONE POPS IN, ASKS HOW I'M FEELING AND OFFERS ME A ZINC LOZENGE.
WHY DON'T YOU GO HOME?
WHY WOULD I DO THAT?
Tissue
Tissue
Tissue

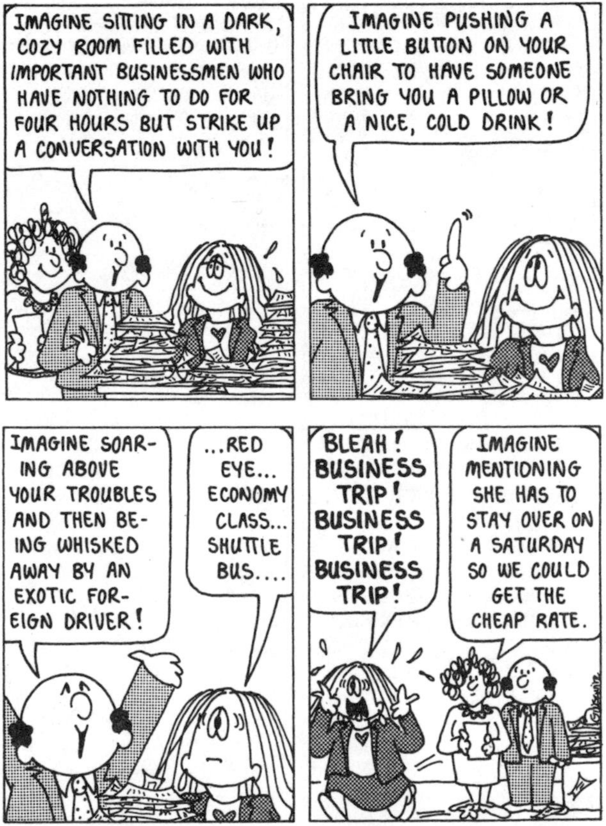
IMAGINE SITTING IN A DARK, COZY ROOM FILLED WITH IMPORTANT BUSINESSMEN WHO HAVE NOTHING TO DO FOR FOUR HOURS BUT STRIKE UP A CONVERSATION WITH YOU!
IMAGINE PUSHING A LITTLE BUTTON ON YOUR CHAIR TO HAVE SOMEONE BRING YOU A PILLOW OR A NICE, COLD DRINK!
IMAGINE SOARING ABOVE YOUR TROUBLES AND THEN BEING WHISKED AWAY BY AN EXOTIC FOREIGN DRIVER!
...RED EYE... ECONOMY CLASS... SHUTTLE BUS....
BLEAH! BUSINESS TRIP! BUSINESS TRIP! BUSINESS TRIP!
IMAGINE MENTIONING SHE HAS TO STAY OVER ON A SATURDAY SO WE COULD GET THE CHEAP RATE.

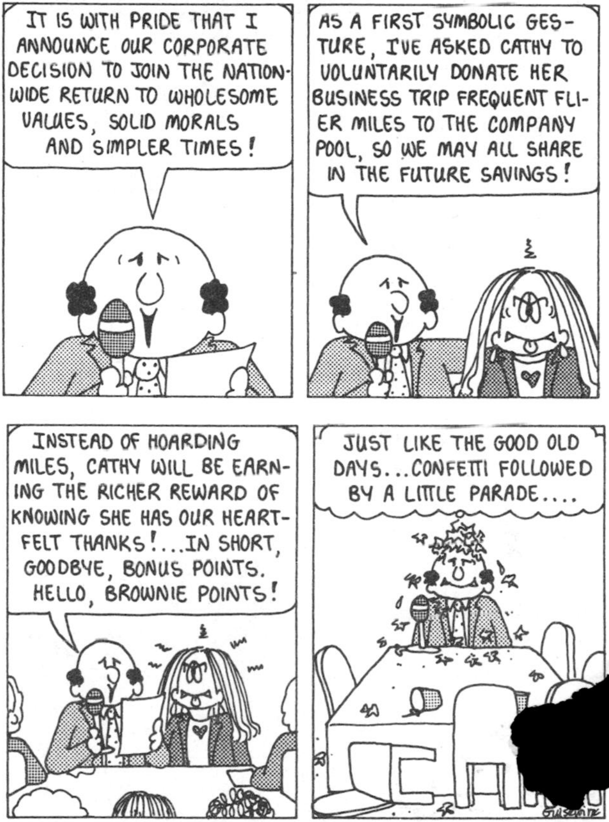
IT IS WITH PRIDE THAT I ANNOUNCE OUR CORPORATE DECISION TO JOIN THE NATION-WIDE RETURN TO WHOLESOME VALUES, SOLID MORALS AND SIMPLER TIMES!
AS A FIRST SYMBOLIC GESTURE, I'VE ASKED CATHY TO VOLUNTARILY DONATE HER BUSINESS TRIP FREQUENT FLIER MILES TO THE COMPANY POOL, SO WE MAY ALL SHARE IN THE FUTURE SAVINGS!
INSTEAD OF HOARDING MILES, CATHY WILL BE EARNING THE RICHER REWARD OF KNOWING SHE HAS OUR HEARTFELT THANKS!...IN SHORT, GOODBYE, BONUS POINTS. HELLO, BROWNIE POINTS!
JUST LIKE THE GOOD OLD DAYS...CONFETTI FOLLOWED BY A LITTLE PARADE....

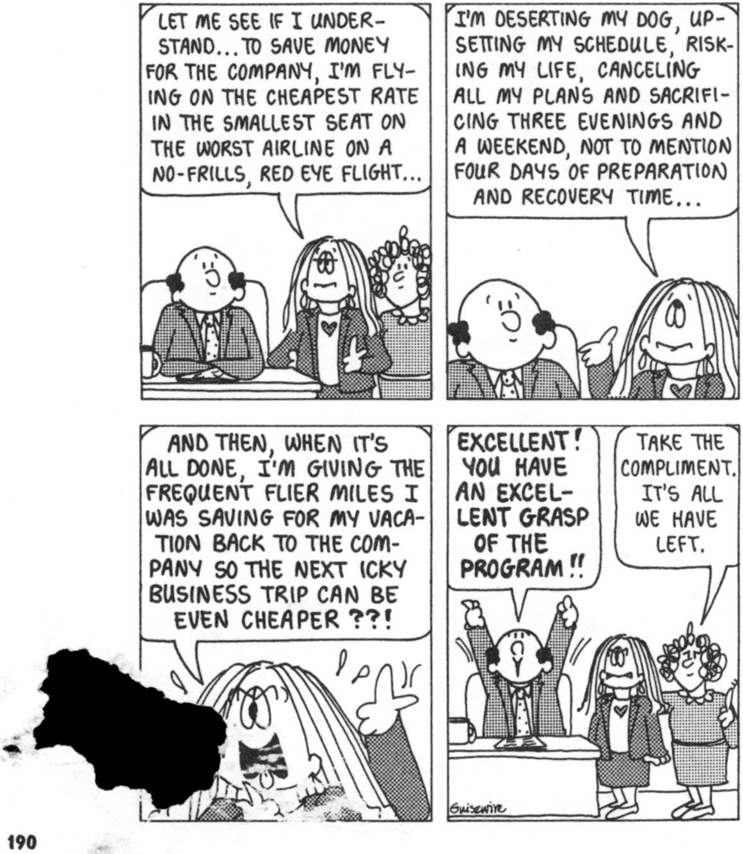
LET ME SEE IF I UNDERSTAND... TO SAVE MONEY FOR THE COMPANY, I'M FLYING ON THE CHEAPEST RATE IN THE SMALLEST SEAT ON THE WORST AIRLINE ON A NO-FRILLS, RED EYE FLIGHT...
I'M DESERTING MY DOG, UPSETTING MY SCHEDULE, RISKING MY LIFE, CANCELING ALL MY PLANS AND SACRIFICING THREE EVENINGS AND A WEEKEND, NOT TO MENTION FOUR DAYS OF PREPARATION AND RECOVERY TIME...
AND THEN, WHEN IT'S ALL DONE, I'M GIVING THE FREQUENT FLIER MILES I WAS SAVING FOR MY VACATION BACK TO THE COMPANY SO THE NEXT ICKY BUSINESS TRIP CAN BE EVEN CHEAPER ??!
EXCELLENT! YOU HAVE AN EXCELLENT GRASP OF THE PROGRAM!!
TAKE THE COMPLIMENT. IT'S ALL WE HAVE LEFT.
Guisewite

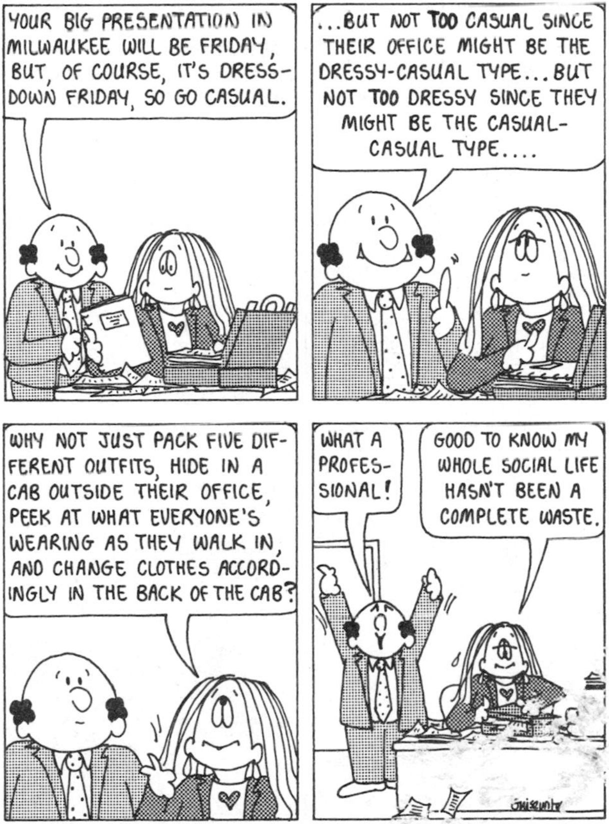

YOUR BIG PRESENTATION IN MILWAUKEE WILL BE FRIDAY, BUT, OF COURSE, IT'S DRESS-DOWN FRIDAY, SO GO CASUAL.
...BUT NOT TOO CASUAL SINCE THEIR OFFICE MIGHT BE THE DRESSY-CASUAL TYPE... BUT NOT TOO DRESSY SINCE THEY MIGHT BE THE CASUAL-CASUAL TYPE....
WHY NOT JUST PACK FIVE DIFFERENT OUTFITS, HIDE IN A CAB OUTSIDE THEIR OFFICE, PEEK AT WHAT EVERYONE'S WEARING AS THEY WALK IN, AND CHANGE CLOTHES ACCORDINGLY IN THE BACK OF THE CAB?
WHAT A PROFESSIONAL!
GOOD TO KNOW MY WHOLE SOCIAL LIFE HASN'T BEEN A COMPLETE WASTE.
Guisewite

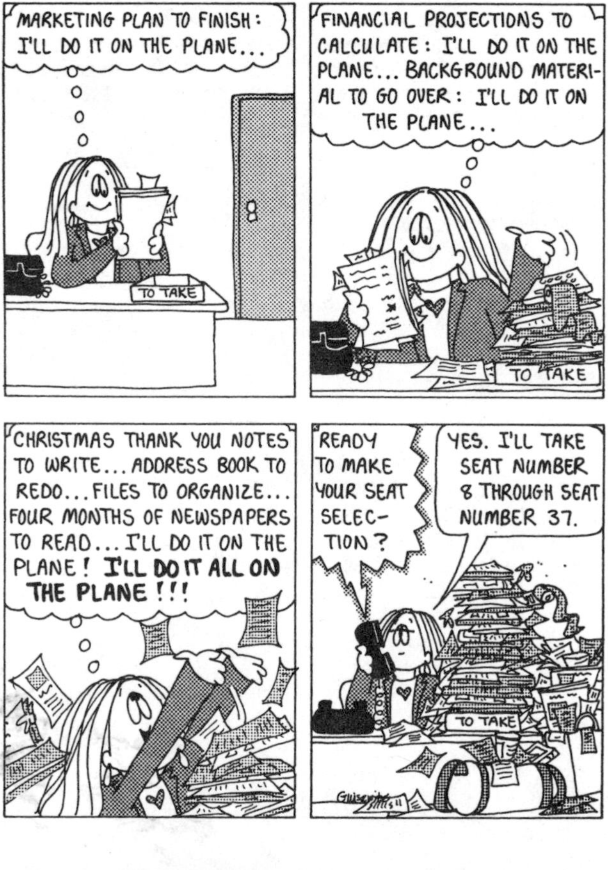
MARKETING PLAN TO FINISH: I'LL DO IT ON THE PLANE...
FINANCIAL PROJECTIONS TO CALCULATE: I'LL DO IT ON THE PLANE... BACKGROUND MATERIAL TO GO OVER: I'LL DO IT ON THE PLANE...
TO TAKE
CHRISTMAS THANK YOU NOTES TO WRITE... ADDRESS BOOK TO REDO... FILES TO ORGANIZE... FOUR MONTHS OF NEWSPAPERS TO READ... I'LL DO IT ON THE PLANE! I'LL DO IT ALL ON THE PLANE!!!
READY TO MAKE YOUR SEAT SELECTION?
YES. I'LL TAKE SEAT NUMBER 8 THROUGH SEAT NUMBER 37.
TO TAKE

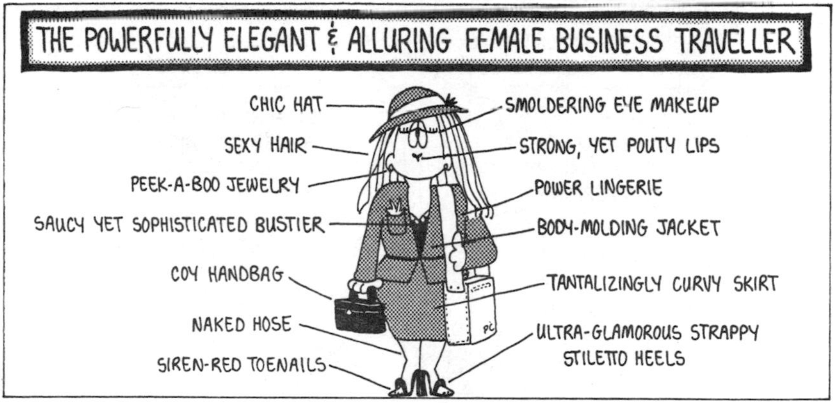
THE POWERFULLY ELEGANT & ALLURING FEMALE BUSINESS TRAVELLER
CHIC HAT
SEXY HAIR
PEEK-A-BOO JEWELRY
SAUCY YET SOPHISTICATED BUSTIER
COY HANDBAG
NAKED HOSE
SIREN-RED TOENAILS
SMOLDERING EYE MAKEUP
STRONG, YET POUTY LIPS
POWER LINGERIE
BODY-MOLDING JACKET
TANTALIZINGLY CURVY SKIRT
ULTRA-GLAMOROUS STRAPPY STILETTO HEELS
PC

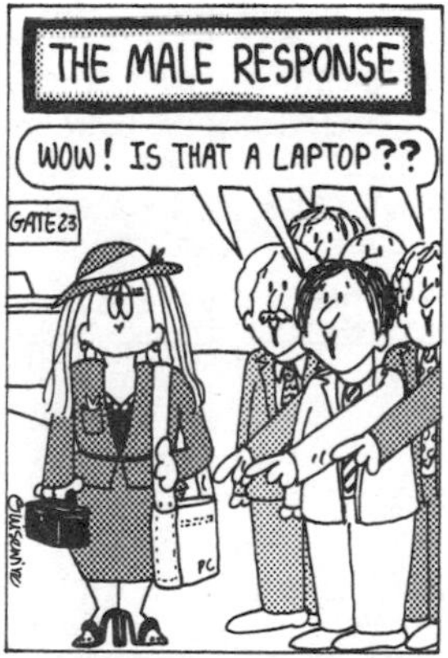
THE MALE RESPONSE
WOW! IS THAT A LAPTOP??
GATE 23
PC

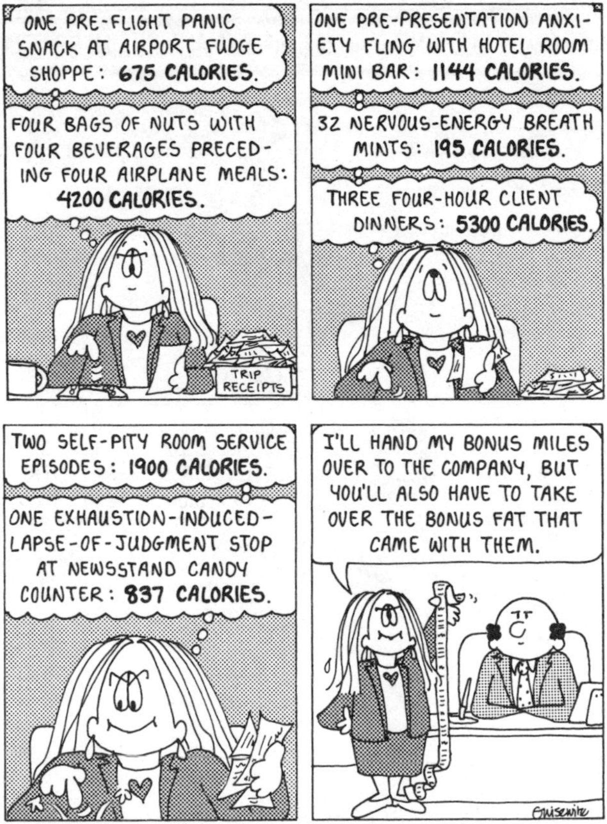
ONE PRE-FLIGHT PANIC SNACK AT AIRPORT FUDGE SHOPPE: 675 CALORIES.
FOUR BAGS OF NUTS WITH FOUR BEVERAGES PRECEDING FOUR AIRPLANE MEALS: 4200 CALORIES.
TRIP RECEIPTS
ONE PRE-PRESENTATION ANXIETY FLING WITH HOTEL ROOM MINI BAR: 1144 CALORIES.
32 NERVOUS-ENERGY BREATH MINTS: 195 CALORIES.
THREE FOUR-HOUR CLIENT DINNERS: 5300 CALORIES.
TWO SELF-PITY ROOM SERVICE EPISODES: 1900 CALORIES.
ONE EXHAUSTION-INDUCED-LAPSE-OF-JUDGMENT STOP AT NEWSSTAND CANDY COUNTER: 837 CALORIES.
I'LL HAND MY BONUS MILES OVER TO THE COMPANY, BUT YOU'LL ALSO HAVE TO TAKE OVER THE BONUS FAT THAT CAME WITH THEM.
Guisewite

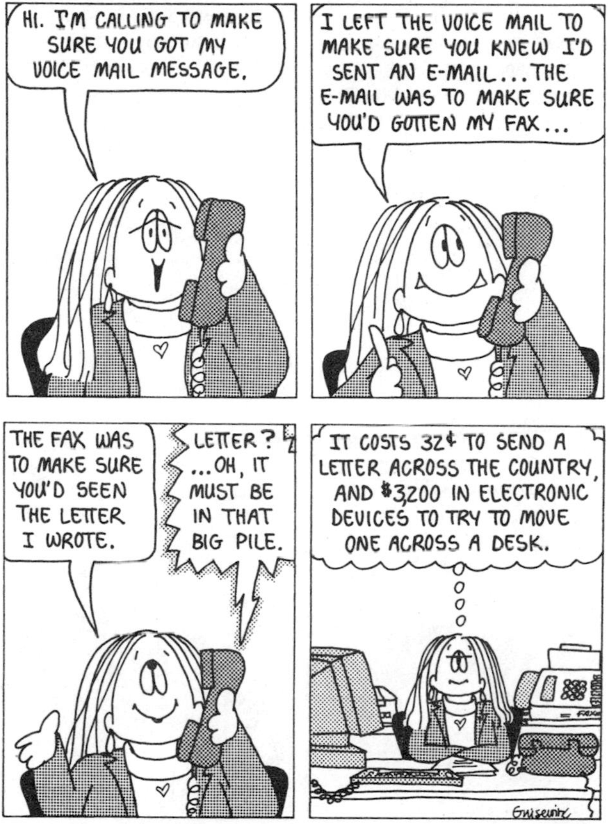
HI. I'M CALLING TO MAKE SURE YOU GOT MY VOICE MAIL MESSAGE.
I LEFT THE VOICE MAIL TO MAKE SURE YOU KNEW I'D SENT AN E-MAIL... THE E-MAIL WAS TO MAKE SURE YOU'D GOTTEN MY FAX...
THE FAX WAS TO MAKE SURE YOU'D SEEN THE LETTER I WROTE.
LETTER? ...OH, IT MUST BE IN THAT BIG PILE.
IT COSTS 32¢ TO SEND A LETTER ACROSS THE COUNTRY, AND $3,200 IN ELECTRONIC DEVICES TO TRY TO MOVE ONE ACROSS A DESK.
Guisewite

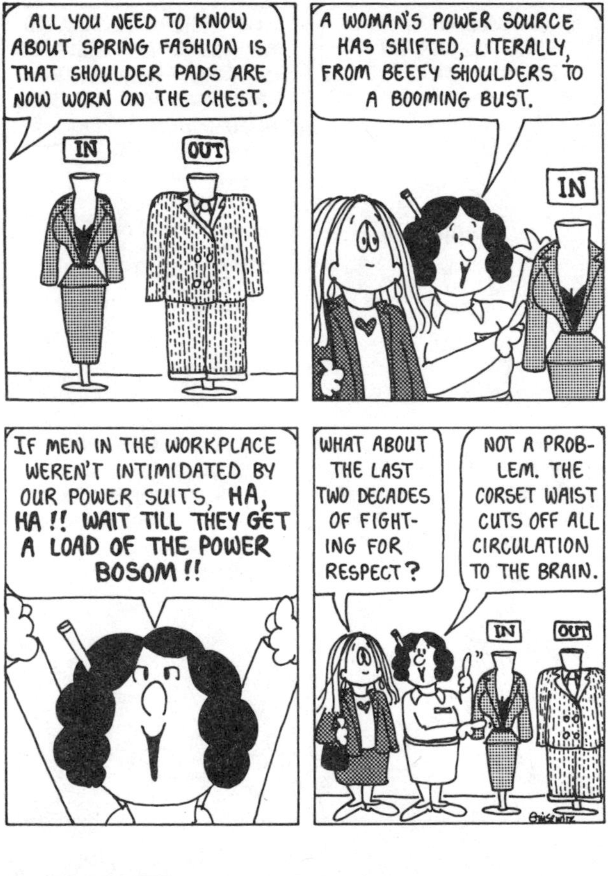
ALL YOU NEED TO KNOW ABOUT SPRING FASHION IS THAT SHOULDER PADS ARE NOW WORN ON THE CHEST.
IN
OUT
A WOMAN'S POWER SOURCE HAS SHIFTED, LITERALLY, FROM BEEFY SHOULDERS TO A BOOMING BUST.
IN
IF MEN IN THE WORKPLACE WEREN'T INTIMIDATED BY OUR POWER SUITS, HA, HA!! WAIT TILL THEY GET A LOAD OF THE POWER BOSOM!!
WHAT ABOUT THE LAST TWO DECADES OF FIGHTING FOR RESPECT?
NOT A PROBLEM. THE CORSET WAIST CUTS OFF ALL CIRCULATION TO THE BRAIN.
IN
OUT

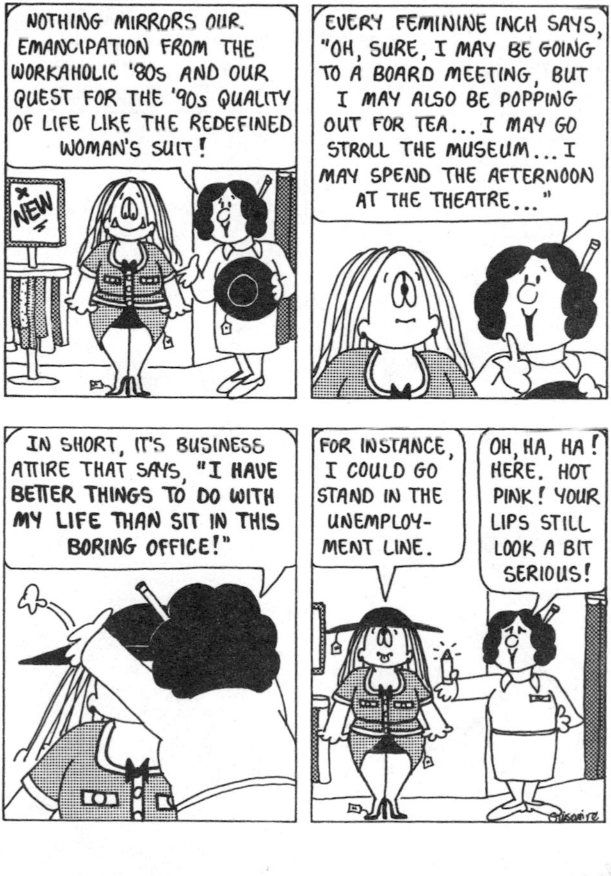
NOTHING MIRRORS OUR EMANCIPATION FROM THE WORKAHOLIC '80s AND OUR QUEST FOR THE '90s QUALITY OF LIFE LIKE THE REDEFINED WOMAN'S SUIT!
NEW
EVERY FEMININE INCH SAYS, "OH, SURE, I MAY BE GOING TO A BOARD MEETING, BUT I MAY ALSO BE POPPING OUT FOR TEA... I MAY GO STROLL THE MUSEUM... I MAY SPEND THE AFTERNOON AT THE THEATRE..."
IN SHORT, IT'S BUSINESS ATTIRE THAT SAYS, "I HAVE BETTER THINGS TO DO WITH MY LIFE THAN SIT IN THIS BORING OFFICE!"
FOR INSTANCE, I COULD GO STAND IN THE UNEMPLOY-MENT LINE.
OH, HA, HA! HERE. HOT PINK! YOUR LIPS STILL LOOK A BIT SERIOUS!
Guisewite

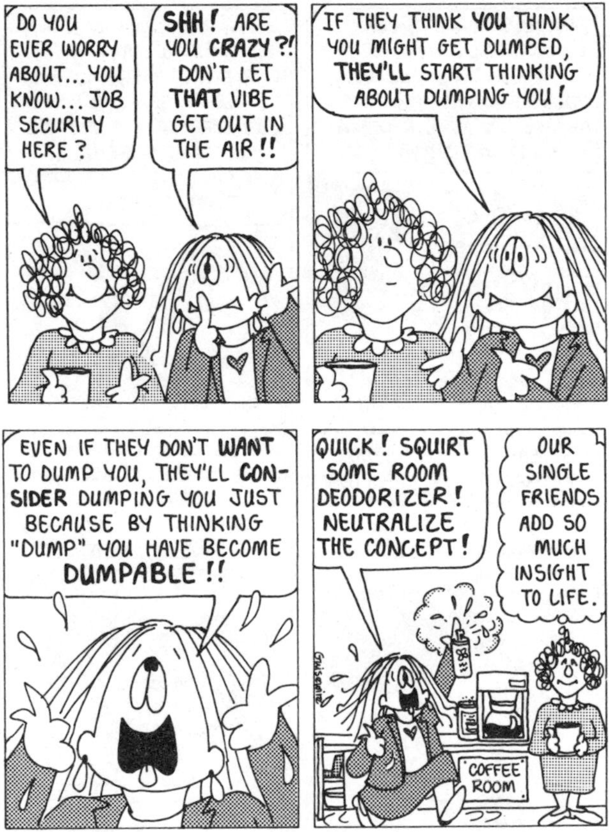

DO YOU EVER WORRY ABOUT... YOU KNOW... JOB SECURITY HERE?
SHH! ARE YOU CRAZY?! DON'T LET THAT VIBE GET OUT IN THE AIR!!
IF THEY THINK YOU THINK YOU MIGHT GET DUMPED, THEY'LL START THINKING ABOUT DUMPING YOU!
EVEN IF THEY DON'T WANT TO DUMP YOU, THEY'LL CONSIDER DUMPING YOU JUST BECAUSE BY THINKING "DUMP" YOU HAVE BECOME DUMPABLE!!
QUICK! SQUIRT SOME ROOM DEODORIZER! NEUTRALIZE THE CONCEPT!
OUR SINGLE FRIENDS ADD SO MUCH INSIGHT TO LIFE.
COFFEE ROOM
Guisewite

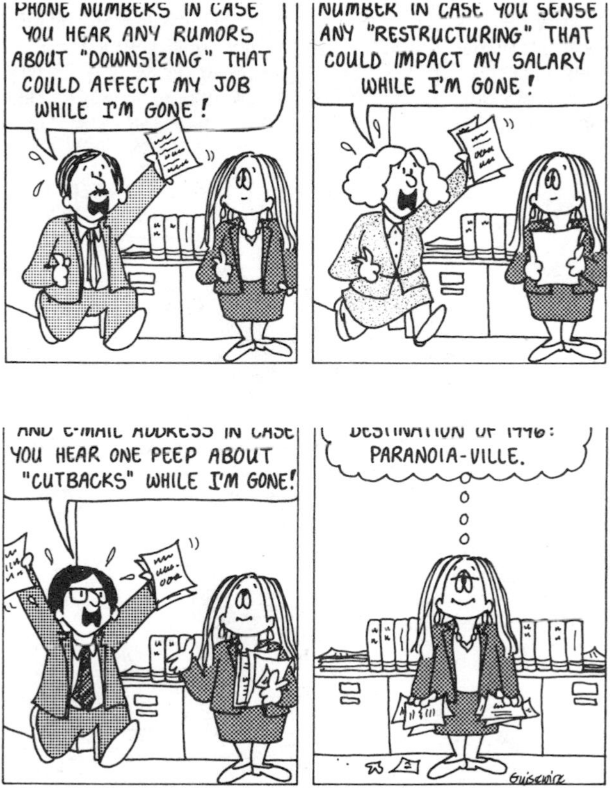

PHONE NUMBERS IN CASE YOU HEAR ANY RUMORS ABOUT "DOWNSIZING" THAT COULD AFFECT MY JOB WHILE I'M GONE!
NUMBER IN CASE YOU SENSE ANY "RESTRUCTURING" THAT COULD IMPACT MY SALARY WHILE I'M GONE!
YOU HEAR ONE PEEP ABOUT "CUTBACKS" WHILE I'M GONE!
PARANOIA-VILLE.

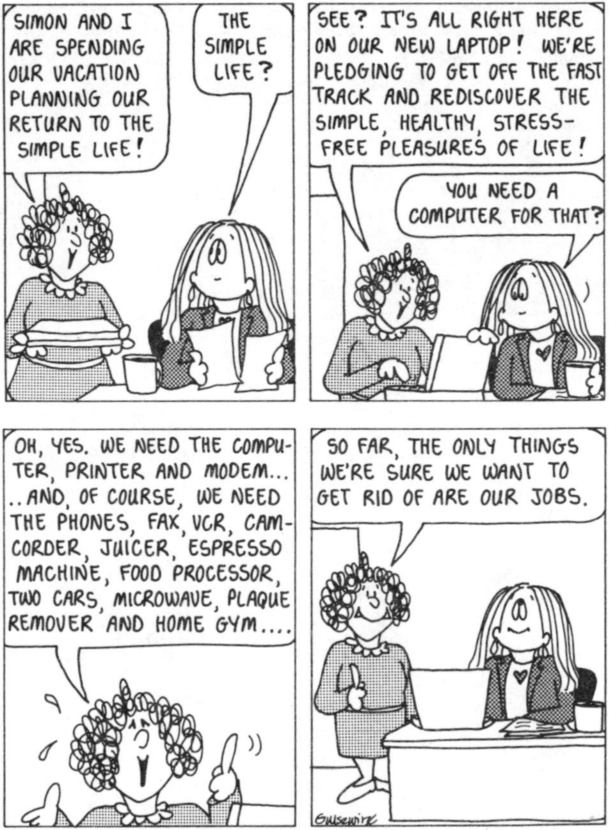
SIMON AND I ARE SPENDING OUR VACATION PLANNING OUR RETURN TO THE SIMPLE LIFE!
THE SIMPLE LIFE?
SEE? IT'S ALL RIGHT HERE ON OUR NEW LAPTOP! WE'RE PLEDGING TO GET OFF THE FAST TRACK AND REDISCOVER THE SIMPLE, HEALTHY, STRESS-FREE PLEASURES OF LIFE!
YOU NEED A COMPUTER FOR THAT?
OH, YES. WE NEED THE COMPUTER, PRINTER AND MODEM... ..AND, OF COURSE, WE NEED THE PHONES, FAX, VCR, CAMCORDER, JUICER, ESPRESSO MACHINE, FOOD PROCESSOR, TWO CARS, MICROWAVE, PLAQUE REMOVER AND HOME GYM....
SO FAR, THE ONLY THINGS WE'RE SURE WE WANT TO GET RID OF ARE OUR JOBS.
GUISEWITE

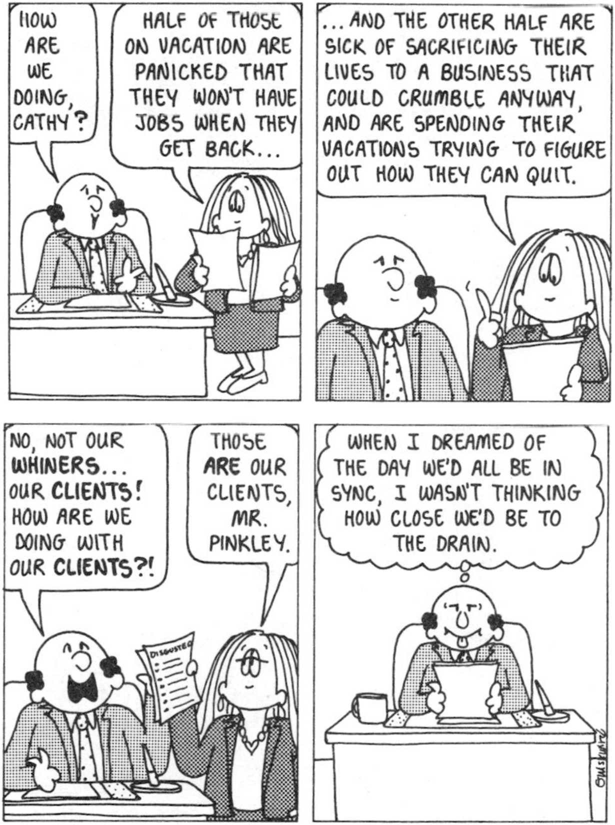
HOW ARE WE DOING, CATHY?
HALF OF THOSE ON VACATION ARE PANICKED THAT THEY WON'T HAVE JOBS WHEN THEY GET BACK...
...AND THE OTHER HALF ARE SICK OF SACRIFICING THEIR LIVES TO A BUSINESS THAT COULD CRUMBLE ANYWAY, AND ARE SPENDING THEIR VACATIONS TRYING TO FIGURE OUT HOW THEY CAN QUIT.
NO, NOT OUR **WHINERS**... OUR **CLIENTS**! HOW ARE WE DOING WITH OUR **CLIENTS**?!
DISGUSTED
THOSE **ARE** OUR CLIENTS, MR. PINKLEY.
WHEN I DREAMED OF THE DAY WE'D ALL BE IN SYNC, I WASN'T THINKING HOW CLOSE WE'D BE TO THE DRAIN.

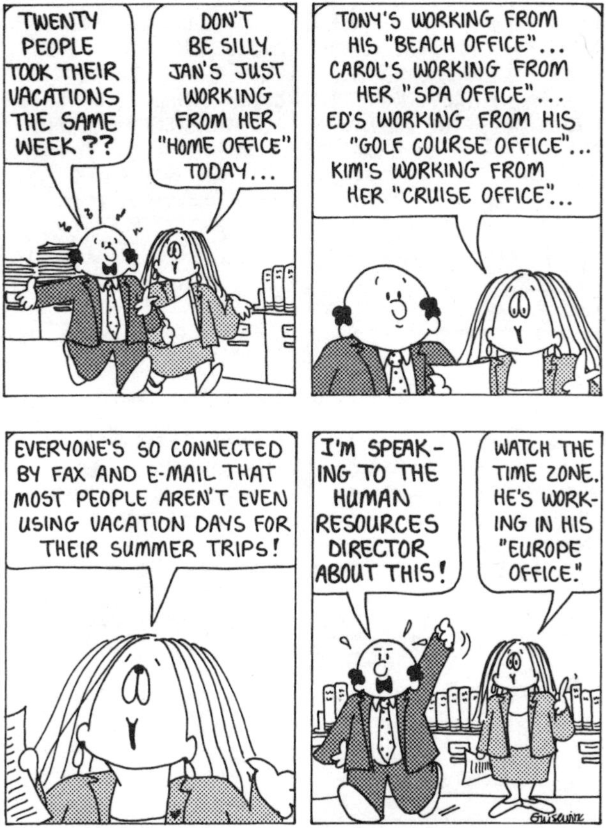
TWENTY PEOPLE TOOK THEIR VACATIONS THE SAME WEEK??
DON'T BE SILLY. JAN'S JUST WORKING FROM HER "HOME OFFICE" TODAY...
TONY'S WORKING FROM HIS "BEACH OFFICE"... CAROL'S WORKING FROM HER "SPA OFFICE"... ED'S WORKING FROM HIS "GOLF COURSE OFFICE"... KIM'S WORKING FROM HER "CRUISE OFFICE"...
EVERYONE'S SO CONNECTED BY FAX AND E-MAIL THAT MOST PEOPLE AREN'T EVEN USING VACATION DAYS FOR THEIR SUMMER TRIPS!
I'M SPEAKING TO THE HUMAN RESOURCES DIRECTOR ABOUT THIS!
WATCH THE TIME ZONE. HE'S WORKING IN HIS "EUROPE OFFICE."
Guisewite

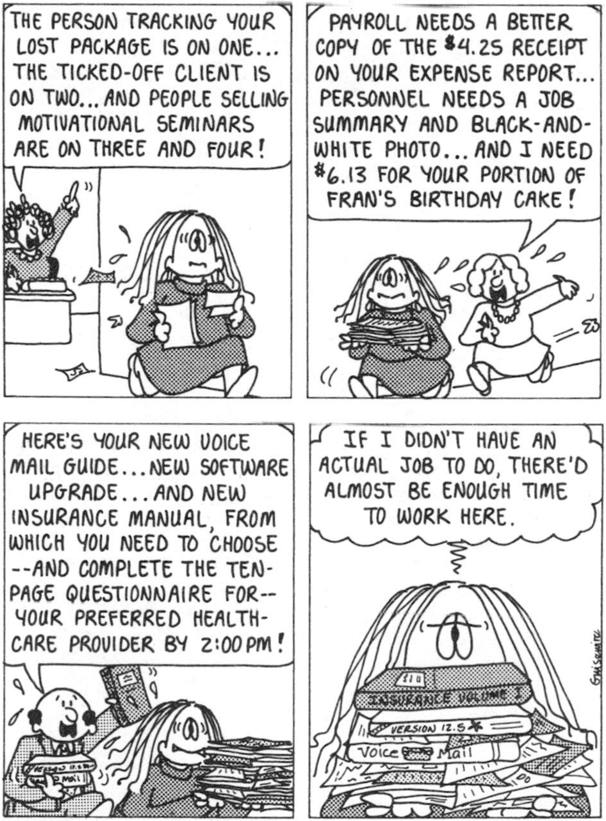
THE PERSON TRACKING YOUR LOST PACKAGE IS ON ONE... THE TICKED-OFF CLIENT IS ON TWO... AND PEOPLE SELLING MOTIVATIONAL SEMINARS ARE ON THREE AND FOUR!
PAYROLL NEEDS A BETTER COPY OF THE $4.25 RECEIPT ON YOUR EXPENSE REPORT... PERSONNEL NEEDS A JOB SUMMARY AND BLACK-AND-WHITE PHOTO... AND I NEED $6.13 FOR YOUR PORTION OF FRAN'S BIRTHDAY CAKE!
HERE'S YOUR NEW VOICE MAIL GUIDE... NEW SOFTWARE UPGRADE... AND NEW INSURANCE MANUAL, FROM WHICH YOU NEED TO CHOOSE --AND COMPLETE THE TEN-PAGE QUESTIONNAIRE FOR-- YOUR PREFERRED HEALTH-CARE PROVIDER BY 2:00 PM!
IF I DIDN'T HAVE AN ACTUAL JOB TO DO, THERE'D ALMOST BE ENOUGH TIME TO WORK HERE.
VERSION 12.5
Voice Mail
GUISEWITE

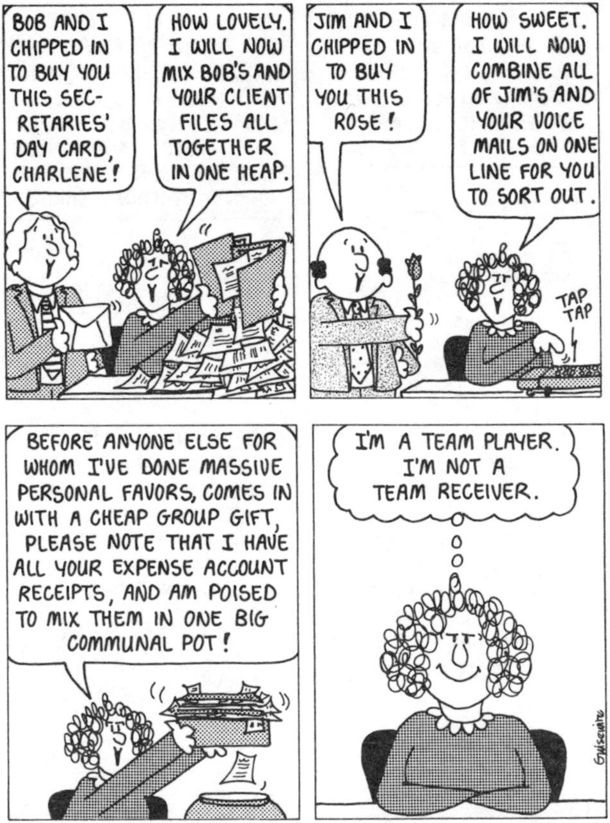
BOB AND I CHIPPED IN TO BUY YOU THIS SEC-RETARIES' DAY CARD, CHARLENE!
HOW LOVELY. I WILL NOW MIX BOB'S AND YOUR CLIENT FILES ALL TOGETHER IN ONE HEAP.
JIM AND I CHIPPED IN TO BUY YOU THIS ROSE!
HOW SWEET. I WILL NOW COMBINE ALL OF JIM'S AND YOUR VOICE MAILS ON ONE LINE FOR YOU TO SORT OUT.
TAP TAP
BEFORE ANYONE ELSE FOR WHOM I'VE DONE MASSIVE PERSONAL FAVORS, COMES IN WITH A CHEAP GROUP GIFT, PLEASE NOTE THAT I HAVE ALL YOUR EXPENSE ACCOUNT RECEIPTS, AND AM POISED TO MIX THEM IN ONE BIG COMMUNAL POT!
I'M A TEAM PLAYER. I'M NOT A TEAM RECEIVER.
Guisewite

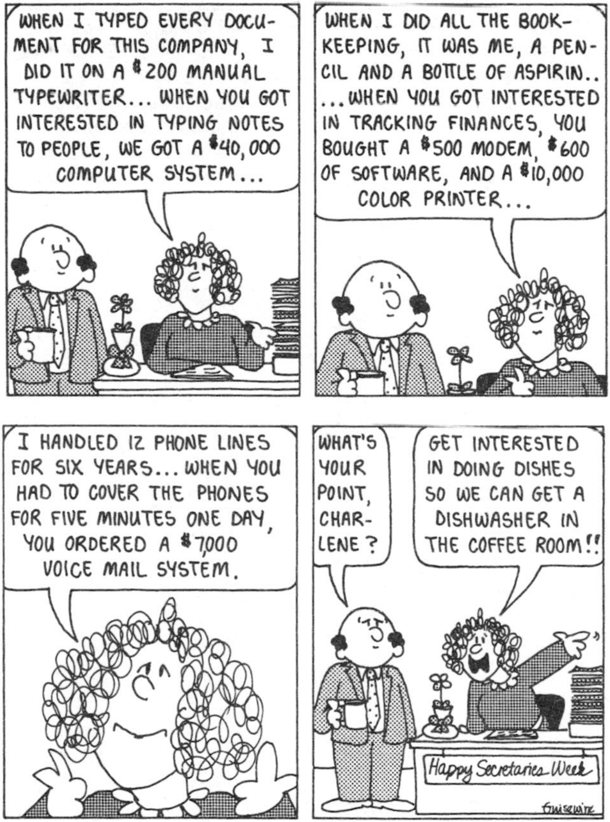
WHEN I TYPED EVERY DOCUMENT FOR THIS COMPANY, I DID IT ON A $200 MANUAL TYPEWRITER... WHEN YOU GOT INTERESTED IN TYPING NOTES TO PEOPLE, WE GOT A $40,000 COMPUTER SYSTEM...
WHEN I DID ALL THE BOOKKEEPING, IT WAS ME, A PENCIL AND A BOTTLE OF ASPIRIN.. ...WHEN YOU GOT INTERESTED IN TRACKING FINANCES, YOU BOUGHT A $500 MODEM, $600 OF SOFTWARE, AND A $10,000 COLOR PRINTER...
I HANDLED 12 PHONE LINES FOR SIX YEARS... WHEN YOU HAD TO COVER THE PHONES FOR FIVE MINUTES ONE DAY, YOU ORDERED A $7,000 VOICE MAIL SYSTEM.
WHAT'S YOUR POINT, CHARLENE?
GET INTERESTED IN DOING DISHES SO WE CAN GET A DISHWASHER IN THE COFFEE ROOM!!
Happy Secretaries Week
Guisewite

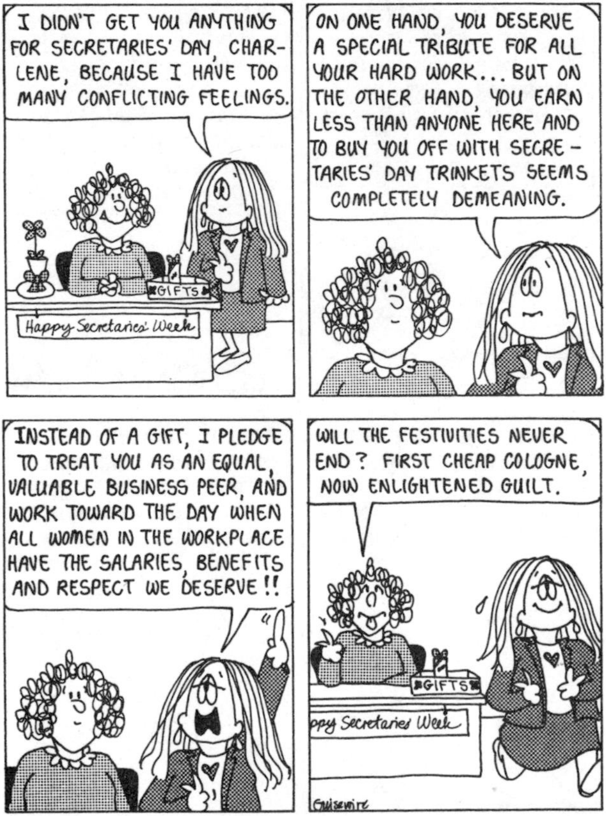
I DIDN'T GET YOU ANYTHING FOR SECRETARIES' DAY, CHARLENE, BECAUSE I HAVE TOO MANY CONFLICTING FEELINGS.
GIFTS
Happy Secretaries' Week
ON ONE HAND, YOU DESERVE A SPECIAL TRIBUTE FOR ALL YOUR HARD WORK... BUT ON THE OTHER HAND, YOU EARN LESS THAN ANYONE HERE AND TO BUY YOU OFF WITH SECRETARIES' DAY TRINKETS SEEMS COMPLETELY DEMEANING.
INSTEAD OF A GIFT, I PLEDGE TO TREAT YOU AS AN EQUAL, VALUABLE BUSINESS PEER, AND WORK TOWARD THE DAY WHEN ALL WOMEN IN THE WORKPLACE HAVE THE SALARIES, BENEFITS AND RESPECT WE DESERVE!!
WILL THE FESTIVITIES NEVER END? FIRST CHEAP COLOGNE, NOW ENLIGHTENED GUILT.
GIFTS
ppy Secretaries Week
Guisewite

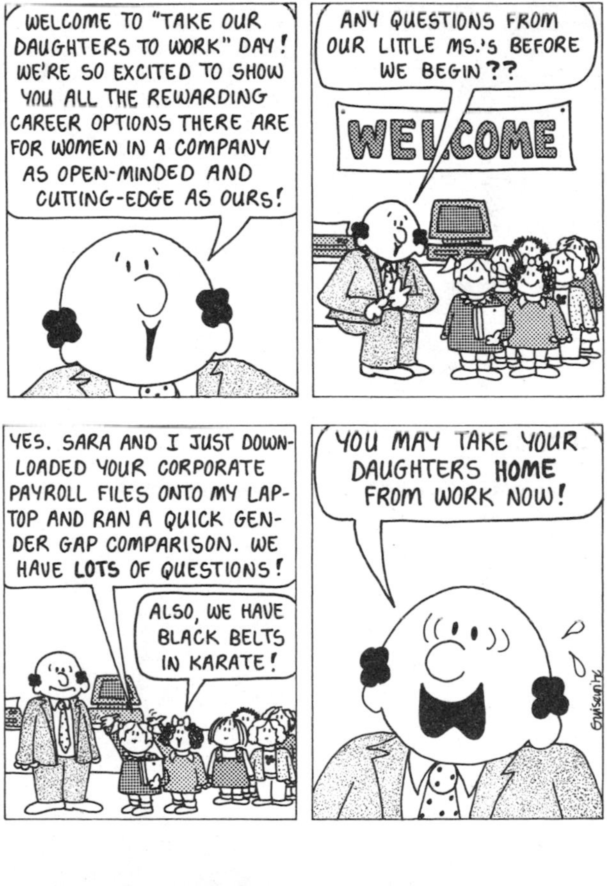
WELCOME TO "TAKE OUR DAUGHTERS TO WORK" DAY! WE'RE SO EXCITED TO SHOW YOU ALL THE REWARDING CAREER OPTIONS THERE ARE FOR WOMEN IN A COMPANY AS OPEN-MINDED AND CUTTING-EDGE AS OURS!
ANY QUESTIONS FROM OUR LITTLE MS.'S BEFORE WE BEGIN??
WELCOME
YES. SARA AND I JUST DOWNLOADED YOUR CORPORATE PAYROLL FILES ONTO MY LAPTOP AND RAN A QUICK GENDER GAP COMPARISON. WE HAVE LOTS OF QUESTIONS!
ALSO, WE HAVE BLACK BELTS IN KARATE!
YOU MAY TAKE YOUR DAUGHTERS HOME FROM WORK NOW!
Guisewite

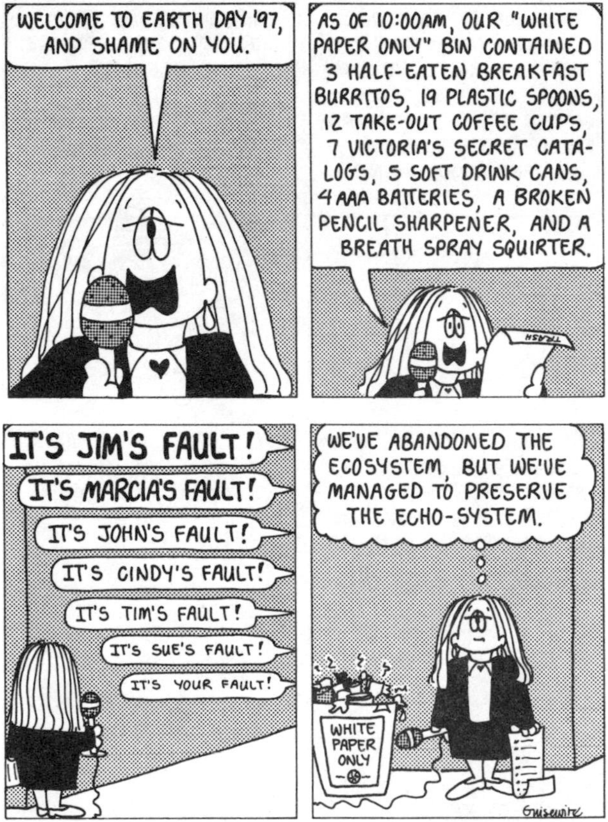
WELCOME TO EARTH DAY '97, AND SHAME ON YOU.
AS OF 10:00AM, OUR "WHITE PAPER ONLY" BIN CONTAINED 3 HALF-EATEN BREAKFAST BURRITOS, 19 PLASTIC SPOONS, 12 TAKE-OUT COFFEE CUPS, 7 VICTORIA'S SECRET CATALOGS, 5 SOFT DRINK CANS, 4 AAA BATTERIES, A BROKEN PENCIL SHARPENER, AND A BREATH SPRAY SQUIRTER.
TRASH
IT'S JIM'S FAULT!
IT'S MARCIA'S FAULT!
IT'S JOHN'S FAULT!
IT'S CINDY'S FAULT!
IT'S TIM'S FAULT!
IT'S SUE'S FAULT!
IT'S YOUR FAULT!
WE'VE ABANDONED THE ECOSYSTEM, BUT WE'VE MANAGED TO PRESERVE THE ECHO-SYSTEM.
WHITE PAPER ONLY
Guisewite

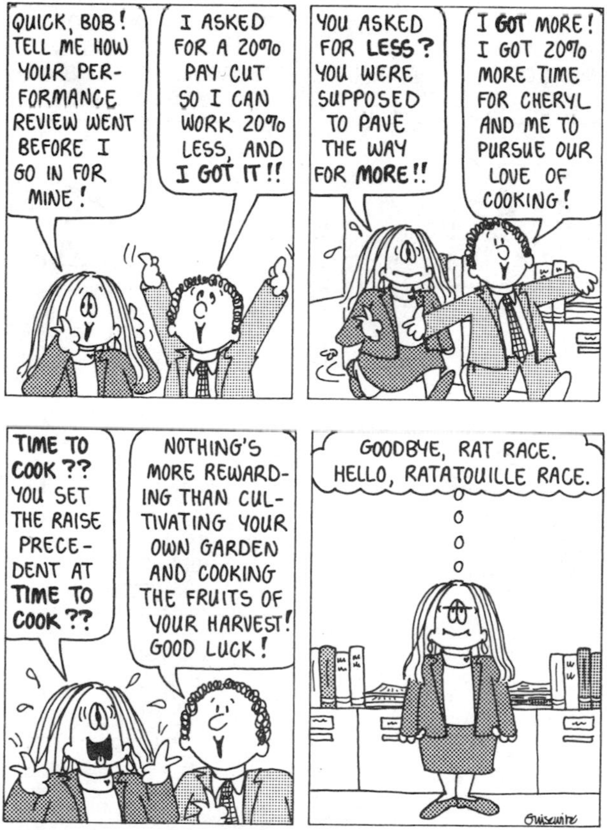
QUICK, BOB! TELL ME HOW YOUR PERFORMANCE REVIEW WENT BEFORE I GO IN FOR MINE!
I ASKED FOR A 20% PAY CUT SO I CAN WORK 20% LESS, AND I GOT IT!!
YOU ASKED FOR LESS? YOU WERE SUPPOSED TO PAVE THE WAY FOR MORE!!
I GOT MORE! I GOT 20% MORE TIME FOR CHERYL AND ME TO PURSUE OUR LOVE OF COOKING!
TIME TO COOK?? YOU SET THE RAISE PRECEDENT AT TIME TO COOK??
NOTHING'S MORE REWARDING THAN CULTIVATING YOUR OWN GARDEN AND COOKING THE FRUITS OF YOUR HARVEST! GOOD LUCK!
GOODBYE, RAT RACE. HELLO, RATATOUILLE RACE.
Guisewite

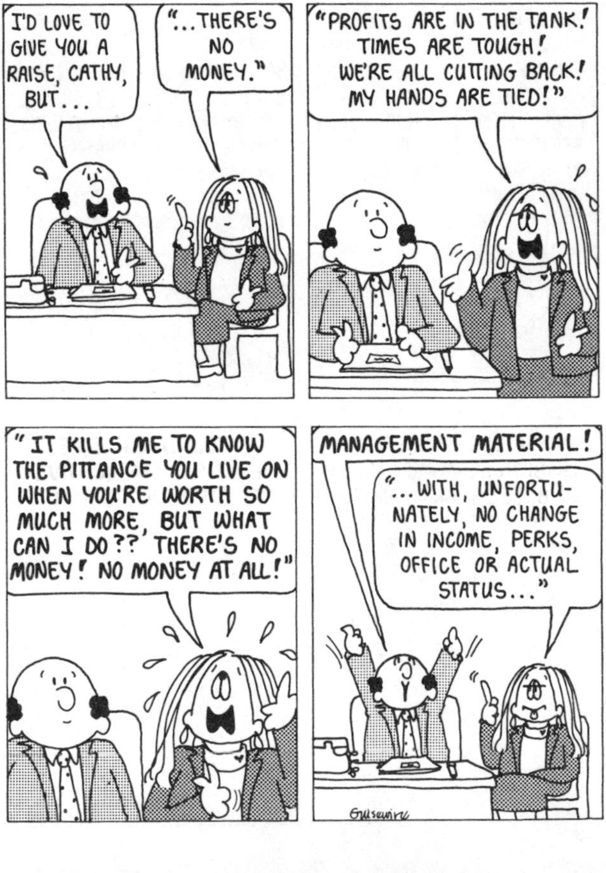
I'D LOVE TO GIVE YOU A RAISE, CATHY, BUT...
"...THERE'S NO MONEY."
"PROFITS ARE IN THE TANK! TIMES ARE TOUGH! WE'RE ALL CUTTING BACK! MY HANDS ARE TIED!"
"IT KILLS ME TO KNOW THE PITTANCE YOU LIVE ON WHEN YOU'RE WORTH SO MUCH MORE, BUT WHAT CAN I DO?? THERE'S NO MONEY! NO MONEY AT ALL!"
MANAGEMENT MATERIAL!
"...WITH, UNFORTUNATELY, NO CHANGE IN INCOME, PERKS, OFFICE OR ACTUAL STATUS..."
Guisewite

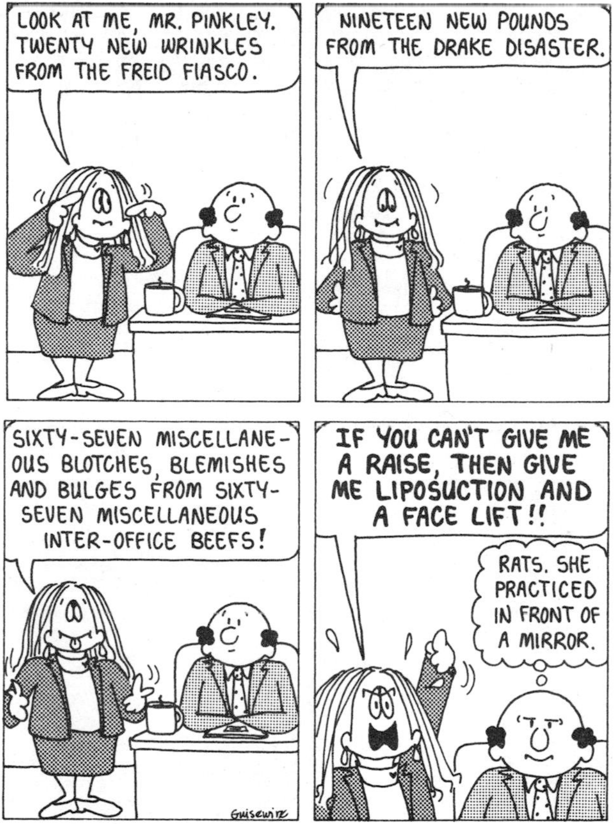
LOOK AT ME, MR. PINKLEY. TWENTY NEW WRINKLES FROM THE FREID FIASCO.
NINETEEN NEW POUNDS FROM THE DRAKE DISASTER.
SIXTY-SEVEN MISCELLANEOUS BLOTCHES, BLEMISHES AND BULGES FROM SIXTY-SEVEN MISCELLANEOUS INTER-OFFICE BEEFS!
IF YOU CAN'T GIVE ME A RAISE, THEN GIVE ME LIPOSUCTION AND A FACE LIFT!!
RATS. SHE PRACTICED IN FRONT OF A MIRROR.
GUISEWITE

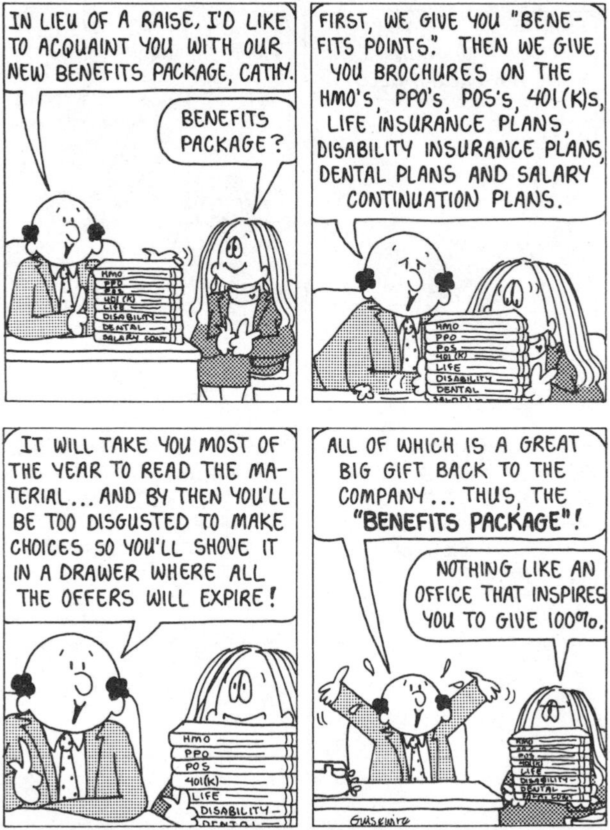
IN LIEU OF A RAISE, I'D LIKE TO ACQUAINT YOU WITH OUR NEW BENEFITS PACKAGE, CATHY.
BENEFITS PACKAGE?
HMO
PPO
POS
401(K)
LIFE
DISABILITY
DENTAL
SALARY CONT
FIRST, WE GIVE YOU "BENEFITS POINTS." THEN WE GIVE YOU BROCHURES ON THE HMO'S, PPO'S, POS'S, 401(K)S, LIFE INSURANCE PLANS, DISABILITY INSURANCE PLANS, DENTAL PLANS AND SALARY CONTINUATION PLANS.
IT WILL TAKE YOU MOST OF THE YEAR TO READ THE MATERIAL... AND BY THEN YOU'LL BE TOO DISGUSTED TO MAKE CHOICES SO YOU'LL SHOVE IT IN A DRAWER WHERE ALL THE OFFERS WILL EXPIRE!
ALL OF WHICH IS A GREAT BIG GIFT BACK TO THE COMPANY... THUS, THE "BENEFITS PACKAGE"!
NOTHING LIKE AN OFFICE THAT INSPIRES YOU TO GIVE 100%.
GUISEWITE

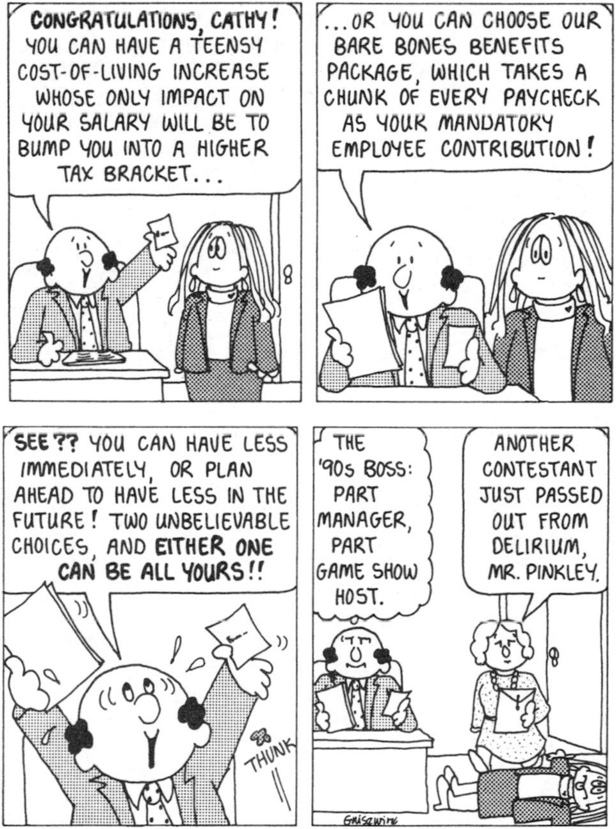
CONGRATULATIONS, CATHY! YOU CAN HAVE A TEENSY COST-OF-LIVING INCREASE WHOSE ONLY IMPACT ON YOUR SALARY WILL BE TO BUMP YOU INTO A HIGHER TAX BRACKET...
...OR YOU CAN CHOOSE OUR BARE BONES BENEFITS PACKAGE, WHICH TAKES A CHUNK OF EVERY PAYCHECK AS YOUR MANDATORY EMPLOYEE CONTRIBUTION!
SEE?? YOU CAN HAVE LESS IMMEDIATELY, OR PLAN AHEAD TO HAVE LESS IN THE FUTURE! TWO UNBELIEVABLE CHOICES, AND EITHER ONE CAN BE ALL YOURS!!
THUNK
THE '90s BOSS: PART MANAGER, PART GAME SHOW HOST.
ANOTHER CONTESTANT JUST PASSED OUT FROM DELIRIUM, MR. PINKLEY.
Guisewite

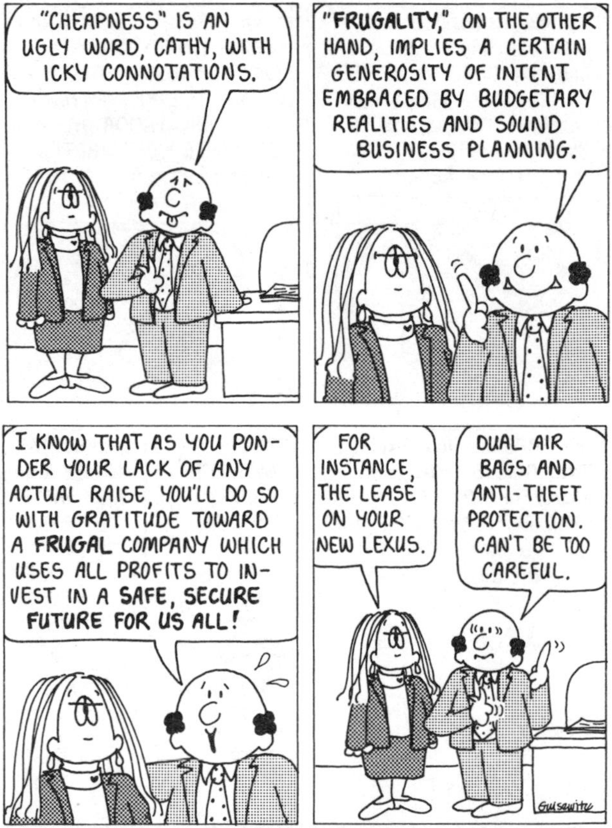
"CHEAPNESS" IS AN UGLY WORD, CATHY, WITH ICKY CONNOTATIONS.
"FRUGALITY," ON THE OTHER HAND, IMPLIES A CERTAIN GENEROSITY OF INTENT EMBRACED BY BUDGETARY REALITIES AND SOUND BUSINESS PLANNING.
I KNOW THAT AS YOU PONDER YOUR LACK OF ANY ACTUAL RAISE, YOU'LL DO SO WITH GRATITUDE TOWARD A FRUGAL COMPANY WHICH USES ALL PROFITS TO INVEST IN A SAFE, SECURE FUTURE FOR US ALL!
FOR INSTANCE, THE LEASE ON YOUR NEW LEXUS.
DUAL AIR BAGS AND ANTI-THEFT PROTECTION. CAN'T BE TOO CAREFUL.
GUISEWITE

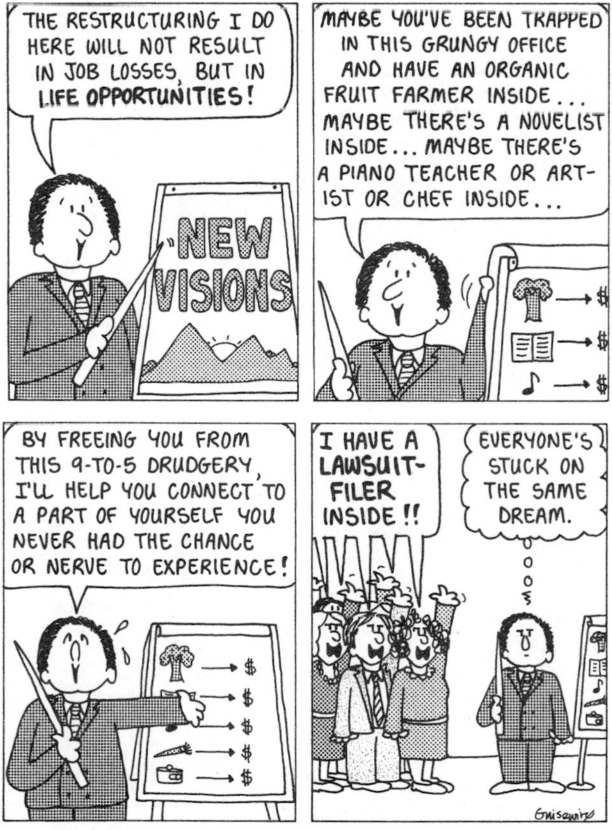
THE RESTRUCTURING I DO HERE WILL NOT RESULT IN JOB LOSSES, BUT IN LIFE OPPORTUNITIES!
NEW VISIONS
MAYBE YOU'VE BEEN TRAPPED IN THIS GRUNGY OFFICE AND HAVE AN ORGANIC FRUIT FARMER INSIDE... MAYBE THERE'S A NOVELIST INSIDE... MAYBE THERE'S A PIANO TEACHER OR ARTIST OR CHEF INSIDE...
BY FREEING YOU FROM THIS 9-TO-5 DRUDGERY, I'LL HELP YOU CONNECT TO A PART OF YOURSELF YOU NEVER HAD THE CHANCE OR NERVE TO EXPERIENCE!
I HAVE A LAWSUIT-FILER INSIDE!!
EVERYONE'S STUCK ON THE SAME DREAM.
Guisewite

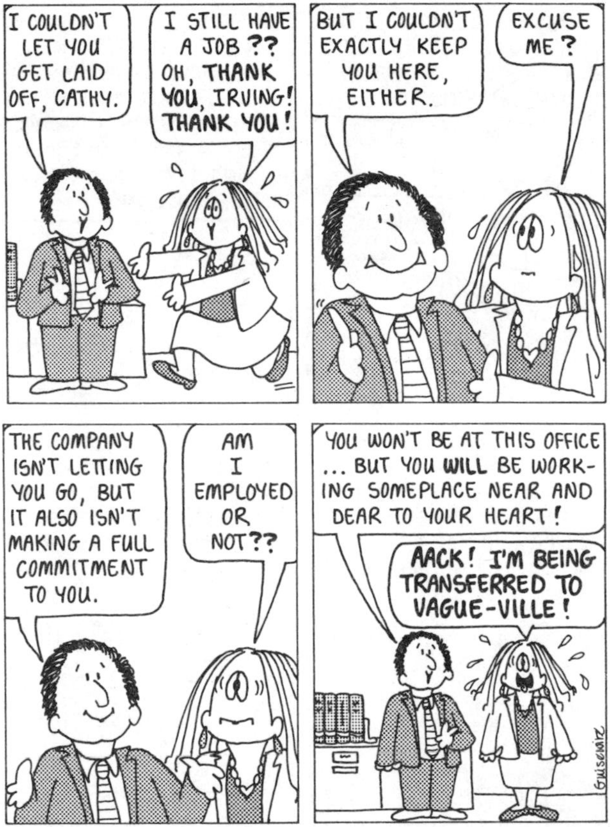
I COULDN'T LET YOU GET LAID OFF, CATHY.
I STILL HAVE A JOB?? OH, THANK YOU, IRVING! THANK YOU!
BUT I COULDN'T EXACTLY KEEP YOU HERE, EITHER.
EXCUSE ME?
THE COMPANY ISN'T LETTING YOU GO, BUT IT ALSO ISN'T MAKING A FULL COMMITMENT TO YOU.
AM I EMPLOYED OR NOT??
YOU WON'T BE AT THIS OFFICE ... BUT YOU WILL BE WORKING SOMEPLACE NEAR AND DEAR TO YOUR HEART!
AACK! I'M BEING TRANSFERRED TO VAGUE-VILLE!
GUISEWITE

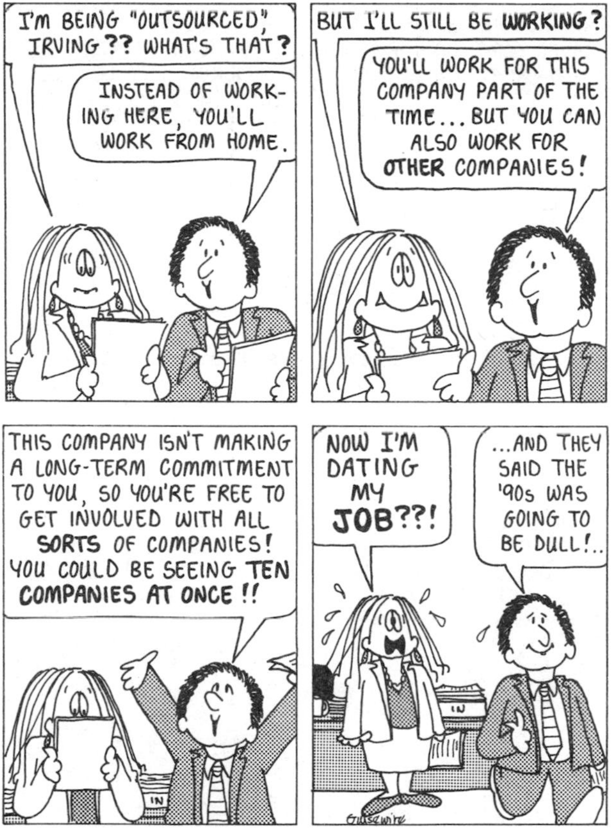
I'M BEING "OUTSOURCED", IRVING?? WHAT'S THAT?
INSTEAD OF WORKING HERE, YOU'LL WORK FROM HOME.
BUT I'LL STILL BE WORKING?
YOU'LL WORK FOR THIS COMPANY PART OF THE TIME... BUT YOU CAN ALSO WORK FOR OTHER COMPANIES!
THIS COMPANY ISN'T MAKING A LONG-TERM COMMITMENT TO YOU, SO YOU'RE FREE TO GET INVOLVED WITH ALL SORTS OF COMPANIES! YOU COULD BE SEEING TEN COMPANIES AT ONCE!!
NOW I'M DATING MY JOB??!
...AND THEY SAID THE '90s WAS GOING TO BE DULL!..
IN
IN
Guisewite

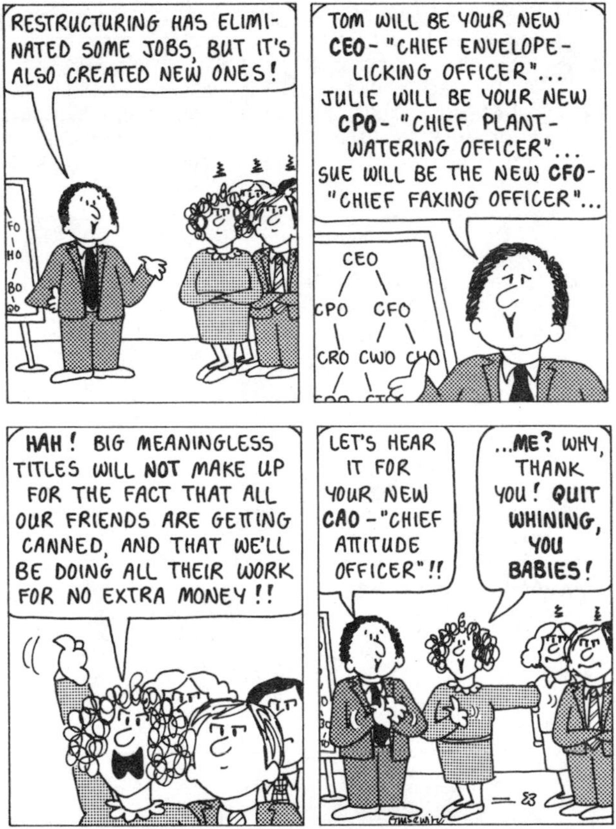

RESTRUCTURING HAS ELIMINATED SOME JOBS, BUT IT'S ALSO CREATED NEW ONES!
TOM WILL BE YOUR NEW **CEO** - "CHIEF ENVELOPE-LICKING OFFICER"... JULIE WILL BE YOUR NEW **CPO** - "CHIEF PLANT-WATERING OFFICER"... SUE WILL BE THE NEW **CFO** - "CHIEF FAXING OFFICER"...
CEO
CPO
CFO
CRO
CWO
HAH! BIG MEANINGLESS TITLES WILL **NOT** MAKE UP FOR THE FACT THAT ALL OUR FRIENDS ARE GETTING CANNED, AND THAT WE'LL BE DOING ALL THEIR WORK FOR NO EXTRA MONEY!!
LET'S HEAR IT FOR YOUR NEW **CAO** - "CHIEF ATTITUDE OFFICER"!!
...**ME?** WHY, THANK YOU! **QUIT WHINING, YOU BABIES!**

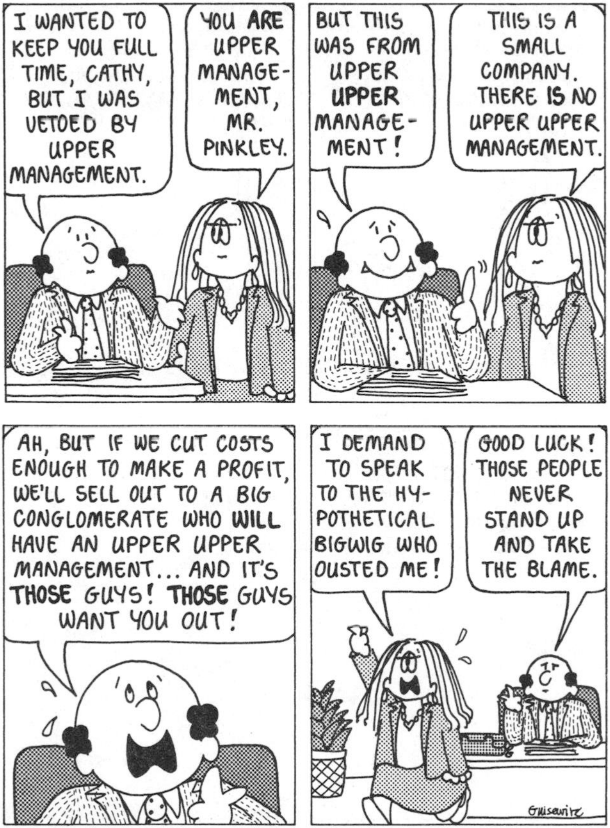
I WANTED TO KEEP YOU FULL TIME, CATHY, BUT I WAS VETOED BY UPPER MANAGEMENT.
YOU **ARE** UPPER MANAGEMENT, MR. PINKLEY.
BUT THIS WAS FROM UPPER **UPPER** MANAGEMENT!
THIS IS A SMALL COMPANY. THERE **IS** NO UPPER UPPER MANAGEMENT.
AH, BUT IF WE CUT COSTS ENOUGH TO MAKE A PROFIT, WE'LL SELL OUT TO A BIG CONGLOMERATE WHO **WILL** HAVE AN UPPER UPPER MANAGEMENT... AND IT'S **THOSE** GUYS! **THOSE** GUYS WANT YOU OUT!
I DEMAND TO SPEAK TO THE HYPOTHETICAL BIGWIG WHO OUSTED ME!
GOOD LUCK! THOSE PEOPLE NEVER STAND UP AND TAKE THE BLAME.
Guisewite

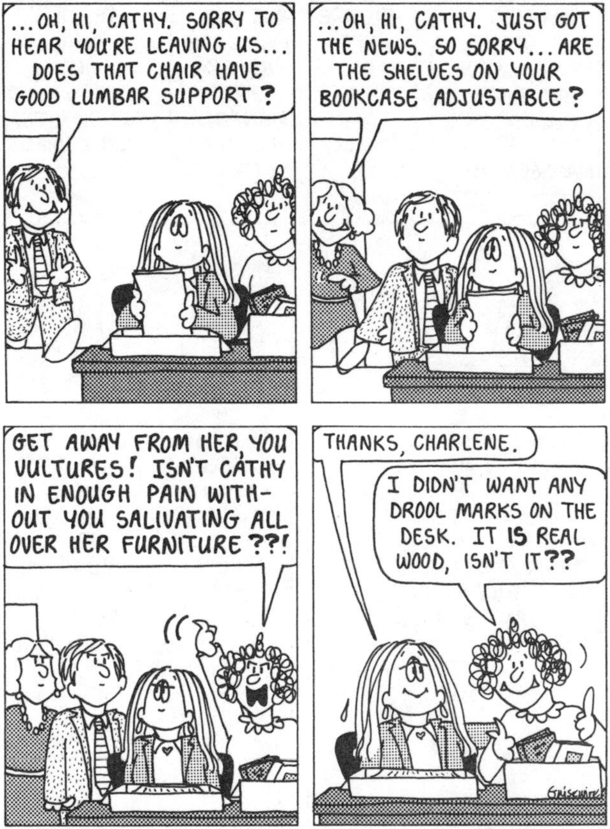
...OH, HI, CATHY. SORRY TO HEAR YOU'RE LEAVING US... DOES THAT CHAIR HAVE GOOD LUMBAR SUPPORT?
...OH, HI, CATHY. JUST GOT THE NEWS. SO SORRY... ARE THE SHELVES ON YOUR BOOKCASE ADJUSTABLE?
GET AWAY FROM HER, YOU VULTURES! ISN'T CATHY IN ENOUGH PAIN WITHOUT YOU SALIVATING ALL OVER HER FURNITURE??!
THANKS, CHARLENE.
I DIDN'T WANT ANY DROOL MARKS ON THE DESK. IT IS REAL WOOD, ISN'T IT??
GUISEWITE

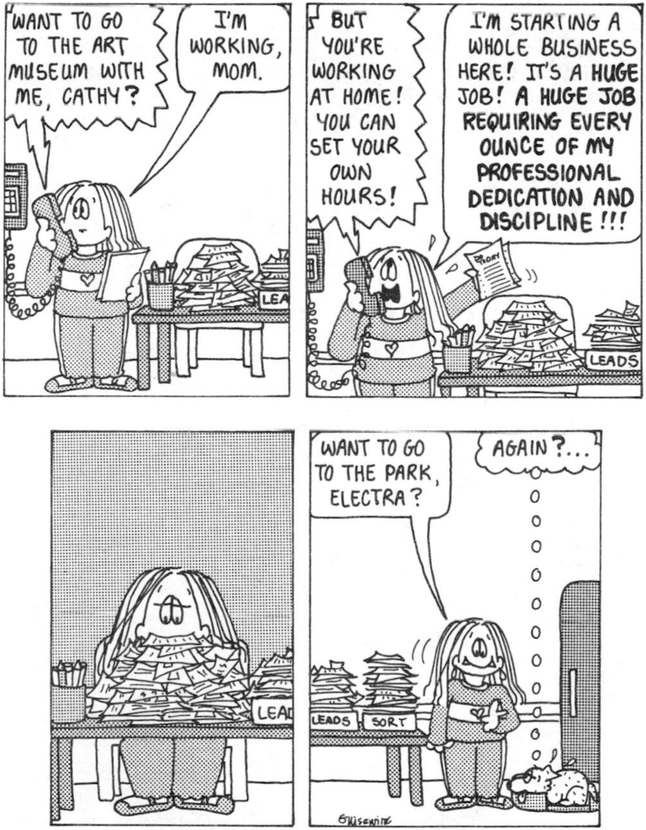
WANT TO GO TO THE ART MUSEUM WITH ME, CATHY?
I'M WORKING, MOM.
BUT YOU'RE WORKING AT HOME! YOU CAN SET YOUR OWN HOURS!
I'M STARTING A WHOLE BUSINESS HERE! IT'S A HUGE JOB! A HUGE JOB REQUIRING EVERY OUNCE OF MY PROFESSIONAL DEDICATION AND DISCIPLINE!!!
LEADS
WANT TO GO TO THE PARK, ELECTRA?
AGAIN?...
LEADS
SORT

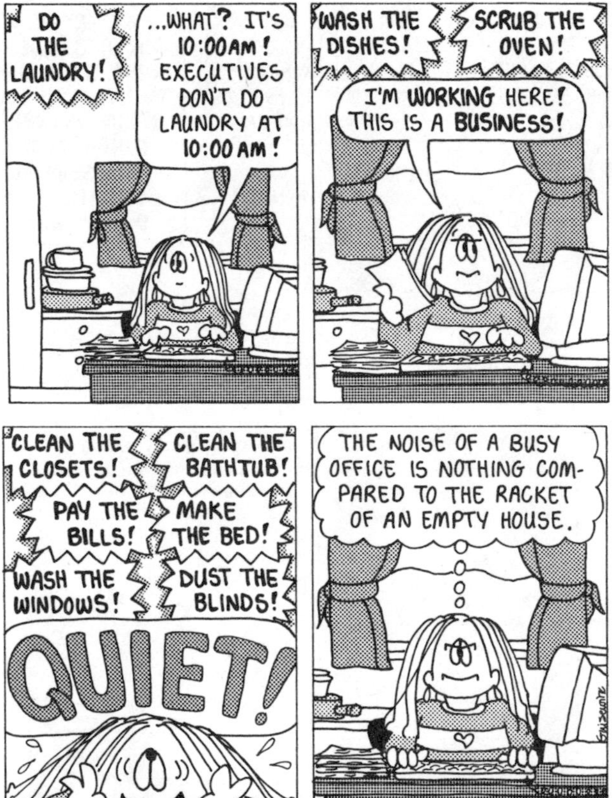
DO THE LAUNDRY!
...WHAT? IT'S 10:00AM! EXECUTIVES DON'T DO LAUNDRY AT 10:00 AM!
WASH THE DISHES!
SCRUB THE OVEN!
I'M WORKING HERE! THIS IS A BUSINESS!
CLEAN THE CLOSETS!
CLEAN THE BATHTUB!
PAY THE BILLS!
MAKE THE BED!
WASH THE WINDOWS!
DUST THE BLINDS!
QUIET!
THE NOISE OF A BUSY OFFICE IS NOTHING COMPARED TO THE RACKET OF AN EMPTY HOUSE.

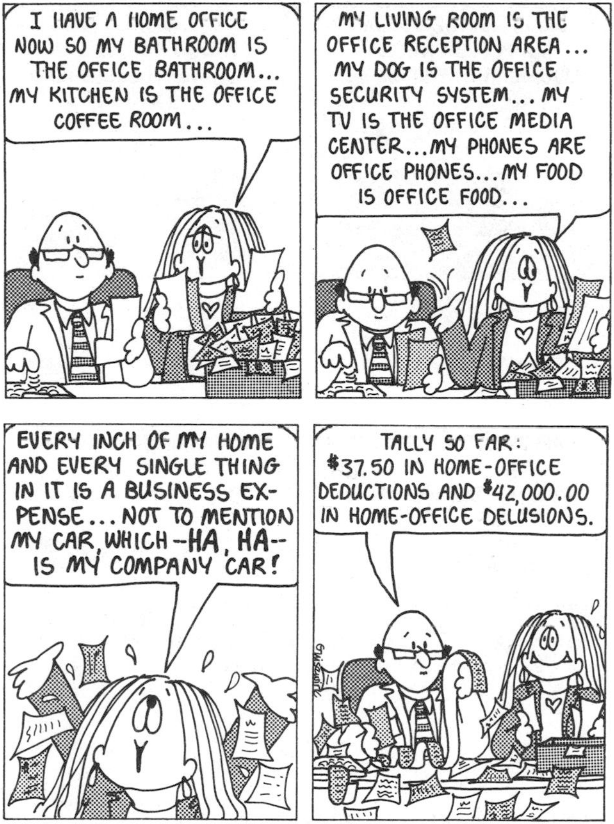
I HAVE A HOME OFFICE NOW SO MY BATHROOM IS THE OFFICE BATHROOM... MY KITCHEN IS THE OFFICE COFFEE ROOM...
MY LIVING ROOM IS THE OFFICE RECEPTION AREA... MY DOG IS THE OFFICE SECURITY SYSTEM... MY TV IS THE OFFICE MEDIA CENTER...MY PHONES ARE OFFICE PHONES... MY FOOD IS OFFICE FOOD...
EVERY INCH OF MY HOME AND EVERY SINGLE THING IN IT IS A BUSINESS EXPENSE... NOT TO MENTION MY CAR, WHICH--HA, HA--IS MY COMPANY CAR!
TALLY SO FAR: $37.50 IN HOME-OFFICE DEDUCTIONS AND $42,000.00 IN HOME-OFFICE DELUSIONS.
GUISEWITE

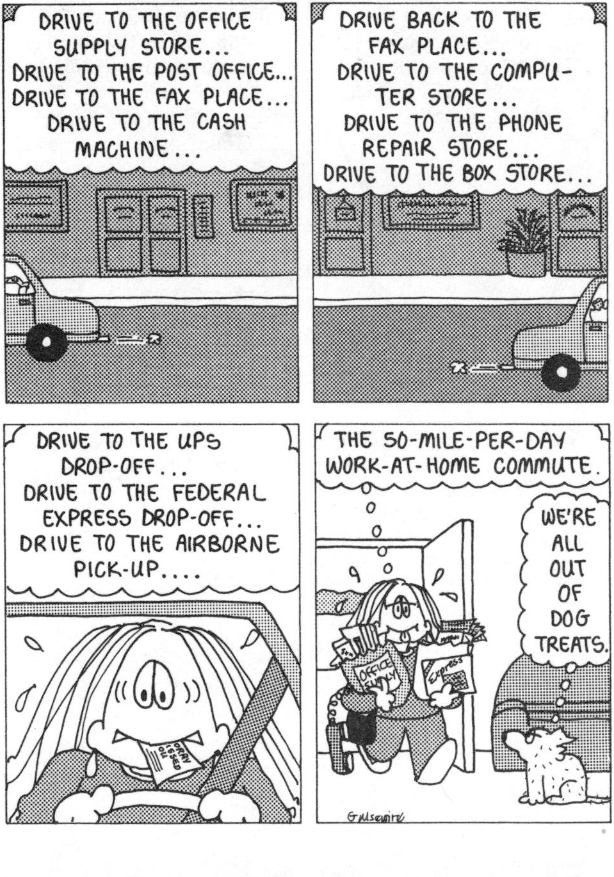
DRIVE TO THE OFFICE SUPPLY STORE... DRIVE TO THE POST OFFICE... DRIVE TO THE FAX PLACE... DRIVE TO THE CASH MACHINE...
DRIVE BACK TO THE FAX PLACE... DRIVE TO THE COMPU-TER STORE... DRIVE TO THE PHONE REPAIR STORE... DRIVE TO THE BOX STORE...
DRIVE TO THE UPS DROP-OFF... DRIVE TO THE FEDERAL EXPRESS DROP-OFF... DRIVE TO THE AIRBORNE PICK-UP....
THE 50-MILE-PER-DAY WORK-AT-HOME COMMUTE.
WE'RE ALL OUT OF DOG TREATS.
OFFICE SUPPLY
Express

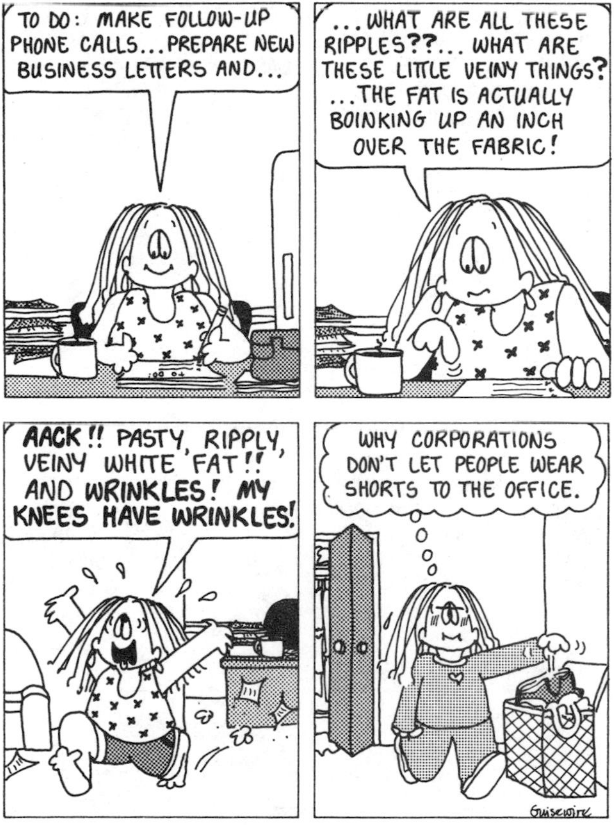

TO DO: MAKE FOLLOW-UP PHONE CALLS... PREPARE NEW BUSINESS LETTERS AND...
TO DO:
...WHAT ARE ALL THESE RIPPLES??... WHAT ARE THESE LITTLE VEINY THINGS? ...THE FAT IS ACTUALLY BOINKING UP AN INCH OVER THE FABRIC!
AACK!! PASTY, RIPPLY, VEINY WHITE FAT!! AND WRINKLES! MY KNEES HAVE WRINKLES!
WHY CORPORATIONS DON'T LET PEOPLE WEAR SHORTS TO THE OFFICE.
Guisewite

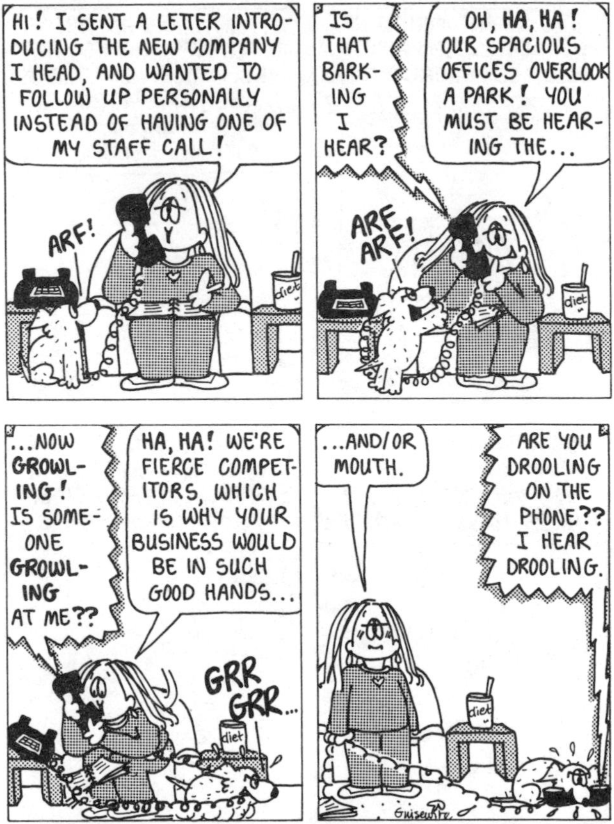
HI! I SENT A LETTER INTRODUCING THE NEW COMPANY I HEAD, AND WANTED TO FOLLOW UP PERSONALLY INSTEAD OF HAVING ONE OF MY STAFF CALL!
ARF!
IS THAT BARKING I HEAR?
OH, HA, HA! OUR SPACIOUS OFFICES OVERLOOK A PARK! YOU MUST BE HEARING THE...
ARF ARF!
...NOW GROWLING! IS SOMEONE GROWLING AT ME??
HA, HA! WE'RE FIERCE COMPETITORS, WHICH IS WHY YOUR BUSINESS WOULD BE IN SUCH GOOD HANDS...
GRR GRR...
...AND/OR MOUTH.
ARE YOU DROOLING ON THE PHONE?? I HEAR DROOLING.
Guisewite

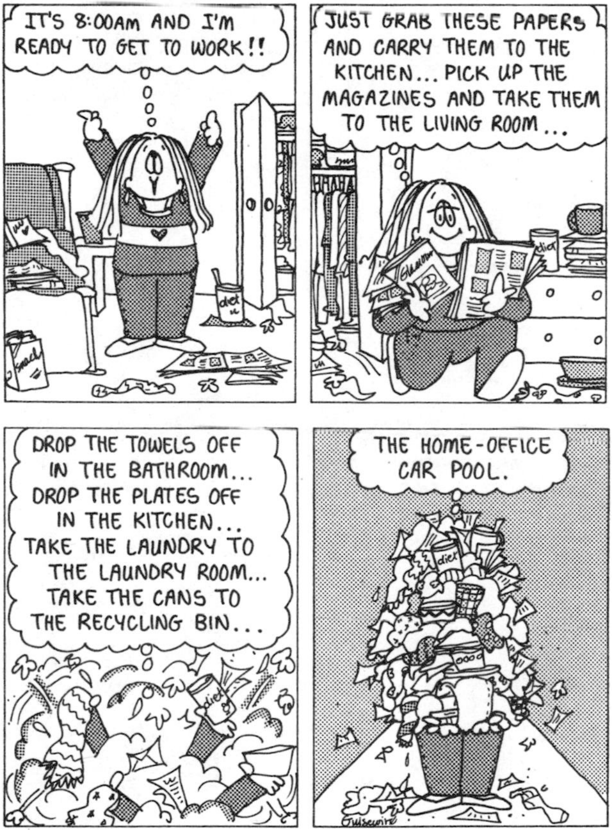
IT'S 8:00AM AND I'M READY TO GET TO WORK!!
JUST GRAB THESE PAPERS AND CARRY THEM TO THE KITCHEN... PICK UP THE MAGAZINES AND TAKE THEM TO THE LIVING ROOM...
DROP THE TOWELS OFF IN THE BATHROOM... DROP THE PLATES OFF IN THE KITCHEN... TAKE THE LAUNDRY TO THE LAUNDRY ROOM... TAKE THE CANS TO THE RECYCLING BIN...
THE HOME-OFFICE CAR POOL.

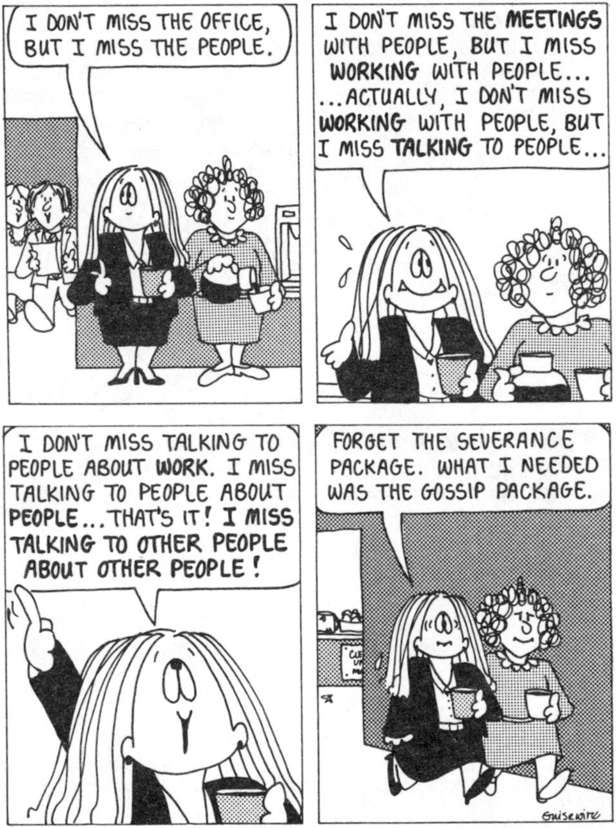
I DON'T MISS THE OFFICE, BUT I MISS THE PEOPLE.
I DON'T MISS THE MEETINGS WITH PEOPLE, BUT I MISS WORKING WITH PEOPLE... ...ACTUALLY, I DON'T MISS WORKING WITH PEOPLE, BUT I MISS TALKING TO PEOPLE...
I DON'T MISS TALKING TO PEOPLE ABOUT WORK. I MISS TALKING TO PEOPLE ABOUT PEOPLE... THAT'S IT! I MISS TALKING TO OTHER PEOPLE ABOUT OTHER PEOPLE!
FORGET THE SEVERANCE PACKAGE. WHAT I NEEDED WAS THE GOSSIP PACKAGE.
Guisewite

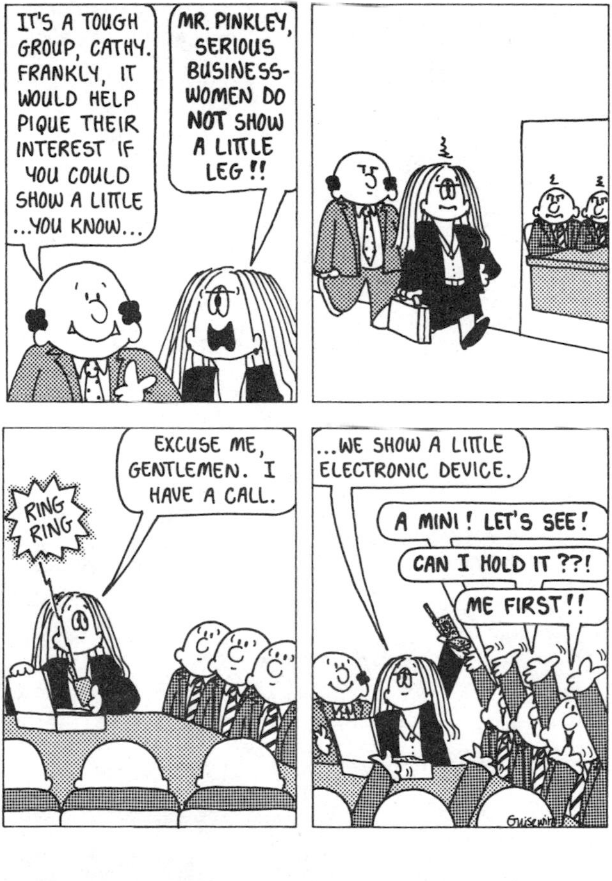
IT'S A TOUGH GROUP, CATHY. FRANKLY, IT WOULD HELP PIQUE THEIR INTEREST IF YOU COULD SHOW A LITTLE ...YOU KNOW...
MR. PINKLEY, SERIOUS BUSINESS-WOMEN DO NOT SHOW A LITTLE LEG!!
RING RING
EXCUSE ME, GENTLEMEN. I HAVE A CALL.
...WE SHOW A LITTLE ELECTRONIC DEVICE.
A MINI! LET'S SEE!
CAN I HOLD IT??!
ME FIRST!!
Guisewite

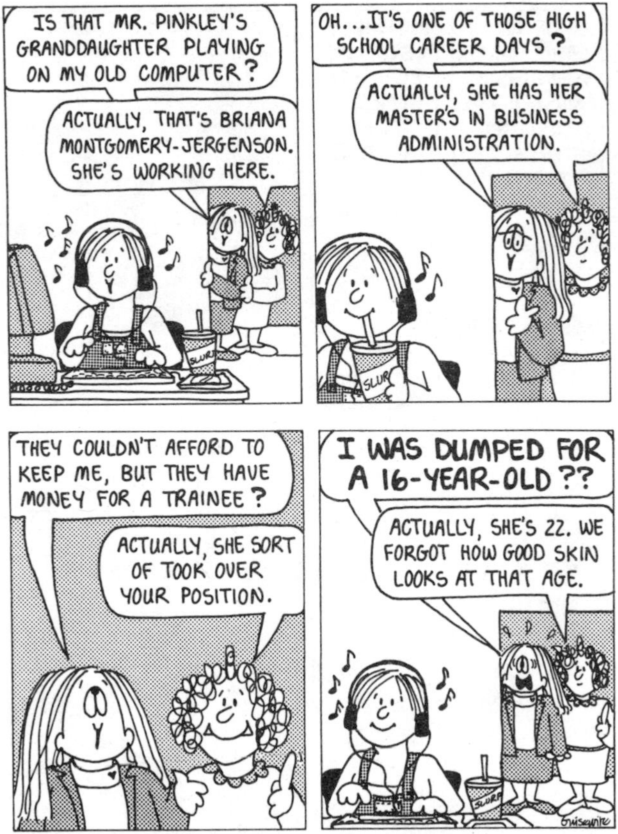
IS THAT MR. PINKLEY'S GRANDDAUGHTER PLAYING ON MY OLD COMPUTER?
ACTUALLY, THAT'S BRIANA MONTGOMERY-JERGENSON. SHE'S WORKING HERE.
SLURP
OH...IT'S ONE OF THOSE HIGH SCHOOL CAREER DAYS?
ACTUALLY, SHE HAS HER MASTER'S IN BUSINESS ADMINISTRATION.
SLURP
THEY COULDN'T AFFORD TO KEEP ME, BUT THEY HAVE MONEY FOR A TRAINEE?
ACTUALLY, SHE SORT OF TOOK OVER YOUR POSITION.
I WAS DUMPED FOR A 16-YEAR-OLD??
ACTUALLY, SHE'S 22. WE FORGOT HOW GOOD SKIN LOOKS AT THAT AGE.
SLURP
Guisewite

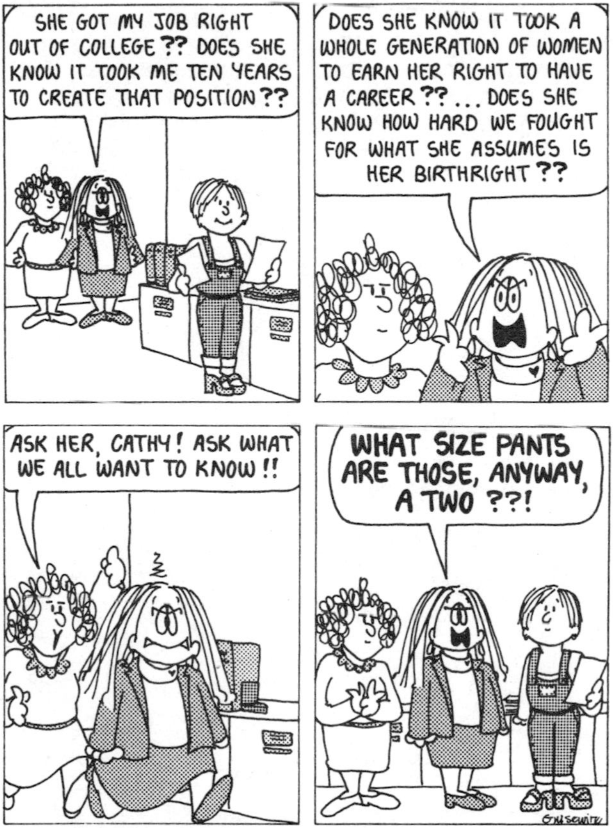
SHE GOT MY JOB RIGHT OUT OF COLLEGE?? DOES SHE KNOW IT TOOK ME TEN YEARS TO CREATE THAT POSITION??
DOES SHE KNOW IT TOOK A WHOLE GENERATION OF WOMEN TO EARN HER RIGHT TO HAVE A CAREER??... DOES SHE KNOW HOW HARD WE FOUGHT FOR WHAT SHE ASSUMES IS HER BIRTHRIGHT??
ASK HER, CATHY! ASK WHAT WE ALL WANT TO KNOW!!
WHAT SIZE PANTS ARE THOSE, ANYWAY, A TWO??!
GUISEWITE

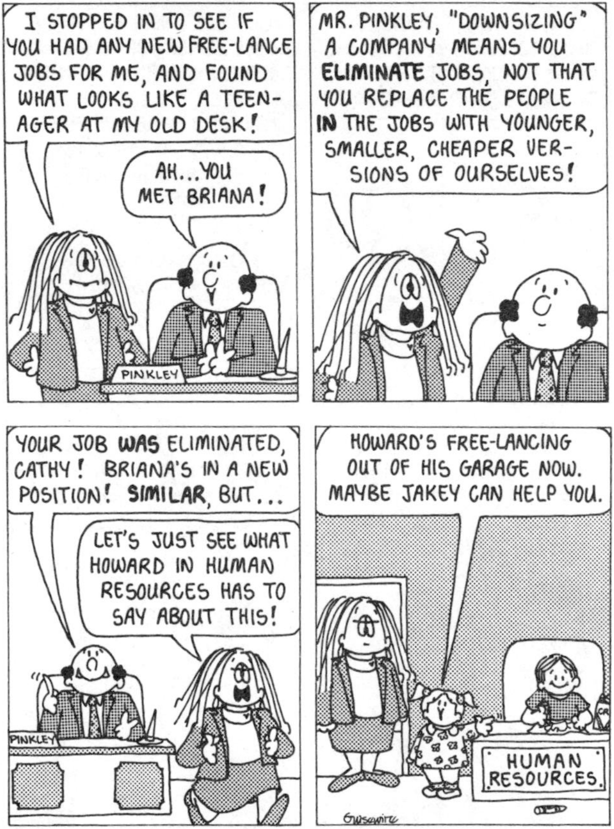
I STOPPED IN TO SEE IF YOU HAD ANY NEW FREE-LANCE JOBS FOR ME, AND FOUND WHAT LOOKS LIKE A TEEN-AGER AT MY OLD DESK!
AH...YOU MET BRIANA!
PINKLEY
MR. PINKLEY, "DOWNSIZING" A COMPANY MEANS YOU **ELIMINATE** JOBS, NOT THAT YOU REPLACE THE PEOPLE **IN** THE JOBS WITH YOUNGER, SMALLER, CHEAPER VERSIONS OF OURSELVES!
YOUR JOB **WAS** ELIMINATED, CATHY! BRIANA'S IN A NEW POSITION! **SIMILAR**, BUT...
LET'S JUST SEE WHAT HOWARD IN HUMAN RESOURCES HAS TO SAY ABOUT THIS!
PINKLEY
HOWARD'S FREE-LANCING OUT OF HIS GARAGE NOW. MAYBE JAKEY CAN HELP YOU.
HUMAN RESOURCES
Guisewite

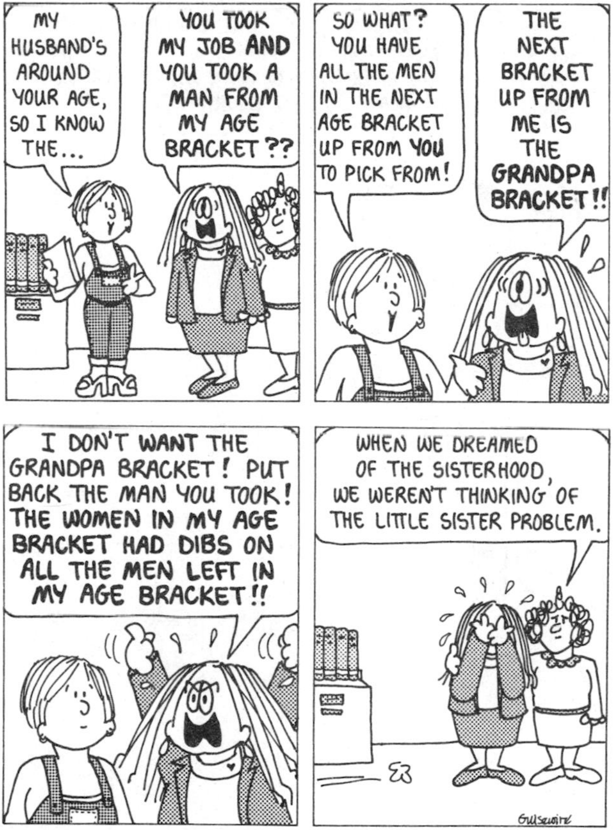
MY HUSBAND'S AROUND YOUR AGE, SO I KNOW THE...
YOU TOOK MY JOB AND YOU TOOK A MAN FROM MY AGE BRACKET??
SO WHAT? YOU HAVE ALL THE MEN IN THE NEXT AGE BRACKET UP FROM YOU TO PICK FROM!
THE NEXT BRACKET UP FROM ME IS THE GRANDPA BRACKET!!
I DON'T WANT THE GRANDPA BRACKET! PUT BACK THE MAN YOU TOOK! THE WOMEN IN MY AGE BRACKET HAD DIBS ON ALL THE MEN LEFT IN MY AGE BRACKET!!
WHEN WE DREAMED OF THE SISTERHOOD, WE WEREN'T THINKING OF THE LITTLE SISTER PROBLEM.
GUISEWITE

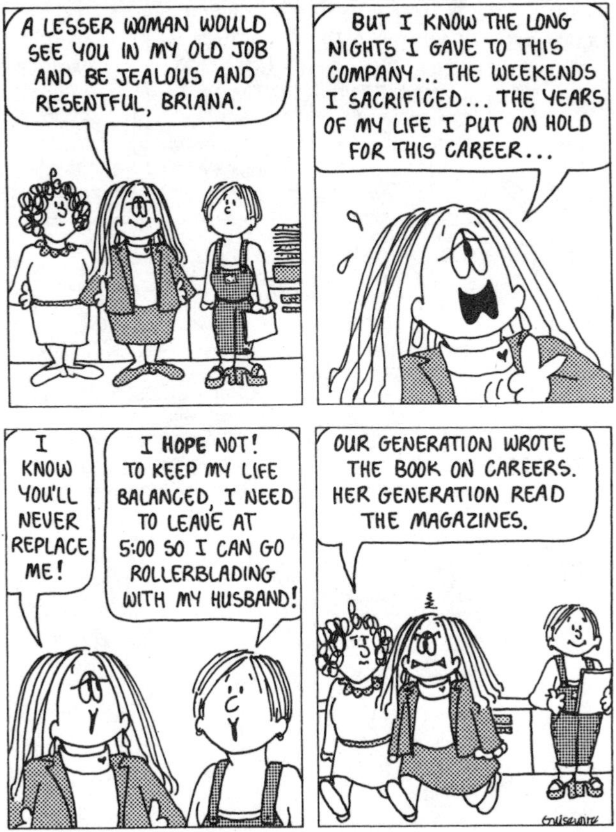
A LESSER WOMAN WOULD SEE YOU IN MY OLD JOB AND BE JEALOUS AND RESENTFUL, BRIANA.
BUT I KNOW THE LONG NIGHTS I GAVE TO THIS COMPANY... THE WEEKENDS I SACRIFICED... THE YEARS OF MY LIFE I PUT ON HOLD FOR THIS CAREER...
I KNOW YOU'LL NEVER REPLACE ME!
I HOPE NOT! TO KEEP MY LIFE BALANCED, I NEED TO LEAVE AT 5:00 SO I CAN GO ROLLERBLADING WITH MY HUSBAND!
OUR GENERATION WROTE THE BOOK ON CAREERS. HER GENERATION READ THE MAGAZINES.

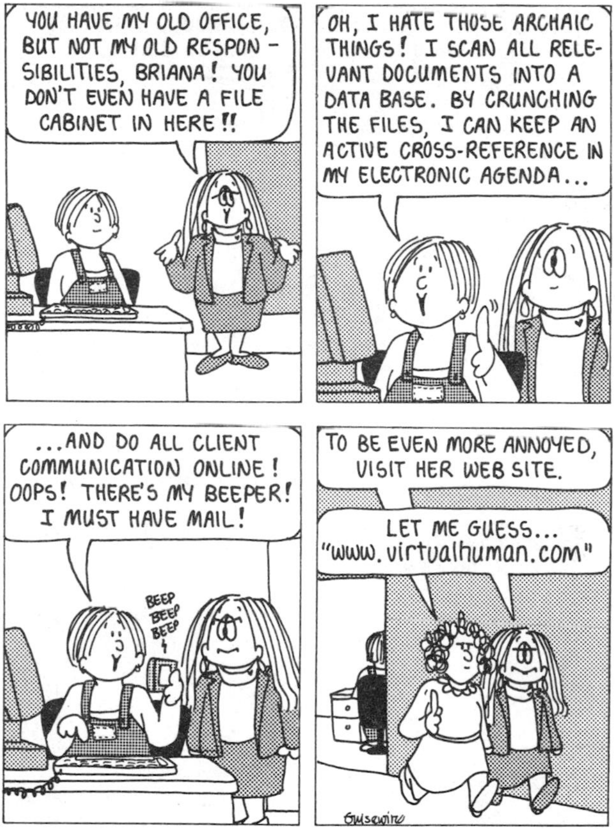
YOU HAVE MY OLD OFFICE, BUT NOT MY OLD RESPON-SIBILITIES, BRIANA! YOU DON'T EVEN HAVE A FILE CABINET IN HERE!!
OH, I HATE THOSE ARCHAIC THINGS! I SCAN ALL RELE-VANT DOCUMENTS INTO A DATA BASE. BY CRUNCHING THE FILES, I CAN KEEP AN ACTIVE CROSS-REFERENCE IN MY ELECTRONIC AGENDA...
...AND DO ALL CLIENT COMMUNICATION ONLINE! OOPS! THERE'S MY BEEPER! I MUST HAVE MAIL!
BEEP BEEP BEEP
TO BE EVEN MORE ANNOYED, VISIT HER WEB SITE.
LET ME GUESS... "www.virtualhuman.com"
Guisewite

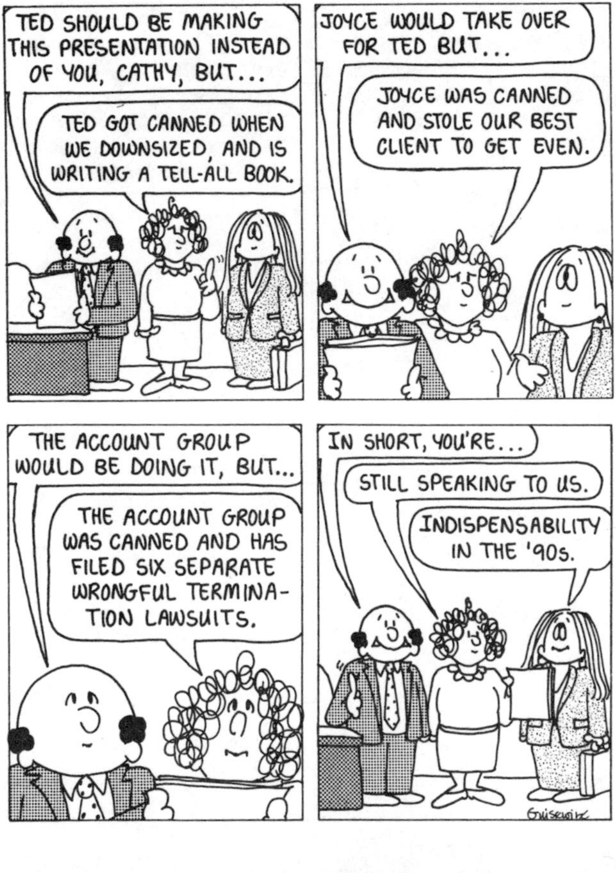
TED SHOULD BE MAKING THIS PRESENTATION INSTEAD OF YOU, CATHY, BUT...
TED GOT CANNED WHEN WE DOWNSIZED, AND IS WRITING A TELL-ALL BOOK.
JOYCE WOULD TAKE OVER FOR TED BUT...
JOYCE WAS CANNED AND STOLE OUR BEST CLIENT TO GET EVEN.
THE ACCOUNT GROUP WOULD BE DOING IT, BUT...
THE ACCOUNT GROUP WAS CANNED AND HAS FILED SIX SEPARATE WRONGFUL TERMINA-TION LAWSUITS.
IN SHORT, YOU'RE...
STILL SPEAKING TO US.
INDISPENSABILITY IN THE '90s.
Guisewite

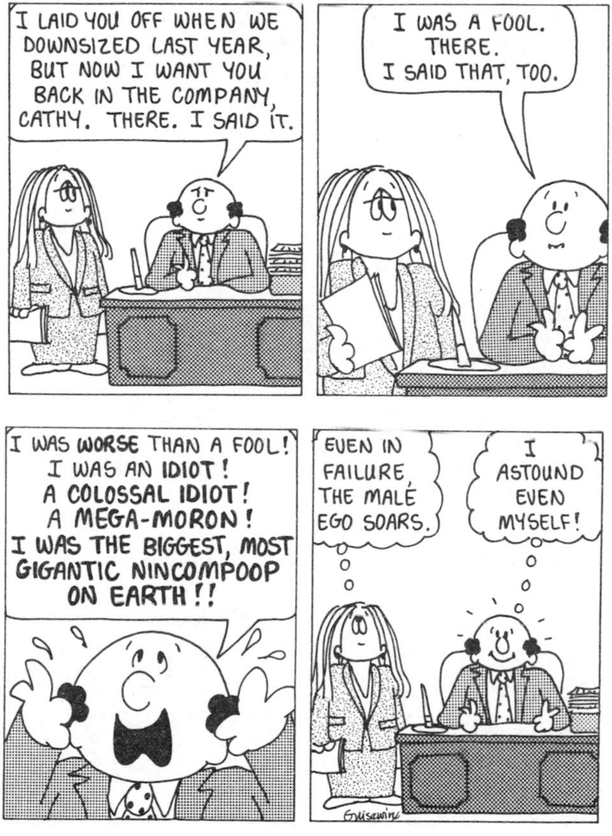
I LAID YOU OFF WHEN WE DOWNSIZED LAST YEAR, BUT NOW I WANT YOU BACK IN THE COMPANY, CATHY. THERE. I SAID IT.
I WAS A FOOL. THERE. I SAID THAT, TOO.
I WAS **WORSE** THAN A FOOL! I WAS AN **IDIOT**! A **COLOSSAL IDIOT**! A **MEGA-MORON**! **I WAS THE BIGGEST, MOST GIGANTIC NINCOMPOOP ON EARTH!!**
EVEN IN FAILURE, THE MALE EGO SOARS.
I ASTOUND EVEN MYSELF!
Guisewite

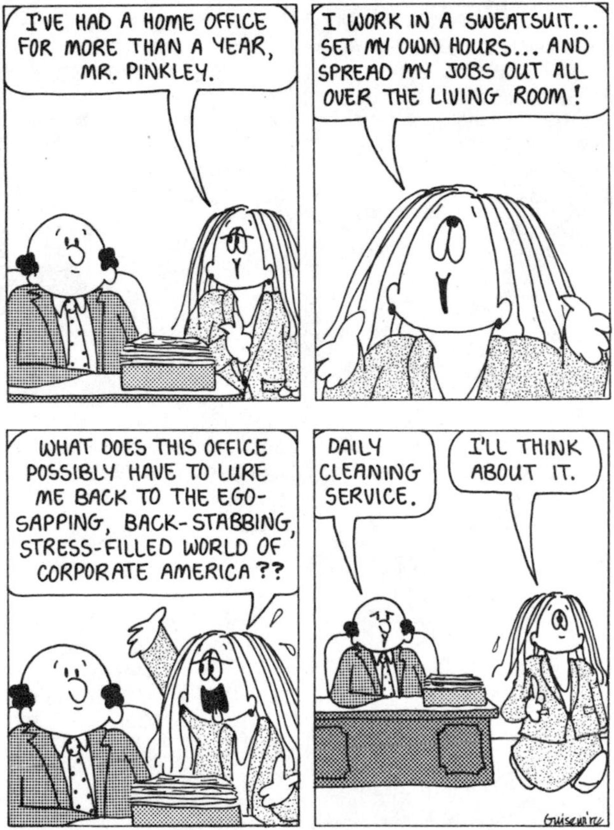
I'VE HAD A HOME OFFICE FOR MORE THAN A YEAR, MR. PINKLEY.
I WORK IN A SWEATSUIT... SET MY OWN HOURS... AND SPREAD MY JOBS OUT ALL OVER THE LIVING ROOM!
WHAT DOES THIS OFFICE POSSIBLY HAVE TO LURE ME BACK TO THE EGO-SAPPING, BACK-STABBING, STRESS-FILLED WORLD OF CORPORATE AMERICA??
DAILY CLEANING SERVICE.
I'LL THINK ABOUT IT.
Guisewite

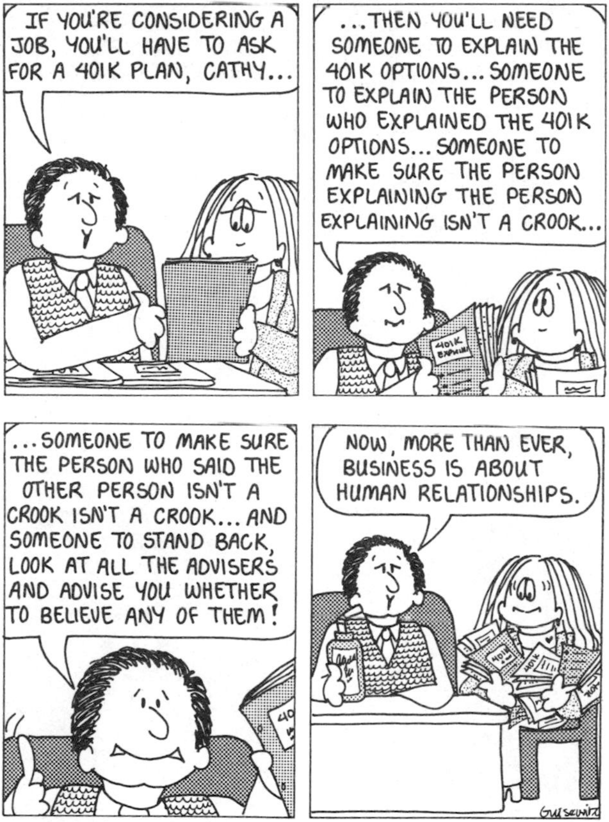
IF YOU'RE CONSIDERING A JOB, YOU'LL HAVE TO ASK FOR A 401K PLAN, CATHY...
...THEN YOU'LL NEED SOMEONE TO EXPLAIN THE 401K OPTIONS... SOMEONE TO EXPLAIN THE PERSON WHO EXPLAINED THE 401K OPTIONS... SOMEONE TO MAKE SURE THE PERSON EXPLAINING THE PERSON EXPLAINING ISN'T A CROOK...
...SOMEONE TO MAKE SURE THE PERSON WHO SAID THE OTHER PERSON ISN'T A CROOK ISN'T A CROOK... AND SOMEONE TO STAND BACK, LOOK AT ALL THE ADVISERS AND ADVISE YOU WHETHER TO BELIEVE ANY OF THEM!
NOW, MORE THAN EVER, BUSINESS IS ABOUT HUMAN RELATIONSHIPS.
GUISEWITE

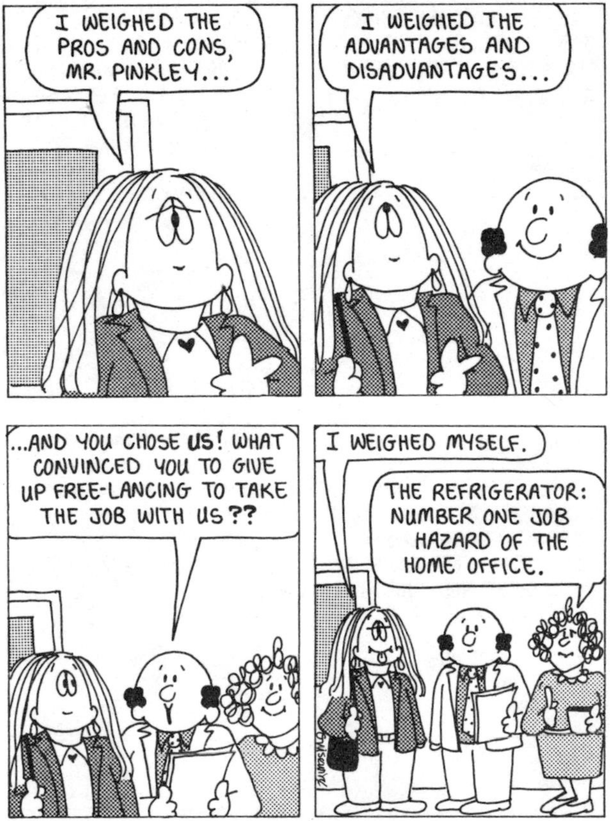
I WEIGHED THE PROS AND CONS, MR. PINKLEY...
I WEIGHED THE ADVANTAGES AND DISADVANTAGES...
...AND YOU CHOSE US! WHAT CONVINCED YOU TO GIVE UP FREE-LANCING TO TAKE THE JOB WITH US??
I WEIGHED MYSELF.
THE REFRIGERATOR: NUMBER ONE JOB HAZARD OF THE HOME OFFICE.

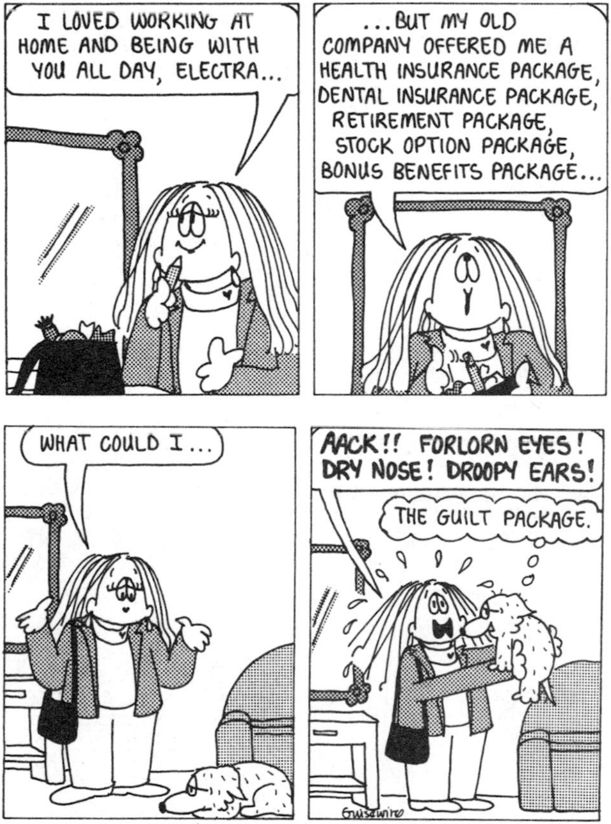
I LOVED WORKING AT HOME AND BEING WITH YOU ALL DAY, ELECTRA...
...BUT MY OLD COMPANY OFFERED ME A HEALTH INSURANCE PACKAGE, DENTAL INSURANCE PACKAGE, RETIREMENT PACKAGE, STOCK OPTION PACKAGE, BONUS BENEFITS PACKAGE...
WHAT COULD I...
AACK!! FORLORN EYES! DRY NOSE! DROOPY EARS!
THE GUILT PACKAGE.
Guisewite

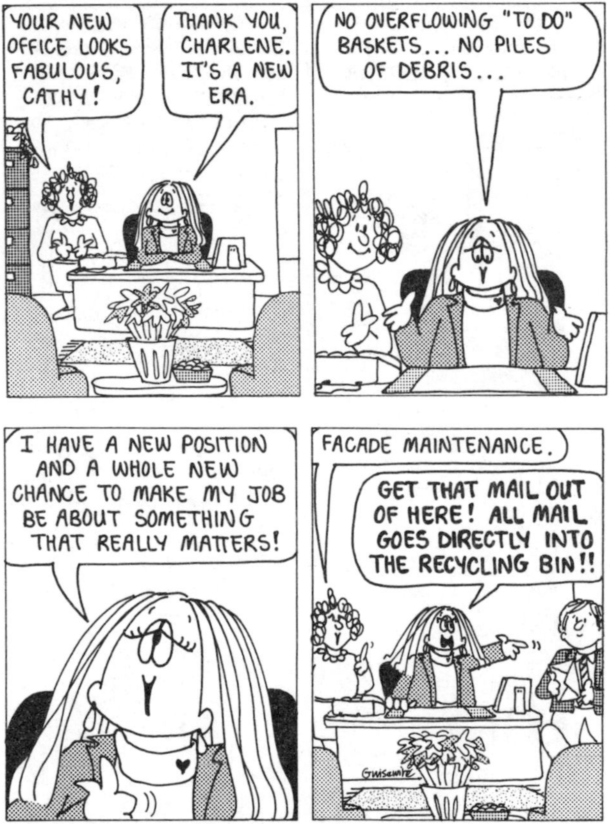
YOUR NEW OFFICE LOOKS FABULOUS, CATHY!
THANK YOU, CHARLENE. IT'S A NEW ERA.
NO OVERFLOWING "TO DO" BASKETS... NO PILES OF DEBRIS...
I HAVE A NEW POSITION AND A WHOLE NEW CHANCE TO MAKE MY JOB BE ABOUT SOMETHING THAT REALLY MATTERS!
FACADE MAINTENANCE.
GET THAT MAIL OUT OF HERE! ALL MAIL GOES DIRECTLY INTO THE RECYCLING BIN!!
Guisewite

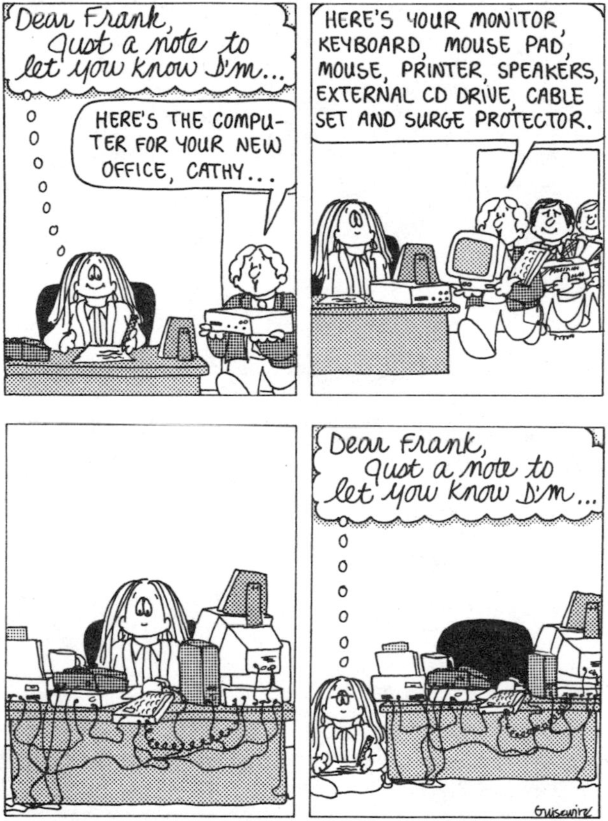
Dear Frank,
Just a note to let you know I'm...
HERE'S THE COMPUTER FOR YOUR NEW OFFICE, CATHY...
HERE'S YOUR MONITOR, KEYBOARD, MOUSE PAD, MOUSE, PRINTER, SPEAKERS, EXTERNAL CD DRIVE, CABLE SET AND SURGE PROTECTOR.
Dear Frank,
Just a note to let you know I'm...
Guisewite

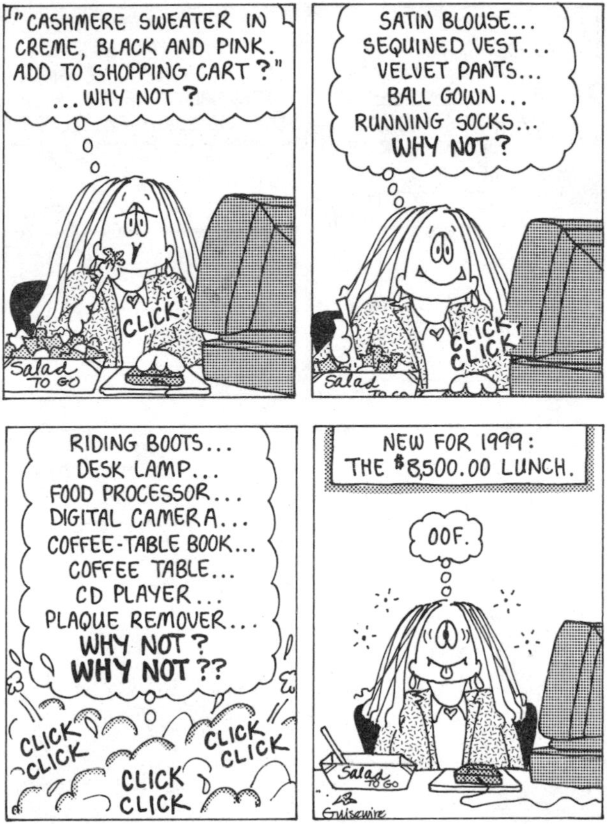
"CASHMERE SWEATER IN CREME, BLACK AND PINK. ADD TO SHOPPING CART?" ...WHY NOT?
CLICK!
Salad TO GO
SATIN BLOUSE... SEQUINED VEST... VELVET PANTS... BALL GOWN... RUNNING SOCKS... WHY NOT?
CLICK CLICK
RIDING BOOTS... DESK LAMP... FOOD PROCESSOR... DIGITAL CAMERA... COFFEE-TABLE BOOK... COFFEE TABLE... CD PLAYER... PLAQUE REMOVER... WHY NOT? WHY NOT??
CLICK CLICK
CLICK CLICK
CLICK CLICK
NEW FOR 1999: THE $8,500.00 LUNCH.
OOF.
Salad TO GO
Guisewite

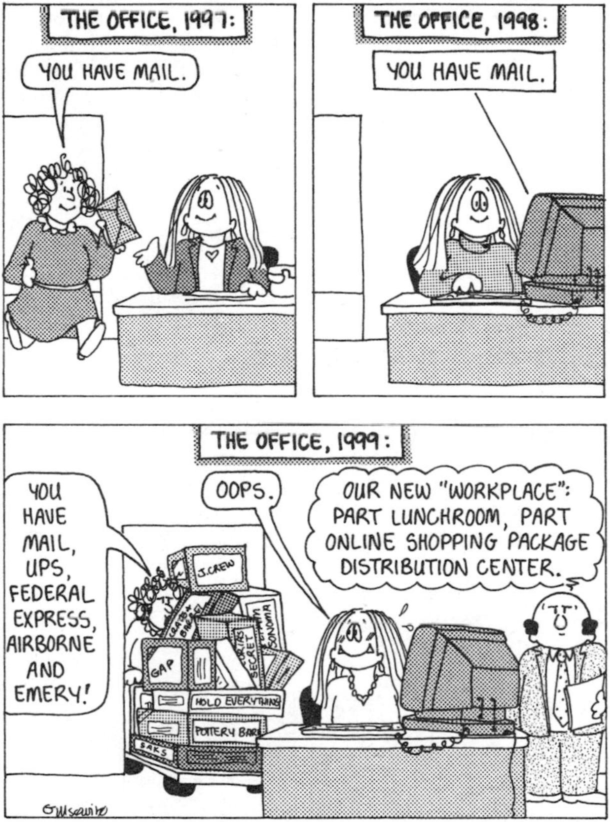
THE OFFICE, 1997:
YOU HAVE MAIL.
THE OFFICE, 1998:
YOU HAVE MAIL.
THE OFFICE, 1999:
YOU HAVE MAIL, UPS, FEDERAL EXPRESS, AIRBORNE AND EMERY!
OOPS.
OUR NEW "WORKPLACE": PART LUNCHROOM, PART ONLINE SHOPPING PACKAGE DISTRIBUTION CENTER.
J.CREW
GAP
HOLD EVERYTHING
SAKS

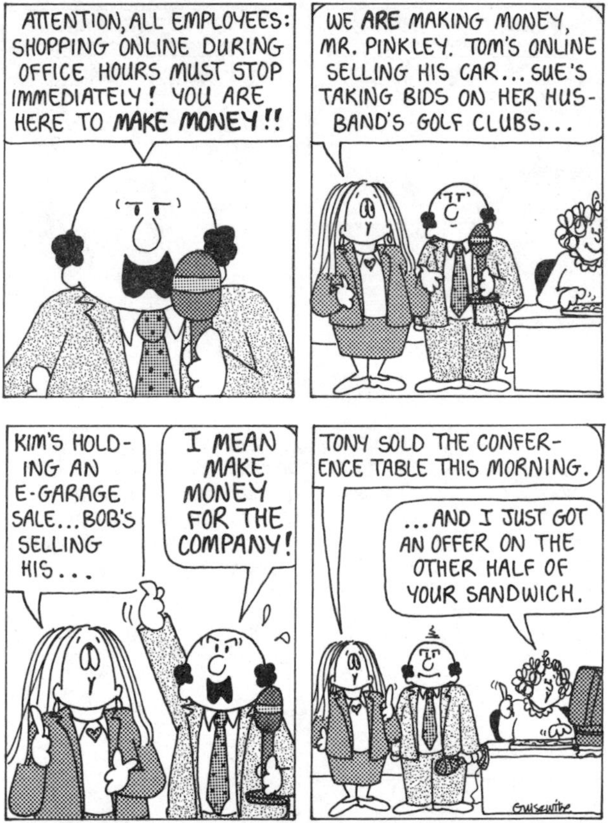
ATTENTION, ALL EMPLOYEES: SHOPPING ONLINE DURING OFFICE HOURS MUST STOP IMMEDIATELY! YOU ARE HERE TO MAKE MONEY!!
WE ARE MAKING MONEY, MR. PINKLEY. TOM'S ONLINE SELLING HIS CAR... SUE'S TAKING BIDS ON HER HUSBAND'S GOLF CLUBS...
KIM'S HOLDING AN E-GARAGE SALE... BOB'S SELLING HIS...
I MEAN MAKE MONEY FOR THE COMPANY!
TONY SOLD THE CONFERENCE TABLE THIS MORNING.
...AND I JUST GOT AN OFFER ON THE OTHER HALF OF YOUR SANDWICH.
Guisewite

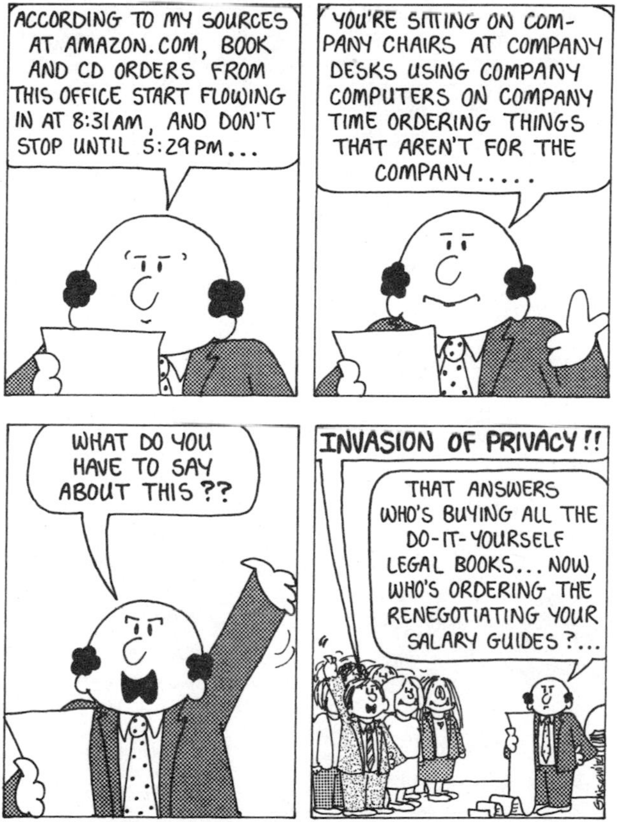
ACCORDING TO MY SOURCES AT AMAZON.COM, BOOK AND CD ORDERS FROM THIS OFFICE START FLOWING IN AT 8:31 AM, AND DON'T STOP UNTIL 5:29 PM...
YOU'RE SITTING ON COMPANY CHAIRS AT COMPANY DESKS USING COMPANY COMPUTERS ON COMPANY TIME ORDERING THINGS THAT AREN'T FOR THE COMPANY.....
WHAT DO YOU HAVE TO SAY ABOUT THIS??
INVASION OF PRIVACY!!
THAT ANSWERS WHO'S BUYING ALL THE DO-IT-YOURSELF LEGAL BOOKS... NOW, WHO'S ORDERING THE RENEGOTIATING YOUR SALARY GUIDES?...

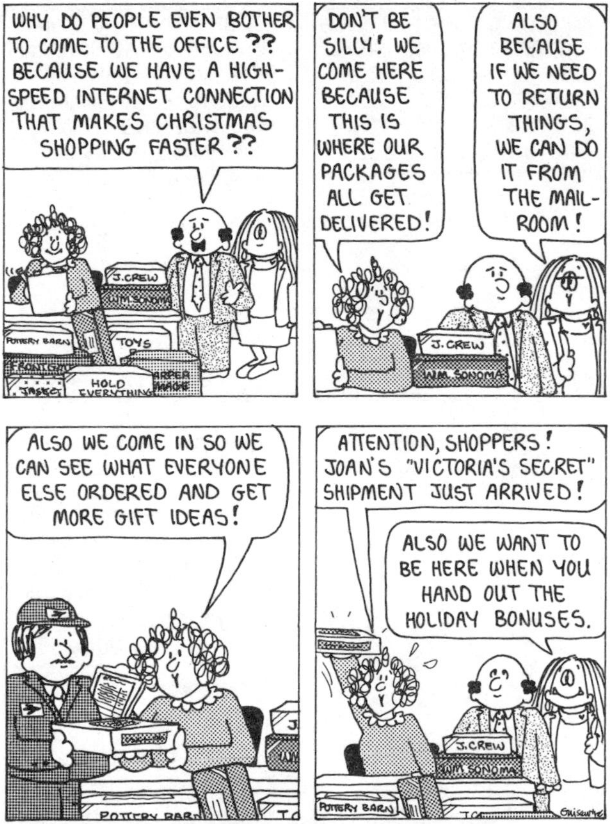
WHY DO PEOPLE EVEN BOTHER TO COME TO THE OFFICE ?? BECAUSE WE HAVE A HIGH-SPEED INTERNET CONNECTION THAT MAKES CHRISTMAS SHOPPING FASTER ??
J.CREW
POTTERY BARN
TOYS
HOLD EVERYTHING
DON'T BE SILLY! WE COME HERE BECAUSE THIS IS WHERE OUR PACKAGES ALL GET DELIVERED!
ALSO BECAUSE IF WE NEED TO RETURN THINGS, WE CAN DO IT FROM THE MAIL-ROOM!
J. CREW
WM. SONOMA
ALSO WE COME IN SO WE CAN SEE WHAT EVERYONE ELSE ORDERED AND GET MORE GIFT IDEAS!
ATTENTION, SHOPPERS! JOAN'S "VICTORIA'S SECRET" SHIPMENT JUST ARRIVED!
ALSO WE WANT TO BE HERE WHEN YOU HAND OUT THE HOLIDAY BONUSES.
J.CREW
WM. SONOMA
POTTERY BARN
Guisewite

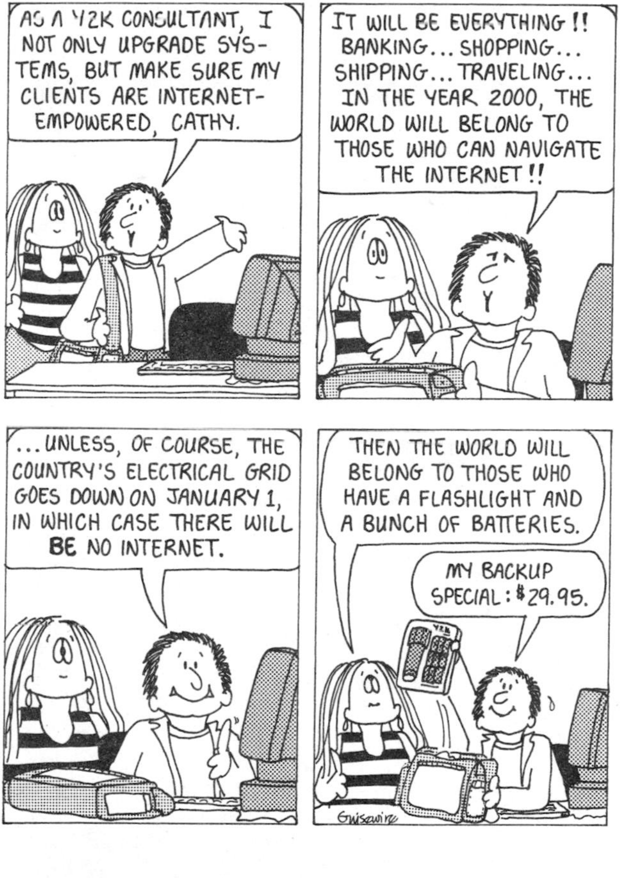
AS A Y2K CONSULTANT, I NOT ONLY UPGRADE SYSTEMS, BUT MAKE SURE MY CLIENTS ARE INTERNET-EMPOWERED, CATHY.
IT WILL BE EVERYTHING!! BANKING... SHOPPING... SHIPPING... TRAVELING... IN THE YEAR 2000, THE WORLD WILL BELONG TO THOSE WHO CAN NAVIGATE THE INTERNET!!
...UNLESS, OF COURSE, THE COUNTRY'S ELECTRICAL GRID GOES DOWN ON JANUARY 1, IN WHICH CASE THERE WILL **BE** NO INTERNET.
THEN THE WORLD WILL BELONG TO THOSE WHO HAVE A FLASHLIGHT AND A BUNCH OF BATTERIES.
MY BACKUP SPECIAL: $29.95.

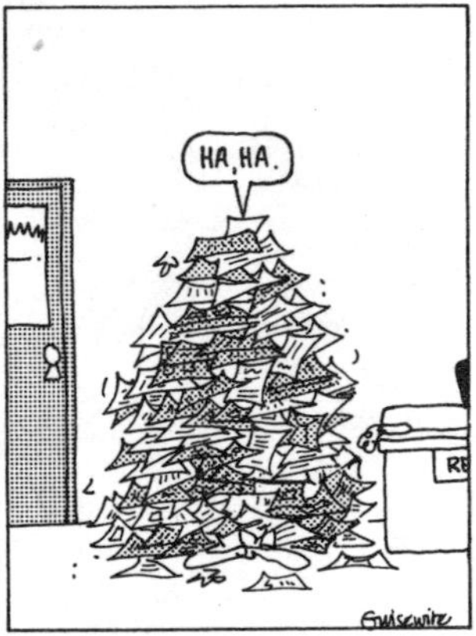
HA, HA.
RE

2000 and Beyond

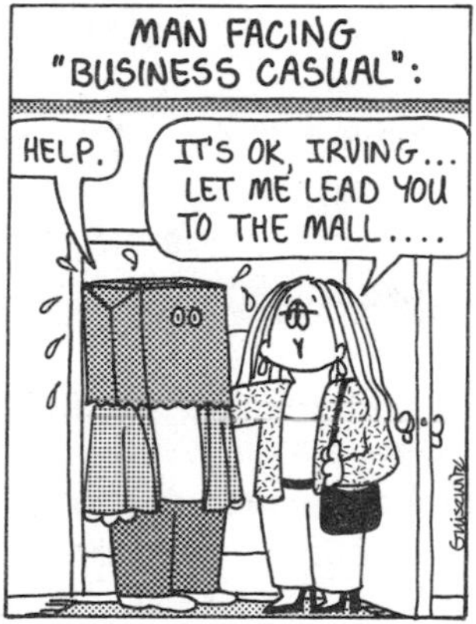
MAN FACING "BUSINESS CASUAL":
HELP.
IT'S OK, IRVING... LET ME LEAD YOU TO THE MALL....

In my 25 years in business, nothing has thrilled me quite as much as watching men try to figure out what to wear on "Casual Friday."

Women—who almost always have had a fraction of the disposable time and income that men have—have always had to dress for success in clothes that go out of style every six weeks.

Men's traditional work uniform has been unchanged for the last 75 years. Everything a man needs—from neckties to socks to shoes to underwear—is sold in a small one-stop-shopping department, which traditionally even does alterations for free.

The equivalent outfit for women requires a four-floor search of a 65,000-acre mall, hundreds of dollars more, and the need to make a whole other stop to get the pants shortened . . . that is, after the woman locates the right shoes, and has an idea of how tall she'll be when wearing this particular suit.

"Business casual" didn't exactly level the playing field, but it made it a lot more entertaining.

As I write this, men are in a complete state of confusion. Does dressing in bike shorts and Cartoon Network tank tops define them as young, edgy entrepreneurs like it did in 1999? Or now that so many dot-coms have gone belly-up, do flip-flops suggest the wearer is broke and can no longer afford shoes?

Does dressing in a traditional suit still mean "out-of-touch geezer," or does it stand for a reassuring return to old-world stability, not to mention, distance the wearer from any unpleasant Internet association?

Does the new "safe" uniform of khakis and white shirt look exactly as wishy-washy as it is?

Businessmen have started carrying "back-up outfits" in the trunks of their cars. They've started tucking a sport coat behind the door, the same way businesswomen, whenever possible, have at least one extra pair of shoes stashed in the desk drawer.

Men want to peek in the conference room and "see how casual the men from the other company think casual is". . . just like women dream of parking in front of a house and watching all the "holiday casual" outfits go in before we commit to what we're going to wear.

Men have been freed from the strangling noose of neckties and experienced the complete debilitation of free choice.

We can only dream that one day businessmen will spend some lunch hours in the same sort of Swimwear Department Hysteria that women do, and will know how it feels to try to conduct an empowered business meeting after experiencing fluorescent lights at noon in March.

With executives in Hawaiian print shirts, bankers in strappy tank tops, insurance agents in everything from shredded jeans to tuxedo jackets, it's hard to imagine how the rest of the twenty-first century will look.

Everyone I know is trying to reclaim a life outside the office, yet calls in more. "Quality of life" is most people's top priority, but "keeping the job so I can pay off last decade's Visa bill" is right up there with it.

Work has been how a lot of us have connected to the world for a long time. We dream of being free of it, but the office is almost always in the top three numbers of the auto-dialer.

Like the office superstore, we're pretty much open 24 hours a day. Documents are received Saturday morning on the home fax. We get paged at Chuck 'E' Cheese. We roll our eyes when others get a business call in the produce aisle, but when it happens to us, we feel needed and sort of important.

Everyone's reachable. Everyone's accessible. Everyone wants to feel connected to something 24/7.

Unless you look back to where we started.

It seems as though, in spite of global access to a worldwide network . . . in spite of instant communication with everyone and everything in the universe . . . in spite of our deep, human need to reach out and to be reached . . . the sink in the office coffee room will forever remain uncontacted.

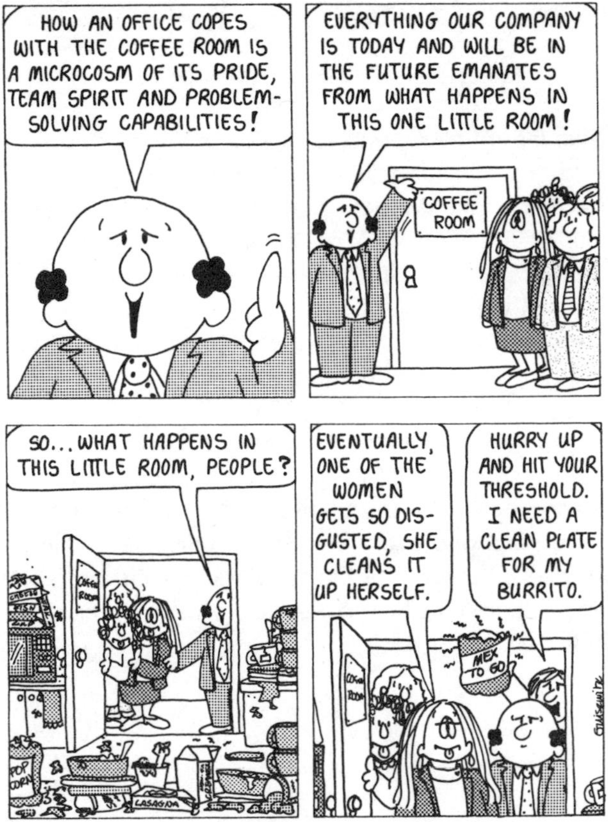
HOW AN OFFICE COPES WITH THE COFFEE ROOM IS A MICROCOSM OF ITS PRIDE, TEAM SPIRIT AND PROBLEM-SOLVING CAPABILITIES!
EVERYTHING OUR COMPANY IS TODAY AND WILL BE IN THE FUTURE EMANATES FROM WHAT HAPPENS IN THIS ONE LITTLE ROOM!
COFFEE ROOM
SO... WHAT HAPPENS IN THIS LITTLE ROOM, PEOPLE?
POP CORN
LASAGNA
EVENTUALLY, ONE OF THE WOMEN GETS SO DISGUSTED, SHE CLEANS IT UP HERSELF.
HURRY UP AND HIT YOUR THRESHOLD. I NEED A CLEAN PLATE FOR MY BURRITO.
MEX TO GO
GUISEWITE

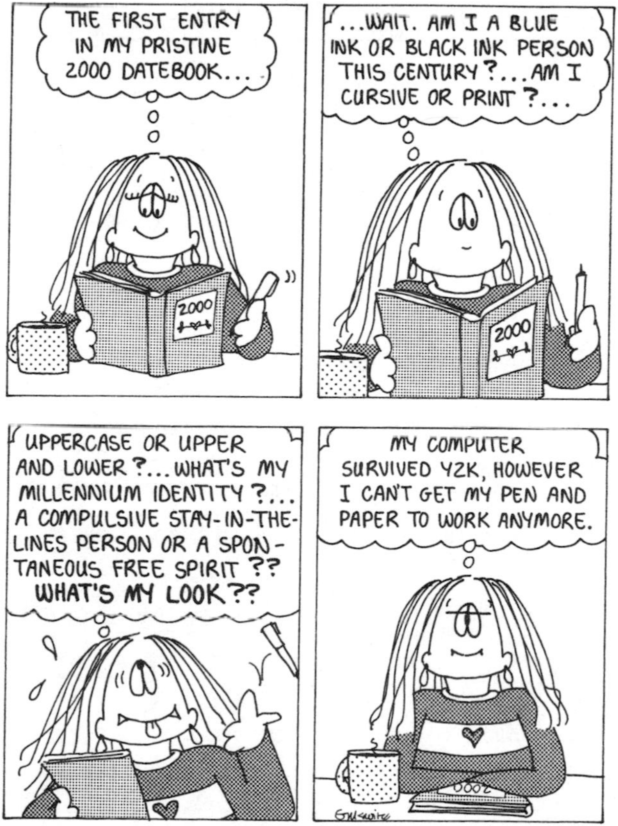
THE FIRST ENTRY IN MY PRISTINE 2000 DATEBOOK...
2000
...WAIT. AM I A BLUE INK OR BLACK INK PERSON THIS CENTURY?...AM I CURSIVE OR PRINT?...
2000
UPPERCASE OR UPPER AND LOWER?...WHAT'S MY MILLENNIUM IDENTITY?... A COMPULSIVE STAY-IN-THE-LINES PERSON OR A SPONTANEOUS FREE SPIRIT?? WHAT'S MY LOOK??
MY COMPUTER SURVIVED Y2K, HOWEVER I CAN'T GET MY PEN AND PAPER TO WORK ANYMORE.

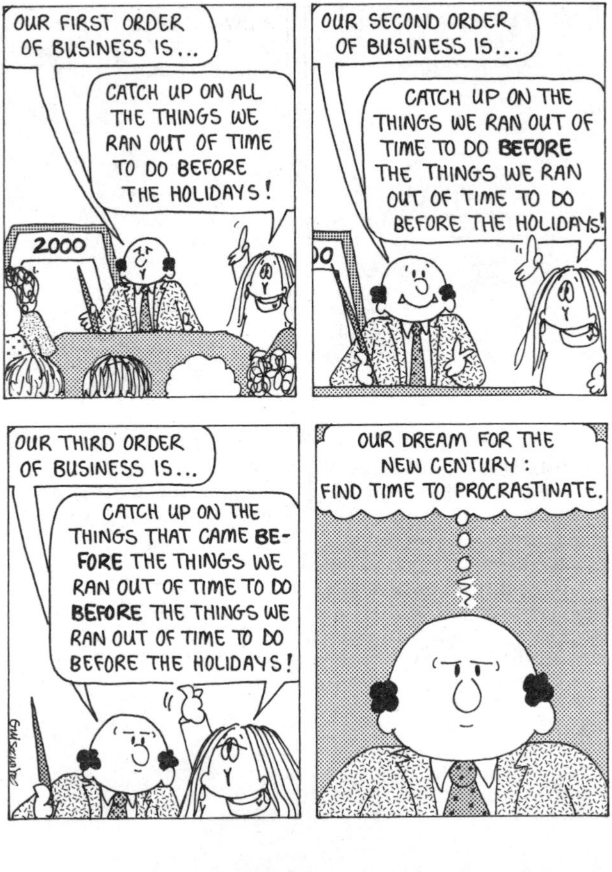
OUR FIRST ORDER OF BUSINESS IS...
CATCH UP ON ALL THE THINGS WE RAN OUT OF TIME TO DO BEFORE THE HOLIDAYS!
2000
OUR SECOND ORDER OF BUSINESS IS...
CATCH UP ON THE THINGS WE RAN OUT OF TIME TO DO **BEFORE** THE THINGS WE RAN OUT OF TIME TO DO BEFORE THE HOLIDAYS!
OUR THIRD ORDER OF BUSINESS IS...
CATCH UP ON THE THINGS THAT CAME **BE-FORE** THE THINGS WE RAN OUT OF TIME TO DO **BEFORE** THE THINGS WE RAN OUT OF TIME TO DO BEFORE THE HOLIDAYS!
OUR DREAM FOR THE NEW CENTURY: FIND TIME TO PROCRASTINATE.

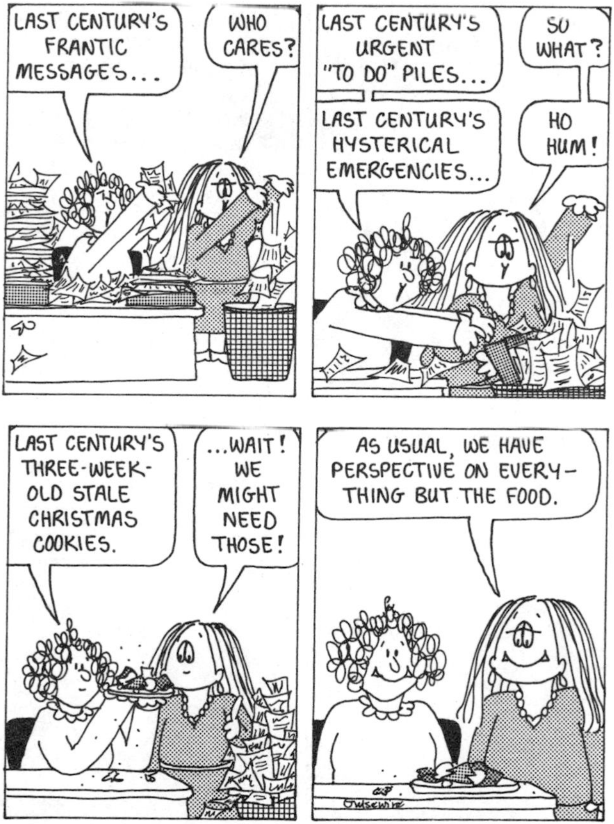
LAST CENTURY'S FRANTIC MESSAGES...
WHO CARES?
LAST CENTURY'S URGENT "TO DO" PILES...
SO WHAT?
LAST CENTURY'S HYSTERICAL EMERGENCIES...
HO HUM!
LAST CENTURY'S THREE-WEEK-OLD STALE CHRISTMAS COOKIES.
...WAIT! WE MIGHT NEED THOSE!
AS USUAL, WE HAVE PERSPECTIVE ON EVERYTHING BUT THE FOOD.

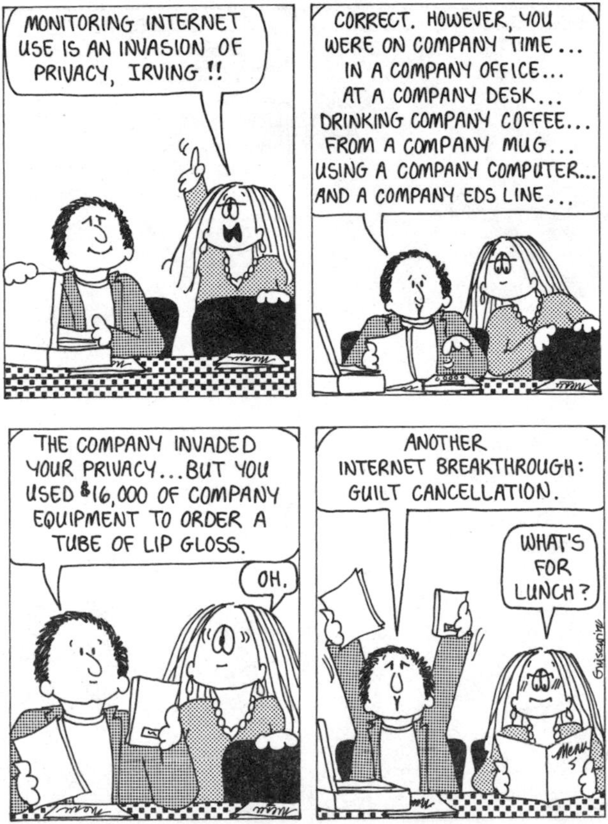
MONITORING INTERNET USE IS AN INVASION OF PRIVACY, IRVING !!
CORRECT. HOWEVER, YOU WERE ON COMPANY TIME... IN A COMPANY OFFICE... AT A COMPANY DESK... DRINKING COMPANY COFFEE... FROM A COMPANY MUG... USING A COMPANY COMPUTER... AND A COMPANY EDS LINE...
THE COMPANY INVADED YOUR PRIVACY...BUT YOU USED $16,000 OF COMPANY EQUIPMENT TO ORDER A TUBE OF LIP GLOSS.
OH.
ANOTHER INTERNET BREAKTHROUGH: GUILT CANCELLATION.
WHAT'S FOR LUNCH?
Menu
Guisewite

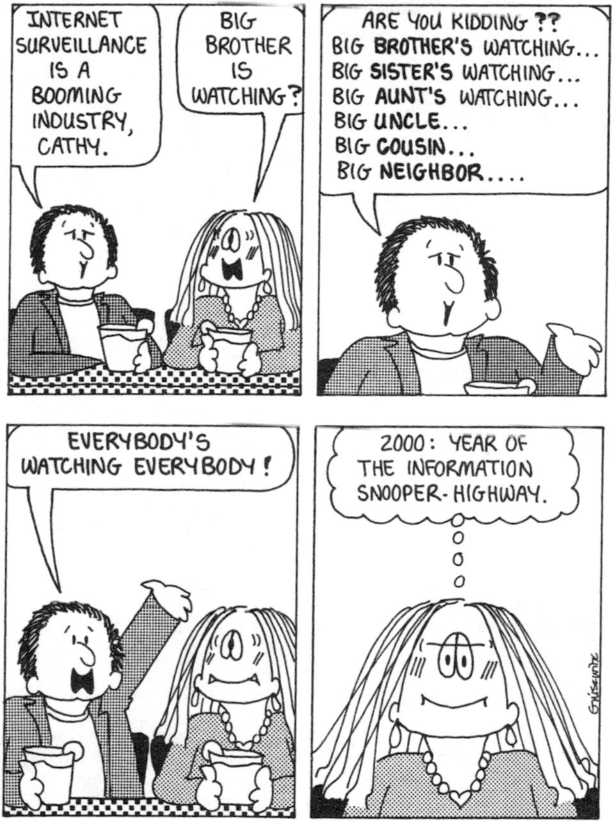
INTERNET SURVEILLANCE IS A BOOMING INDUSTRY, CATHY.
BIG BROTHER IS WATCHING?
ARE YOU KIDDING ?? BIG BROTHER'S WATCHING... BIG SISTER'S WATCHING... BIG AUNT'S WATCHING... BIG UNCLE... BIG COUSIN... BIG NEIGHBOR....
EVERYBODY'S WATCHING EVERYBODY!
2000: YEAR OF THE INFORMATION SNOOPER-HIGHWAY.
GUISEWITE

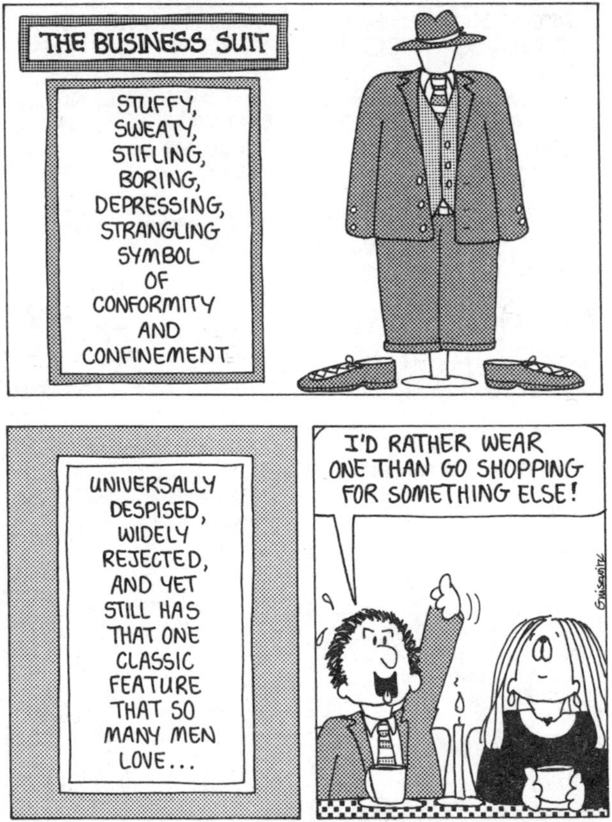

THE BUSINESS SUIT
STUFFY, SWEATY, STIFLING, BORING, DEPRESSING, STRANGLING SYMBOL OF CONFORMITY AND CONFINEMENT
UNIVERSALLY DESPISED, WIDELY REJECTED, AND YET STILL HAS THAT ONE CLASSIC FEATURE THAT SO MANY MEN LOVE...
I'D RATHER WEAR ONE THAN GO SHOPPING FOR SOMETHING ELSE!
GUISEWITE

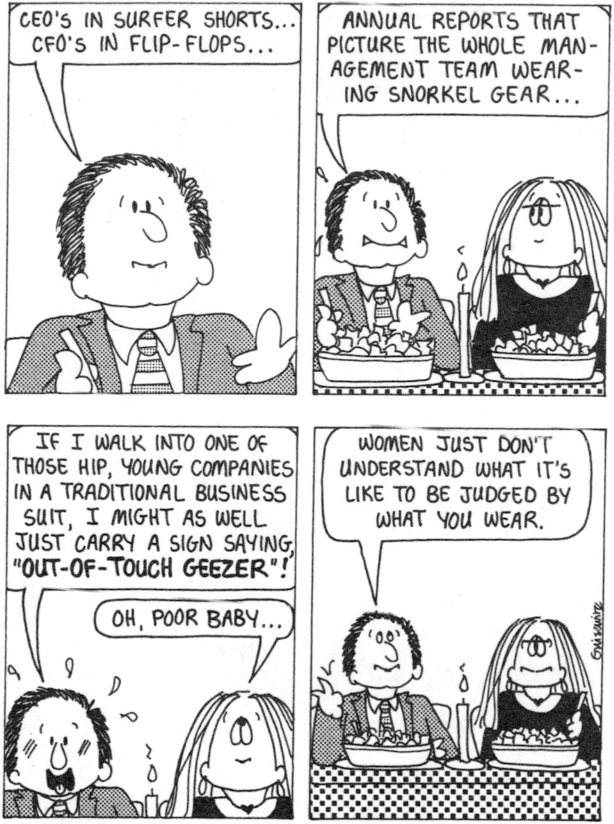
CEO'S IN SURFER SHORTS... CFO'S IN FLIP-FLOPS...
ANNUAL REPORTS THAT PICTURE THE WHOLE MANAGEMENT TEAM WEARING SNORKEL GEAR...
IF I WALK INTO ONE OF THOSE HIP, YOUNG COMPANIES IN A TRADITIONAL BUSINESS SUIT, I MIGHT AS WELL JUST CARRY A SIGN SAYING, "OUT-OF-TOUCH GEEZER"!
OH, POOR BABY...
WOMEN JUST DON'T UNDERSTAND WHAT IT'S LIKE TO BE JUDGED BY WHAT YOU WEAR.

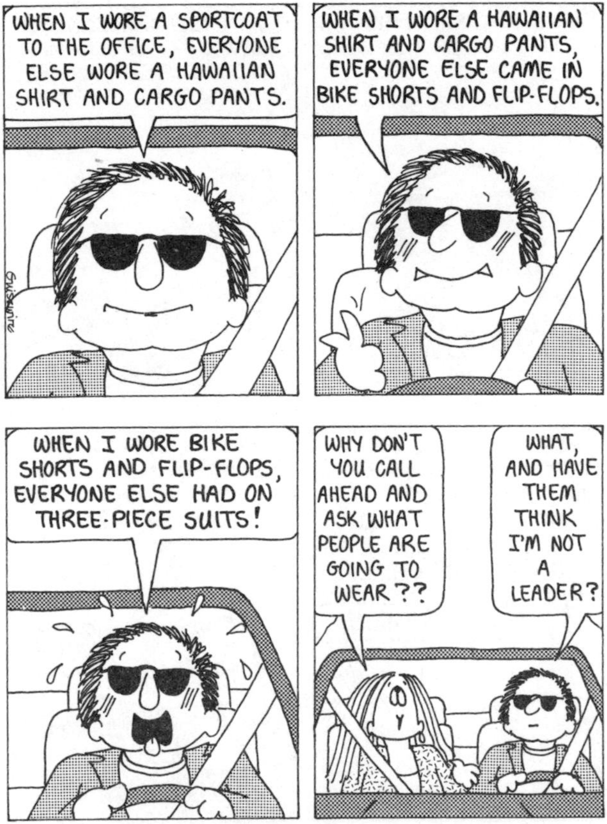
WHEN I WORE A SPORTCOAT TO THE OFFICE, EVERYONE ELSE WORE A HAWAIIAN SHIRT AND CARGO PANTS.
GUISEWITE
WHEN I WORE A HAWAIIAN SHIRT AND CARGO PANTS, EVERYONE ELSE CAME IN BIKE SHORTS AND FLIP-FLOPS.
WHEN I WORE BIKE SHORTS AND FLIP-FLOPS, EVERYONE ELSE HAD ON THREE-PIECE SUITS!
WHY DON'T YOU CALL AHEAD AND ASK WHAT PEOPLE ARE GOING TO WEAR??
WHAT, AND HAVE THEM THINK I'M NOT A LEADER?

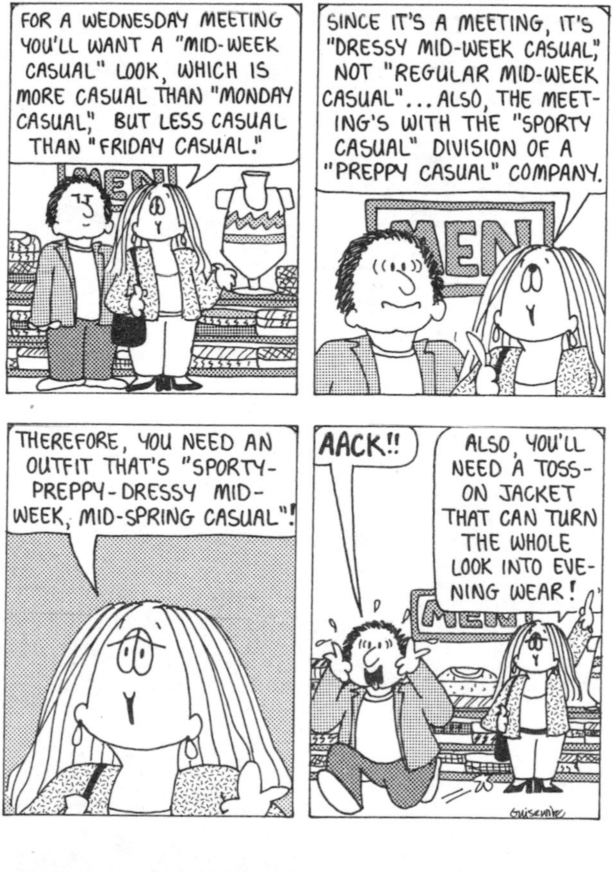
FOR A WEDNESDAY MEETING YOU'LL WANT A "MID-WEEK CASUAL" LOOK, WHICH IS MORE CASUAL THAN "MONDAY CASUAL," BUT LESS CASUAL THAN "FRIDAY CASUAL."
MEN
SINCE IT'S A MEETING, IT'S "DRESSY MID-WEEK CASUAL," NOT "REGULAR MID-WEEK CASUAL"... ALSO, THE MEETING'S WITH THE "SPORTY CASUAL" DIVISION OF A "PREPPY CASUAL" COMPANY.
MEN
THEREFORE, YOU NEED AN OUTFIT THAT'S "SPORTY-PREPPY-DRESSY MID-WEEK, MID-SPRING CASUAL"!
AACK!!
ALSO, YOU'LL NEED A TOSS-ON JACKET THAT CAN TURN THE WHOLE LOOK INTO EVENING WEAR!
Guisewite

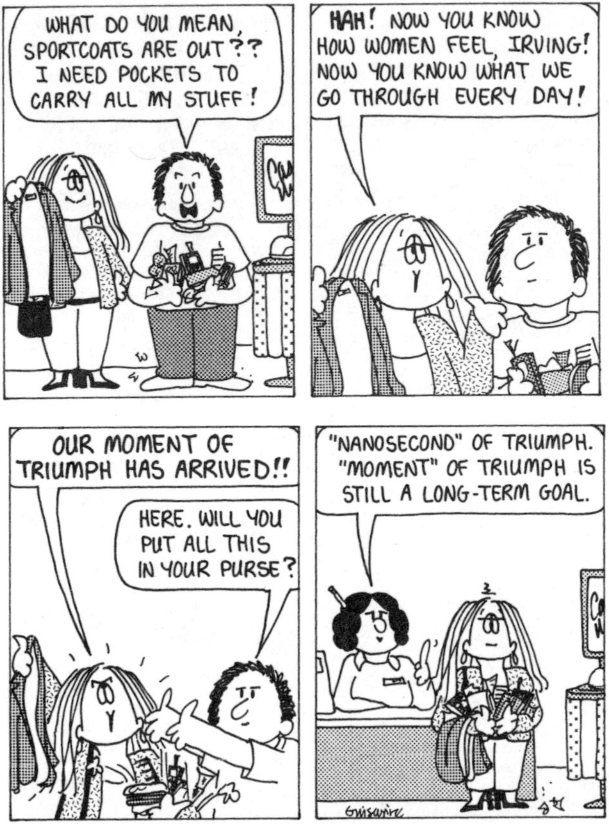
WHAT DO YOU MEAN, SPORTCOATS ARE OUT?? I NEED POCKETS TO CARRY ALL MY STUFF!
HAH! NOW YOU KNOW HOW WOMEN FEEL, IRVING! NOW YOU KNOW WHAT WE GO THROUGH EVERY DAY!
OUR MOMENT OF TRIUMPH HAS ARRIVED!!
HERE. WILL YOU PUT ALL THIS IN YOUR PURSE?
"NANOSECOND" OF TRIUMPH. "MOMENT" OF TRIUMPH IS STILL A LONG-TERM GOAL.
Guisewite

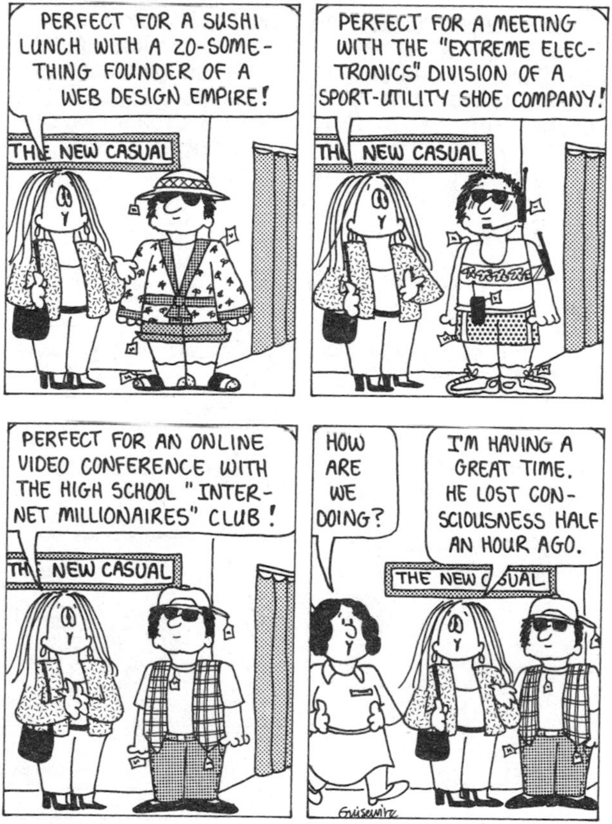
PERFECT FOR A SUSHI LUNCH WITH A 20-SOMETHING FOUNDER OF A WEB DESIGN EMPIRE!
THE NEW CASUAL
PERFECT FOR A MEETING WITH THE "EXTREME ELECTRONICS" DIVISION OF A SPORT-UTILITY SHOE COMPANY!
THE NEW CASUAL
PERFECT FOR AN ONLINE VIDEO CONFERENCE WITH THE HIGH SCHOOL "INTERNET MILLIONAIRES" CLUB!
THE NEW CASUAL
HOW ARE WE DOING?
I'M HAVING A GREAT TIME. HE LOST CONSCIOUSNESS HALF AN HOUR AGO.
THE NEW CASUAL
Guisewite

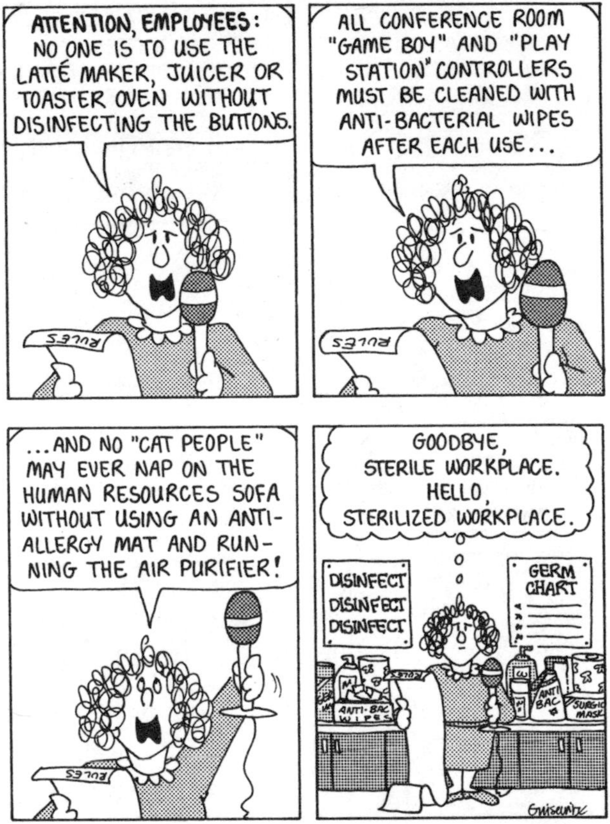
ATTENTION, EMPLOYEES: NO ONE IS TO USE THE LATTÉ MAKER, JUICER OR TOASTER OVEN WITHOUT DISINFECTING THE BUTTONS.
ALL CONFERENCE ROOM "GAME BOY" AND "PLAY STATION" CONTROLLERS MUST BE CLEANED WITH ANTI-BACTERIAL WIPES AFTER EACH USE...
...AND NO "CAT PEOPLE" MAY EVER NAP ON THE HUMAN RESOURCES SOFA WITHOUT USING AN ANTI-ALLERGY MAT AND RUNNING THE AIR PURIFIER!
GOODBYE, STERILE WORKPLACE. HELLO, STERILIZED WORKPLACE.
DISINFECT DISINFECT DISINFECT
GERM CHART
ANTI-BAC WIPES
ANTI BAC

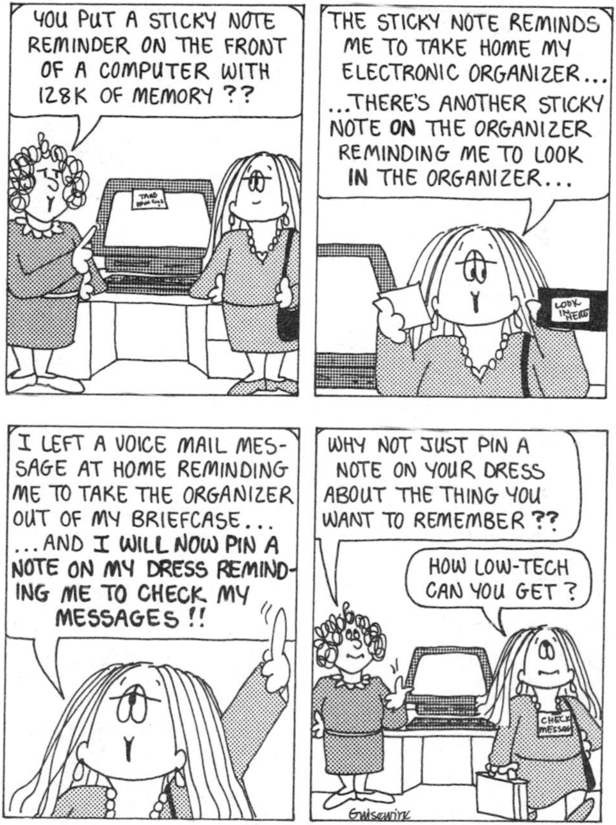

YOU PUT A STICKY NOTE REMINDER ON THE FRONT OF A COMPUTER WITH 128K OF MEMORY ??
THE STICKY NOTE REMINDS ME TO TAKE HOME MY ELECTRONIC ORGANIZER... ...THERE'S ANOTHER STICKY NOTE **ON** THE ORGANIZER REMINDING ME TO LOOK **IN** THE ORGANIZER...
LOOK IN HERE
I LEFT A VOICE MAIL MESSAGE AT HOME REMINDING ME TO TAKE THE ORGANIZER OUT OF MY BRIEFCASE... ...AND **I WILL NOW PIN A NOTE ON MY DRESS REMINDING ME TO CHECK MY MESSAGES !!**
WHY NOT JUST PIN A NOTE ON YOUR DRESS ABOUT THE THING YOU WANT TO REMEMBER ??
HOW LOW-TECH CAN YOU GET ?
Guisewite

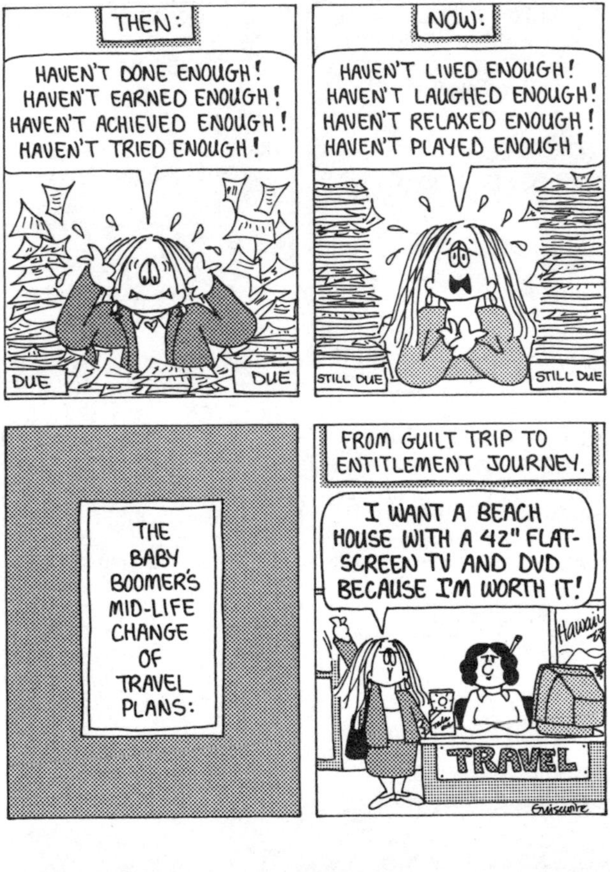
THEN:
HAVEN'T DONE ENOUGH! HAVEN'T EARNED ENOUGH! HAVEN'T ACHIEVED ENOUGH! HAVEN'T TRIED ENOUGH!
DUE
DUE
NOW:
HAVEN'T LIVED ENOUGH! HAVEN'T LAUGHED ENOUGH! HAVEN'T RELAXED ENOUGH! HAVEN'T PLAYED ENOUGH!
STILL DUE
STILL DUE
THE BABY BOOMER'S MID-LIFE CHANGE OF TRAVEL PLANS:
FROM GUILT TRIP TO ENTITLEMENT JOURNEY.
I WANT A BEACH HOUSE WITH A 42" FLAT-SCREEN TV AND DVD BECAUSE I'M WORTH IT!
Hawaii
TRAVEL
Guisewite

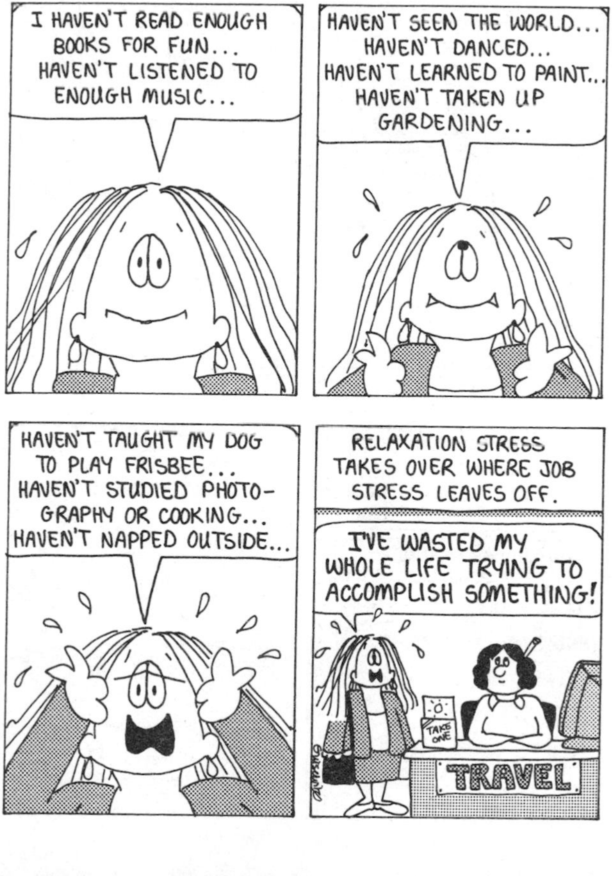
I HAVEN'T READ ENOUGH BOOKS FOR FUN... HAVEN'T LISTENED TO ENOUGH MUSIC...
HAVEN'T SEEN THE WORLD... HAVEN'T DANCED... HAVEN'T LEARNED TO PAINT... HAVEN'T TAKEN UP GARDENING...
HAVEN'T TAUGHT MY DOG TO PLAY FRISBEE... HAVEN'T STUDIED PHOTO-GRAPHY OR COOKING... HAVEN'T NAPPED OUTSIDE...
RELAXATION STRESS TAKES OVER WHERE JOB STRESS LEAVES OFF.
I'VE WASTED MY WHOLE LIFE TRYING TO ACCOMPLISH SOMETHING!
TAKE ONE
TRAVEL

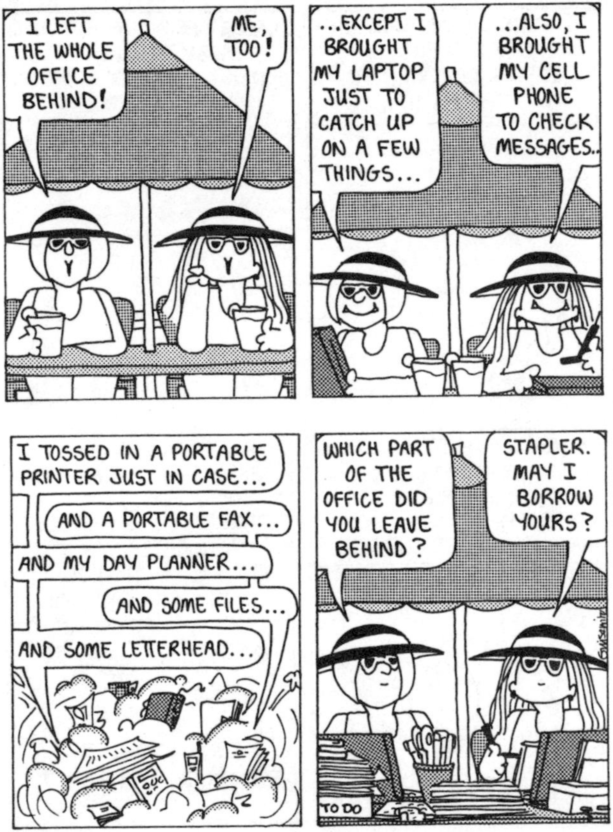
I LEFT THE WHOLE OFFICE BEHIND!
ME, TOO!
...EXCEPT I BROUGHT MY LAPTOP JUST TO CATCH UP ON A FEW THINGS...
...ALSO, I BROUGHT MY CELL PHONE TO CHECK MESSAGES...
I TOSSED IN A PORTABLE PRINTER JUST IN CASE...
AND A PORTABLE FAX...
AND MY DAY PLANNER...
AND SOME FILES...
AND SOME LETTERHEAD...
WHICH PART OF THE OFFICE DID YOU LEAVE BEHIND?
STAPLER. MAY I BORROW YOURS?
TO DO

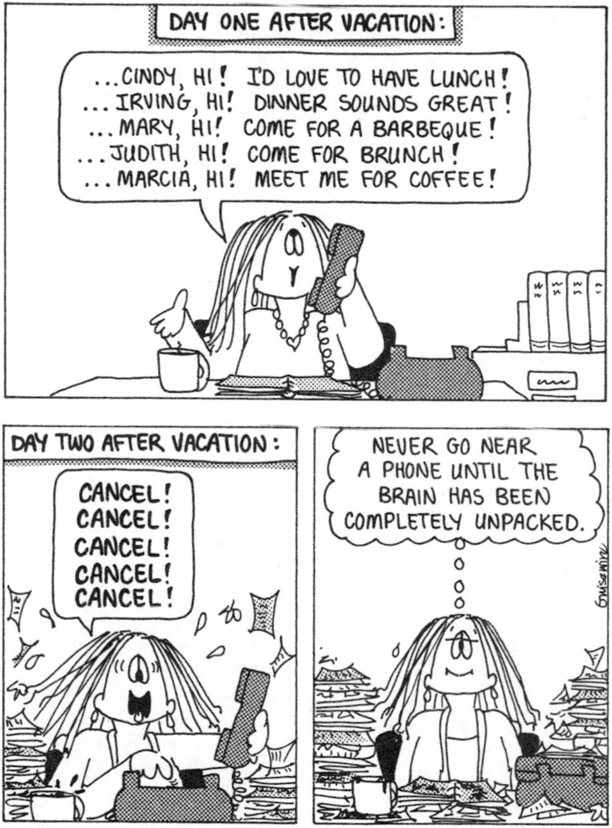
DAY ONE AFTER VACATION:
...CINDY, HI! I'D LOVE TO HAVE LUNCH! ...IRVING, HI! DINNER SOUNDS GREAT! ...MARY, HI! COME FOR A BARBEQUE! ...JUDITH, HI! COME FOR BRUNCH! ...MARCIA, HI! MEET ME FOR COFFEE!
DAY TWO AFTER VACATION:
CANCEL! CANCEL! CANCEL! CANCEL! CANCEL!
NEVER GO NEAR A PHONE UNTIL THE BRAIN HAS BEEN COMPLETELY UNPACKED.

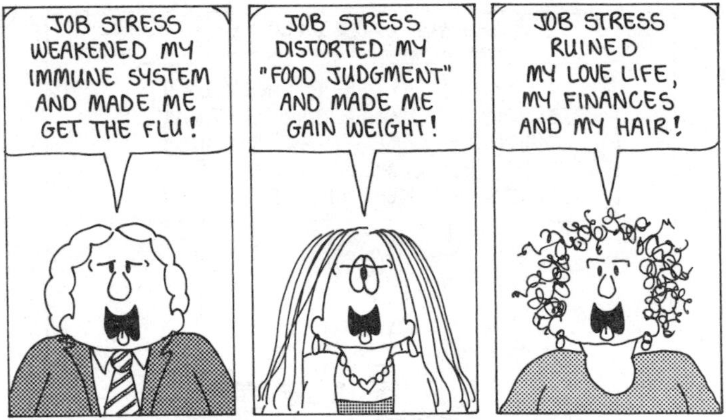
JOB STRESS WEAKENED MY IMMUNE SYSTEM AND MADE ME GET THE FLU!
JOB STRESS DISTORTED MY "FOOD JUDGMENT" AND MADE ME GAIN WEIGHT!
JOB STRESS RUINED MY LOVE LIFE, MY FINANCES AND MY HAIR!

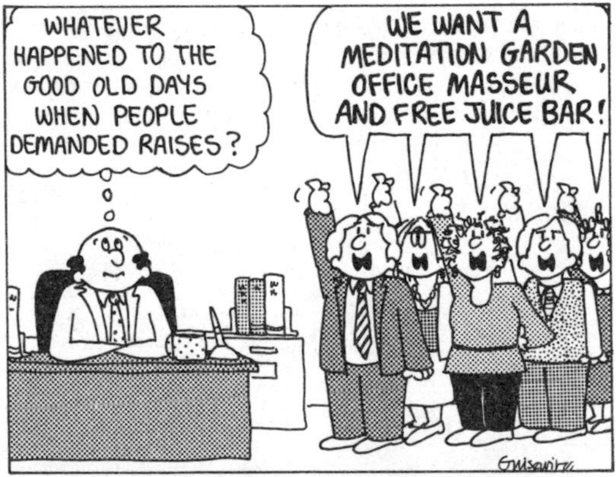
WE WANT A MEDITATION GARDEN, OFFICE MASSEUR AND FREE JUICE BAR!
WHATEVER HAPPENED TO THE GOOD OLD DAYS WHEN PEOPLE DEMANDED RAISES?

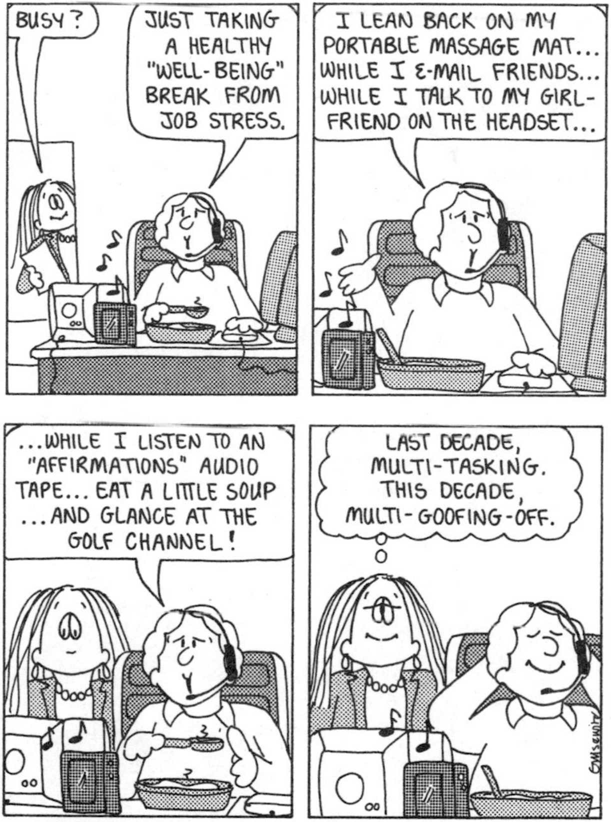

BUSY?
JUST TAKING A HEALTHY "WELL-BEING" BREAK FROM JOB STRESS.
I LEAN BACK ON MY PORTABLE MASSAGE MAT... WHILE I E-MAIL FRIENDS... WHILE I TALK TO MY GIRL-FRIEND ON THE HEADSET...
...WHILE I LISTEN TO AN "AFFIRMATIONS" AUDIO TAPE... EAT A LITTLE SOUP ...AND GLANCE AT THE GOLF CHANNEL!
LAST DECADE, MULTI-TASKING. THIS DECADE, MULTI-GOOFING-OFF.
GUISEWITE

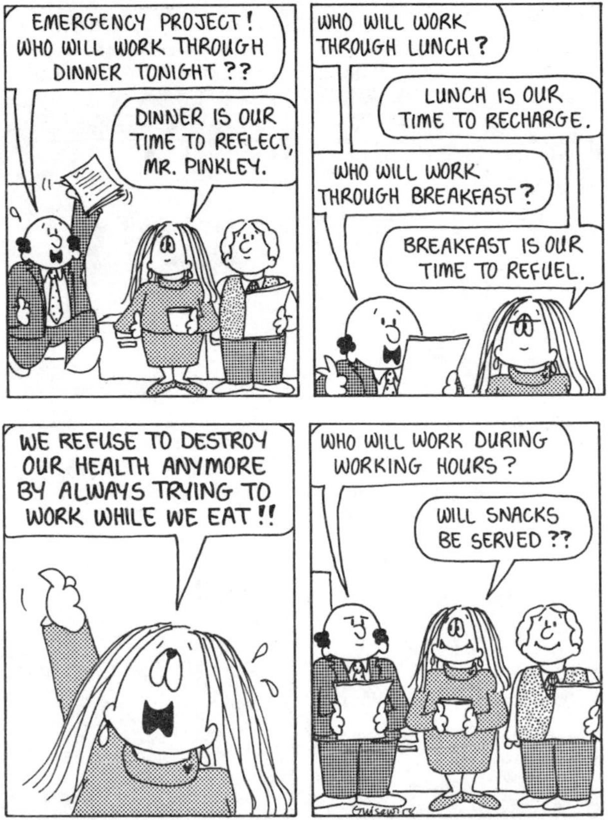
EMERGENCY PROJECT! WHO WILL WORK THROUGH DINNER TONIGHT??
DINNER IS OUR TIME TO REFLECT, MR. PINKLEY.
WHO WILL WORK THROUGH LUNCH?
LUNCH IS OUR TIME TO RECHARGE.
WHO WILL WORK THROUGH BREAKFAST?
BREAKFAST IS OUR TIME TO REFUEL.
WE REFUSE TO DESTROY OUR HEALTH ANYMORE BY ALWAYS TRYING TO WORK WHILE WE EAT!!
WHO WILL WORK DURING WORKING HOURS?
WILL SNACKS BE SERVED??

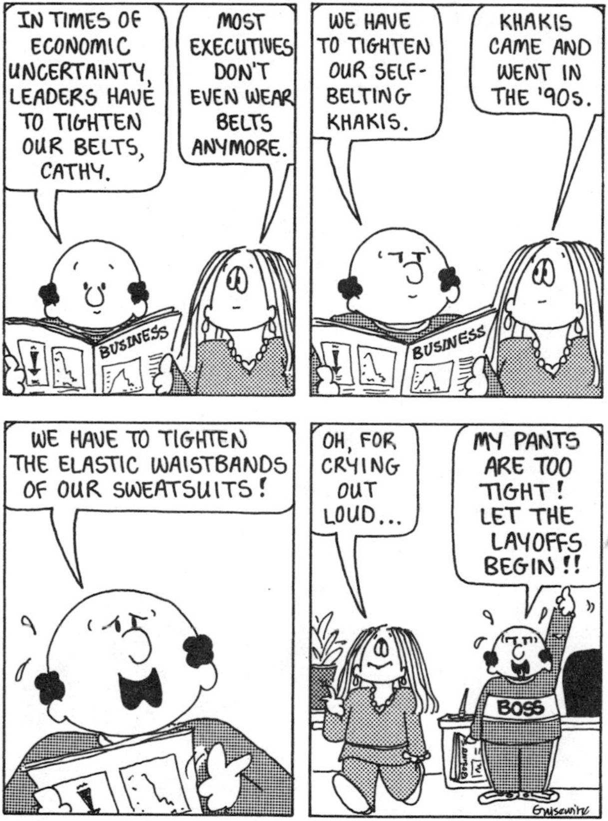
IN TIMES OF ECONOMIC UNCERTAINTY, LEADERS HAVE TO TIGHTEN OUR BELTS, CATHY.
MOST EXECUTIVES DON'T EVEN WEAR BELTS ANYMORE.
BUSINESS
WE HAVE TO TIGHTEN OUR SELF-BELTING KHAKIS.
KHAKIS CAME AND WENT IN THE '90S.
BUSINESS
WE HAVE TO TIGHTEN THE ELASTIC WAISTBANDS OF OUR SWEATSUITS!
OH, FOR CRYING OUT LOUD...
MY PANTS ARE TOO TIGHT! LET THE LAYOFFS BEGIN!!
BOSS
Guisewite

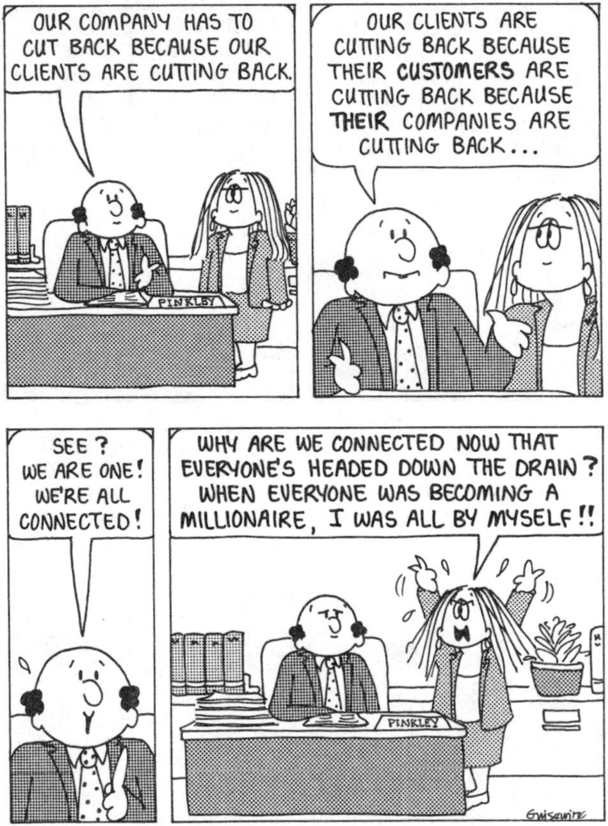
OUR COMPANY HAS TO CUT BACK BECAUSE OUR CLIENTS ARE CUTTING BACK.
PINKLEY
OUR CLIENTS ARE CUTTING BACK BECAUSE THEIR **CUSTOMERS** ARE CUTTING BACK BECAUSE **THEIR** COMPANIES ARE CUTTING BACK...
SEE? WE ARE ONE! WE'RE ALL CONNECTED!
WHY ARE WE CONNECTED NOW THAT EVERYONE'S HEADED DOWN THE DRAIN? WHEN EVERYONE WAS BECOMING A MILLIONAIRE, I WAS ALL BY MYSELF!!
PINKLEY
Guisewite

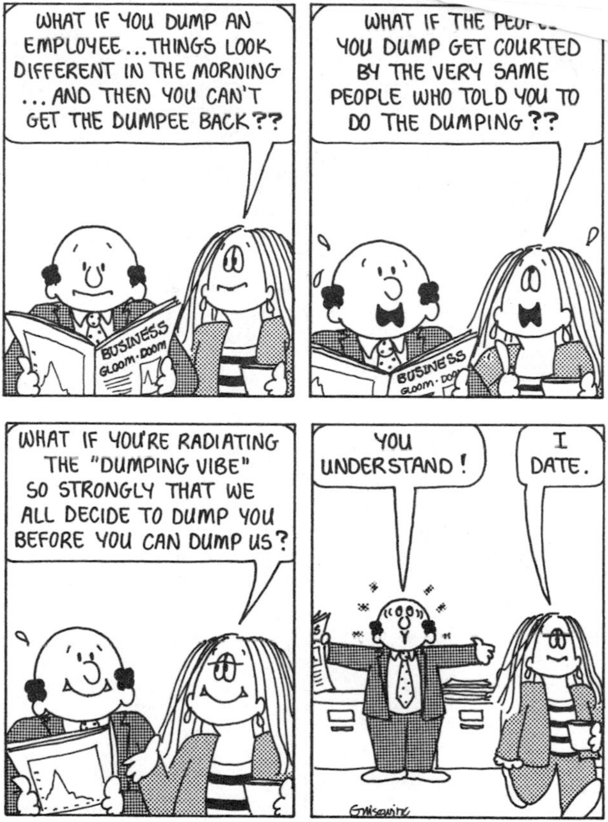
WHAT IF YOU DUMP AN EMPLOYEE... THINGS LOOK DIFFERENT IN THE MORNING ... AND THEN YOU CAN'T GET THE DUMPEE BACK??
BUSINESS
GLOOM-DOOM
WHAT IF THE
YOU DUMP GET COURTED BY THE VERY SAME PEOPLE WHO TOLD YOU TO DO THE DUMPING??
BUSINESS
WHAT IF YOU'RE RADIATING THE "DUMPING VIBE" SO STRONGLY THAT WE ALL DECIDE TO DUMP YOU BEFORE YOU CAN DUMP US?
YOU UNDERSTAND!
I DATE.
GUISEWITE

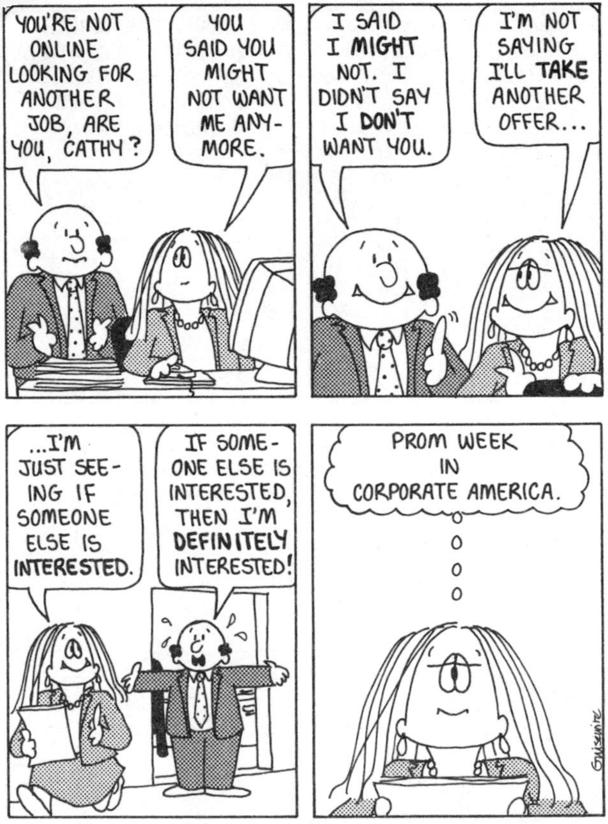
YOU'RE NOT ONLINE LOOKING FOR ANOTHER JOB, ARE YOU, CATHY?
YOU SAID YOU MIGHT NOT WANT ME ANYMORE.
I SAID I **MIGHT** NOT. I DIDN'T SAY I **DON'T** WANT YOU.
I'M NOT SAYING I'LL **TAKE** ANOTHER OFFER...
...I'M JUST SEEING IF SOMEONE ELSE IS **INTERESTED**.
IF SOMEONE ELSE IS INTERESTED, THEN I'M **DEFINITELY** INTERESTED!
PROM WEEK IN CORPORATE AMERICA.

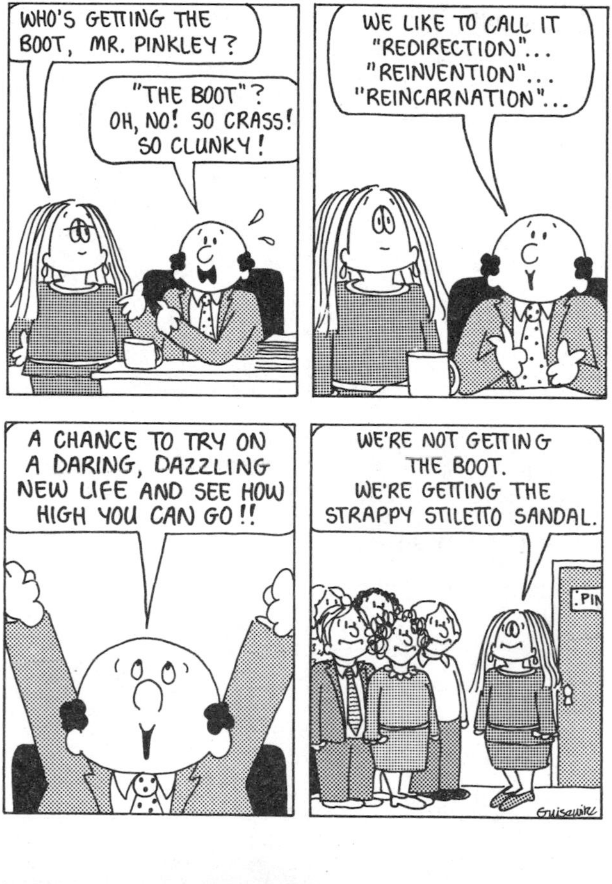
WHO'S GETTING THE BOOT, MR. PINKLEY?
"THE BOOT"? OH, NO! SO CRASS! SO CLUNKY!
WE LIKE TO CALL IT "REDIRECTION"... "REINVENTION"... "REINCARNATION"...
A CHANCE TO TRY ON A DARING, DAZZLING NEW LIFE AND SEE HOW HIGH YOU CAN GO!!
WE'RE NOT GETTING THE BOOT. WE'RE GETTING THE STRAPPY STILETTO SANDAL.
Guisewite

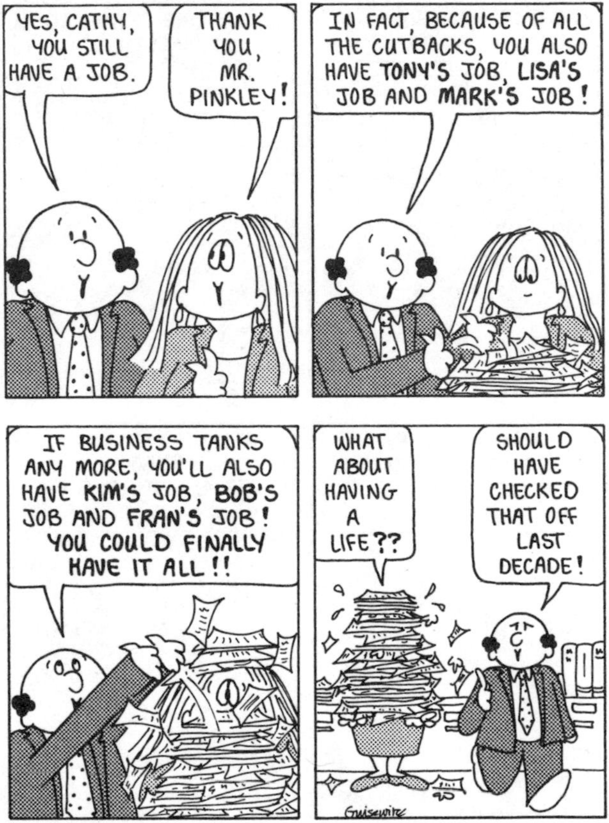
YES, CATHY, YOU STILL HAVE A JOB.
THANK YOU, MR. PINKLEY!
IN FACT, BECAUSE OF ALL THE CUTBACKS, YOU ALSO HAVE TONY'S JOB, LISA'S JOB AND MARK'S JOB!
IF BUSINESS TANKS ANY MORE, YOU'LL ALSO HAVE KIM'S JOB, BOB'S JOB AND FRAN'S JOB! YOU COULD FINALLY HAVE IT ALL!!
WHAT ABOUT HAVING A LIFE??
SHOULD HAVE CHECKED THAT OFF LAST DECADE!
Guisewite

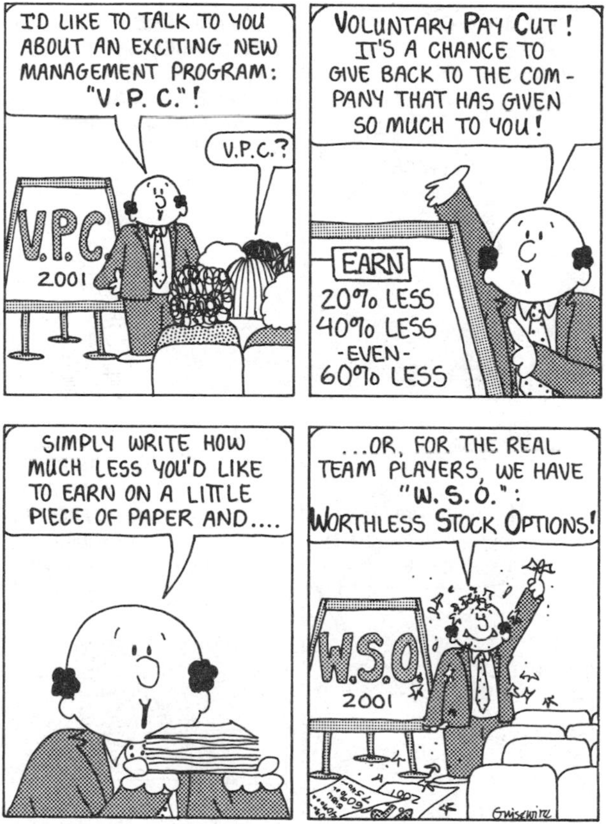
I'D LIKE TO TALK TO YOU ABOUT AN EXCITING NEW MANAGEMENT PROGRAM: "V.P.C."!
V.P.C.?
V.P.C.
2001
VOLUNTARY PAY CUT! IT'S A CHANCE TO GIVE BACK TO THE COM-PANY THAT HAS GIVEN SO MUCH TO YOU!
EARN
20% LESS
40% LESS
-EVEN-
60% LESS
SIMPLY WRITE HOW MUCH LESS YOU'D LIKE TO EARN ON A LITTLE PIECE OF PAPER AND....
...OR, FOR THE REAL TEAM PLAYERS, WE HAVE "W.S.O.": WORTHLESS STOCK OPTIONS!
W.S.O.
2001
Guisewite

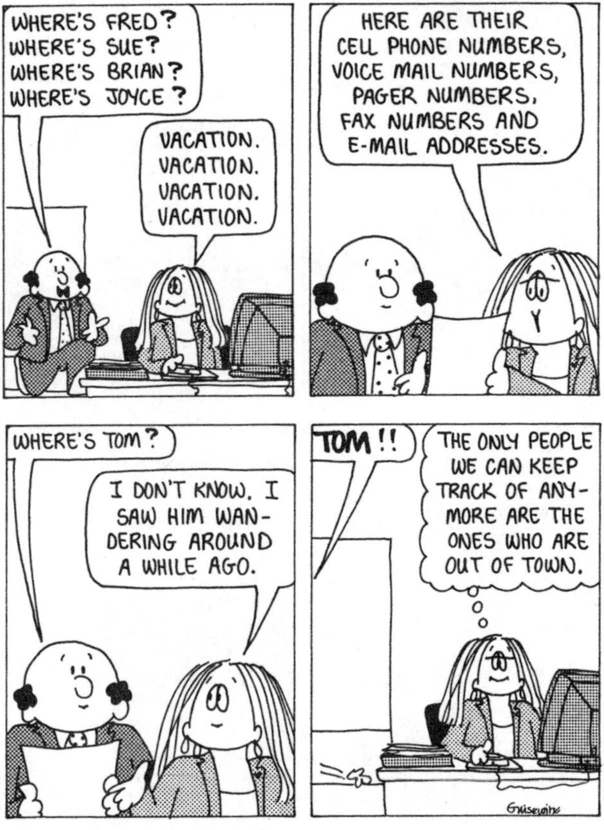
WHERE'S FRED? WHERE'S SUE? WHERE'S BRIAN? WHERE'S JOYCE?
VACATION. VACATION. VACATION. VACATION.
HERE ARE THEIR CELL PHONE NUMBERS, VOICE MAIL NUMBERS, PAGER NUMBERS, FAX NUMBERS AND E-MAIL ADDRESSES.
WHERE'S TOM?
I DON'T KNOW. I SAW HIM WAN-DERING AROUND A WHILE AGO.
TOM!!
THE ONLY PEOPLE WE CAN KEEP TRACK OF ANY-MORE ARE THE ONES WHO ARE OUT OF TOWN.
Guisewite

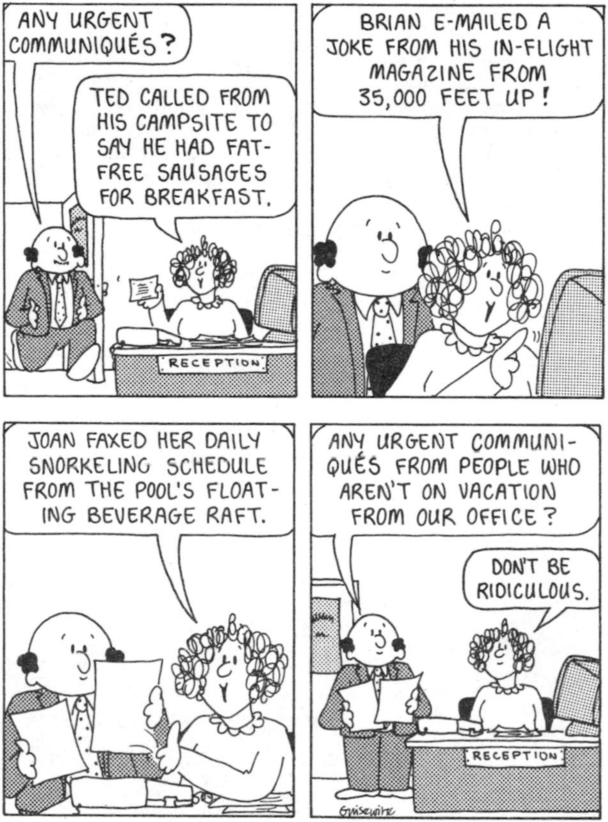
ANY URGENT COMMUNIQUÉS?
TED CALLED FROM HIS CAMPSITE TO SAY HE HAD FAT-FREE SAUSAGES FOR BREAKFAST.
RECEPTION
BRIAN E-MAILED A JOKE FROM HIS IN-FLIGHT MAGAZINE FROM 35,000 FEET UP!
JOAN FAXED HER DAILY SNORKELING SCHEDULE FROM THE POOL'S FLOATING BEVERAGE RAFT.
ANY URGENT COMMUNIQUÉS FROM PEOPLE WHO AREN'T ON VACATION FROM OUR OFFICE?
DON'T BE RIDICULOUS.
RECEPTION
Guisewite

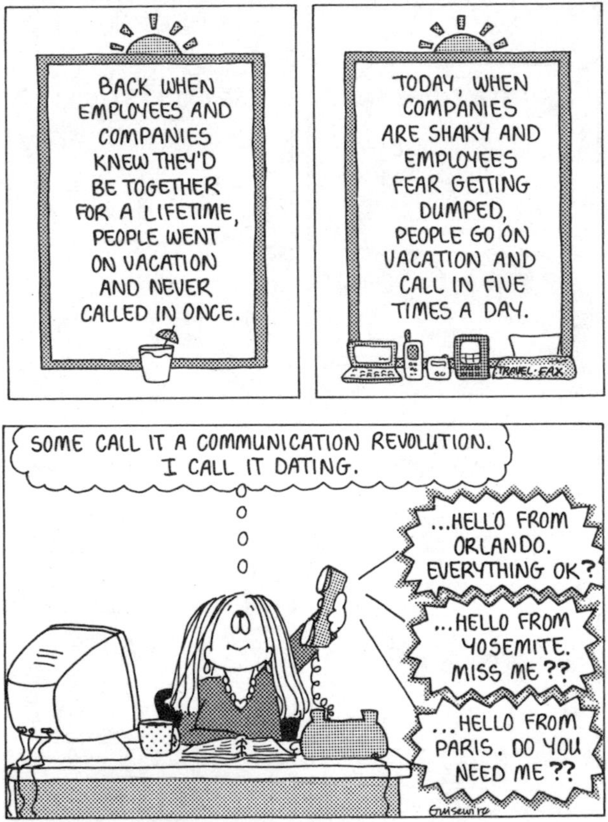
BACK WHEN EMPLOYEES AND COMPANIES KNEW THEY'D BE TOGETHER FOR A LIFETIME, PEOPLE WENT ON VACATION AND NEVER CALLED IN ONCE.
TODAY, WHEN COMPANIES ARE SHAKY AND EMPLOYEES FEAR GETTING DUMPED, PEOPLE GO ON VACATION AND CALL IN FIVE TIMES A DAY.
TRAVEL·FAX
SOME CALL IT A COMMUNICATION REVOLUTION. I CALL IT DATING.
...HELLO FROM ORLANDO. EVERYTHING OK?
...HELLO FROM YOSEMITE. MISS ME??
...HELLO FROM PARIS. DO YOU NEED ME??

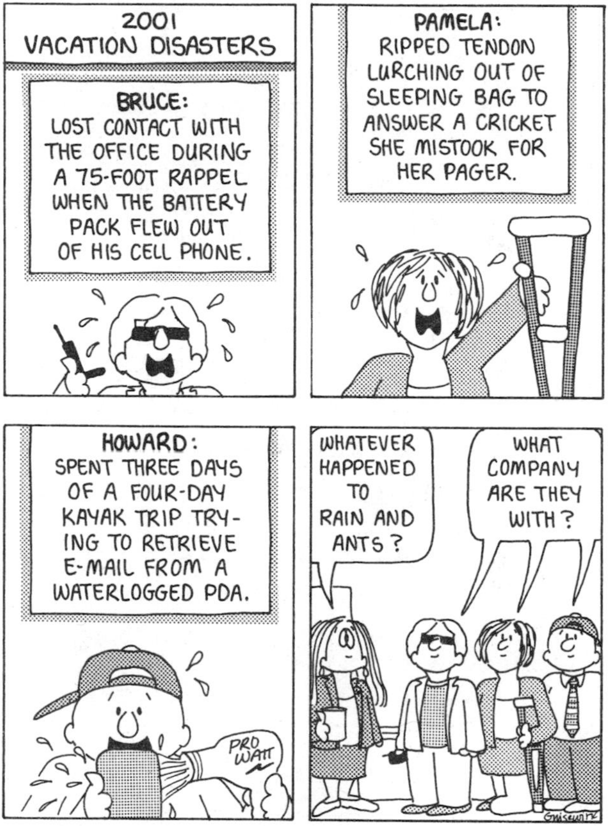
2001
VACATION DISASTERS
BRUCE:
LOST CONTACT WITH THE OFFICE DURING A 75-FOOT RAPPEL WHEN THE BATTERY PACK FLEW OUT OF HIS CELL PHONE.
PAMELA:
RIPPED TENDON LURCHING OUT OF SLEEPING BAG TO ANSWER A CRICKET SHE MISTOOK FOR HER PAGER.
HOWARD:
SPENT THREE DAYS OF A FOUR-DAY KAYAK TRIP TRY-ING TO RETRIEVE E-MAIL FROM A WATERLOGGED PDA.
PRO WATT
WHATEVER HAPPENED TO RAIN AND ANTS?
WHAT COMPANY ARE THEY WITH?

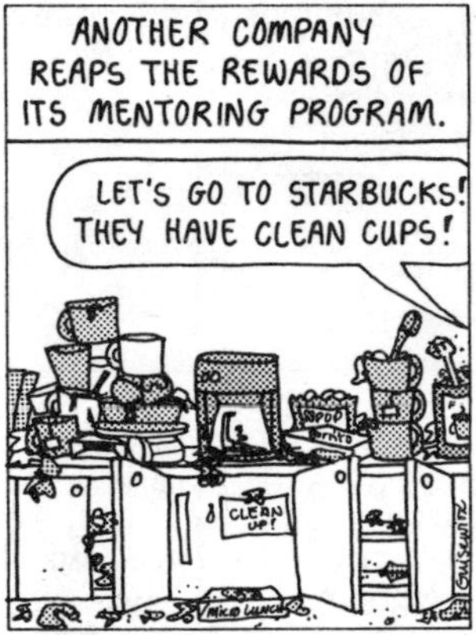
ANOTHER COMPANY REAPS THE REWARDS OF ITS MENTORING PROGRAM.
LET'S GO TO STARBUCKS! THEY HAVE CLEAN CUPS!
CLEAN UP!
GUISEWITE